Tales from an Island

Tales from an Island

Christina Hall

ORIGIN

This edition published in 2018 by
Birlinn Origin, an imprint of
Birlinn Limited
West Newington House
10 Newington Road
Edinburgh
EH9 1QS

www.birlinn.co.uk

First published in 2008 by Birlinn Ltd

ISBN: 978 1 91247 631 2
eBook ISBN: 978 0 85790 280 1

British Library Cataloguing-in-Publication Data
A catalogue record for this book is available from
the British Library

Typeset by Carolyn Griffiths, Cambridge
Printed and bound in Great Britain by Clays Ltd, Elcograf S.p.A.

Contents

Acknowledgements

My grateful thanks to Donald Iain Campbell of Glendale Road, South Uist, and Mary Flora Forrester of the Old House, Kilpheder, South Uist, for helping me to track down old photographs. Thanks also to 'the English soldier' for St Kilda input, maps, commas and cups of tea.

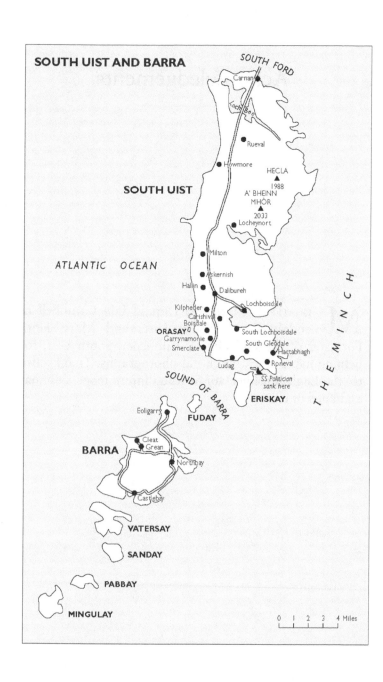

SOUTH UIST AND BARRA

SOUTH FORD

Carnan

Loch Bee

Rueval

Howmore

HECLA
1988
A' BHEINN
MHÒR
2033

SOUTH UIST

Locheynort

ATLANTIC OCEAN

Milton

Askernish

Hallin

Dalibureh

Kilpheder

Lochboisdale

Carishival
Boisdale

ORASAY

South Lochboisdale

Garrynamonie

South Glendale

Smerclate

Hartabhagh

Roneval

Ludag

SS Politician
sank here

SOUND OF BARRA

ERISKAY

THE MINCH

Eoligarry

FUDAY

Cleat
Grean

BARRA

Northbay

Castlebay

VATERSAY

SANDAY

PABBAY

MINGULAY

0   1   2   3   4 Miles

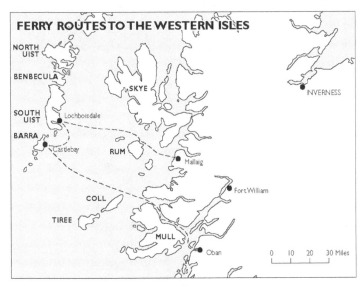

FERRY ROUTES TO THE WESTERN ISLES

NORTH UIST
BENBECULA
SKYE
SOUTH UIST — Lochboisdale
BARRA
Castlebay
RUM
Mallaig
Fort William
COLL
TIREE
MULL
Oban
INVERNESS

0   10   20   30 Miles

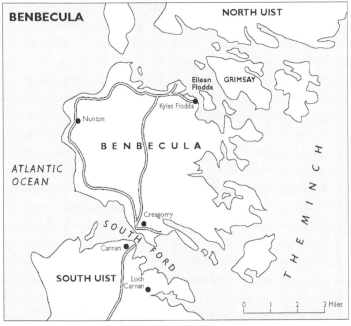

BENBECULA   **NORTH UIST**

Eilean Flodda   GRIMSAY
Kyles Flodda
Nunton
B E N B E C U L A
ATLANTIC OCEAN
Creagorry
SOUTH FORD
Carnan
SOUTH UIST
Loch Carnan
THE MINCH

0   1   2   3 Miles

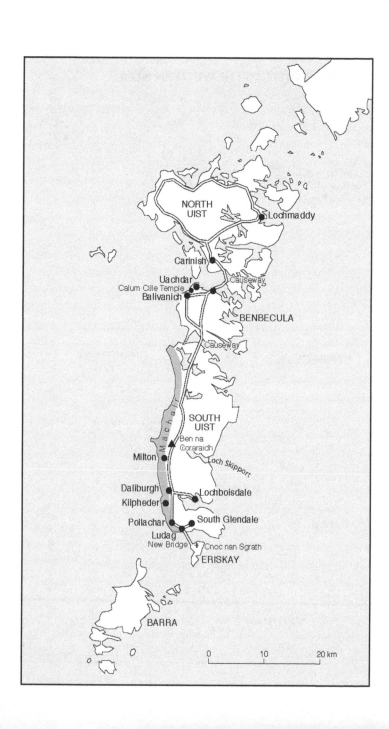

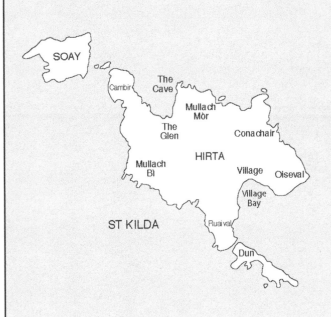

SOAY

Cambir

The
Cave

Mullach
Mòr

The
Glen

Conachair

HIRTA

Mullach
Bì

Village

Oiseval

Village
Bay

ST KILDA

Ruaival

Dun

To the Edge of the Sea

For Colin

An òige

Nuair dh'fhosglas sùil an òg-uain
   bhàin
Ri taobh a mhàthar air an raon,
Seallaidh feannag air a fiaradh
Anns an iarmailt os a chionn.

Tha sligh' a' bhradain cinnteach
   cruaidh
A' dìreadh suas ri eas nan gleann;
Dh'aindeoin riaslaidh, cuileag iasgair
Airson lìon a chur mu cheann.

An tug thu 'n air' air aodann pàiste
'S e na thàmh an cadal trom –
Cuiridh manadh na tha 'n dàn dha
Saighead cràidh is crith na chom.

Nach math nach fiosrach dhuinn nar
   n-òige
Gach lot, gach leòn, gach bròn 's
   gach tàir',
Gach feannag 's iasgair tha gar
   triall-ne,
Gach lìon is riasladh tha air sàil.

Tha clann òg an là an-diugh
Mar bha clann an là an-dè,
Cho beag de chùram ris an druid,
Cho saor de dhragh ri dealain-dè.

Na bi ro throm air an fhear bheag,
Ach crom ri thaobh is bi ris còir,
Oir thig eallach trom an uallaich
Air a ghuailnean tràth gu leòr.

Donald John MacMillan, 1980

Youth

The lamb newborn surveys the world
Close to its mother on the hill;
Above, the crow, behind a cloud
Looks down and notes it for a kill.

The salmon's task is never easy–
He toils against the stream instead:
Despite his guile, the angler's fly
Will cast a net around his head.
Reflect upon an infant's face

So calm and quiet sleeping near
Some ghostly hint of what awaits him
Makes him shake and cry in fear.

What a blessing that in youth
We give no thought to future woes,
The anglers and the crows that trail us –
Each net, each struggle still unknown.

The children that we see today
Are like the child of yesteryear,
As free from worry as the skylark
Like butterflies, they know no fear.

So don't begrudge your child his
   childhood:
Bend down beside him, show him
   love
For life with all its heavy burdens
Will stoop his shoulders soon enough.

Translated by the author

3

Chapter One

WITH SHAKING KNEES AND gasping breath I squeezed myself as far as I could under the kitchen bench. It was a tight fit, warm, in a musty, smelly way. I tried to avoid the shoes and Wellington boots and fend off the welcoming licks of Scot, who was thumping his tail at this unusual invasion of his sleeping quarters. My two brothers were in there too, giggling, the way boys do when they are terrified and loving it. I could see it coming, leaving a fan-shaped track in the fine white sand on the stone floor. Its claw as it passed my father's size-ten boot was exactly the same length! 'It can't get over the rail,' I whispered to my brothers. 'We're safe in here.' At that moment two eyes appeared, two stalks waved over the rail, inches from my face, and I wet myself.

'For the love of God, man, stop playing with that lobster and get it in the pot before it dies of old age.'

We crept out of our hiding place and joined my father and mother admiring the latest victim of his *croman*, the piece of bent wire with which he tickled the lobster, teasing it, until it grabbed the *croman* in its huge claw and was caught. 'Aye, Kate, the Sgeir Mhòr [Big Rock] has hidden him for the last time. Winston Churchill himself won't have a finer dinner today.' The massive lobster was dropped in the pot and we three children breathed again.

I was born in a crofter's thatched cottage, on the Hebridean island of South Uist, the third child in a family of six, roughly one hundred years after Gordon of Cluny's Highland Clearances and a year before the start of Adolf Hitler's world war. On an island predominantly Catholic since St Patrick founded the See of the Isles in the fifth century, it was a matter of pride to fill a whole pew with healthy children, and family planning simply meant working out how many children you could sleep in a bed if you used the head and the foot.

How do I describe the land of my birth? The place where we say up south and down north? The island of South Uist is both beautiful and ugly. A heavenly place on a calm early morning, in Kilpheder, looking across the Gortain and Clach Ghlas towards Carisheval, when the call of the curlew and the distant sigh of the sea seem to be the only sounds left on earth. Travel south and east to the scenic village of South Lochboisdale and right at the tip you will find Rudha. There look across the bay to the busy harbour of North Lochboisdale, where, sheltered by Ben Kenneth, fishing boats, their size diminished by distance, bob at anchor. All around you the rich soil brought from Russia as ballast in empty boats and dumped in what was then the Harbourmaster's yard has produced a lush country garden at odds with the rugged terrain beyond its walls. Go north to Rueaval and drive to the summit; ignore the radar base and instead turn your eyes towards the sea. The islands of the Hebrides rise up before you and you can see the Monachs and St Kilda on a clear day. You will say, 'What a lovely island.'

Wait until a force 10 gale makes your feet take you where you don't want to go and the sky looks as if the sun doesn't live there any more. When the wind abates, walk out to Hartabagh, along the old hill road, and see the ruins of sad little houses once home to crofters driven to the very edge of the island by their landlord's greed. See the evidence of their struggle for survival in the crop scars on the heather-clad hillside and be grateful that the two hours of hill walking which bring you back to twentieth-century Uist are all that is required of you. As you pass the lochs, try not to notice the noble salmon in their man-made watery compounds, leaping in vain as their instincts tell them to swim to freedom, while they wait to be starved, bled and smoked to tempt palates which can afford such delicacies. Comfort yourself by the thought that many islanders benefit financially from this sin against nature, and it is called survival, in a place where your sheep are bought for fifty pence. Beautiful and ugly, it's a place that I love more than I admit even to myself, and if I could give a city child one gift, I would give him or her the gift of a summer in South Uist.

Life was basic but not too difficult by the time I was born, and we certainly never went hungry. Most families had livestock: cattle on the land in the summer, crops with which to feed them in winter, sheep grazing on the hills, hens and ducks and sometimes a horse or two, and the bounty of the sea all around us. Lobsters under rocks, herring, mackerel and many other kinds of fish to buy for pennies when the boats came in. Salmon was not for us, although the rivers bristled with them; they were the property of the Estate and the mainland anglers who could afford the permits. However, that is not to say that we never ate salmon – even a gamekeeper has to sleep sometime.

Running a croft was hard work for the crofter and his wife, and as soon as the children could understand simple instructions they were expected to help. The older children looked after the little ones and allowed the mother to get on with milking and other outside chores – feeding young calves, who had been separated from their mothers, setting the milk in wide basins in the cream shed, skimming off the thick cream from other basins and storing it in crocks for churning, and the many other tasks which running a croft involve. As the children grew, so their workload was increased. If you were big enough to do it, you did it.

This system meant that I came close to death or at least brain damage in early infancy. I was left in a cradle under the supervision of two brothers aged four and three while my mother milked the cows. She was in a byre just behind the house and nearly jumped out of her skin when they rushed in shouting, 'He killed the girl!' 'No, it was him. He killed the girl!' The milk pail went flying and my mother ran into the house to find the cradle up-ended, with its rockers in the air. Fortunately, she had used a harness to strap me in, and there I was dangling upside down, about six inches above the stone floor.

Apparently the boys had been having a rocking competition which had gone wrong. My mother was deeply shocked and asked one of the neighbours how she coped with her brood of toddlers and the outside work. 'I have no trouble,' said the woman. 'I get a piece of rope and tie them all to the bench.' Today's social services would not approve. However, the family in question grew up tall and strong and pillars of the community with no need for counselling.

The island, even then, was no longer an island on its own, as it had been in the early '30s, when my mother was nearly drowned crossing the South Ford, which separated South Uist from its nearest neighbour, the then island of Benbecula. Fed by the Atlantic on one side and the Minch on the other, currents and tides in that sandy stretch were treacherous, and the crossing at low tide was achieved by means of what in those days was called a 'machine'. This was a special horse-drawn carriage used for carrying people and post across from one island to another. The coachman had a mature and experienced horse between one pair of shafts and was breaking in a young horse on the other side. It was a dark evening with a rising wind and he was anxious to complete the journey quickly, as it was dangerously close to the time when one of the channels he had to cross would fill with rushing water and become a death-trap. The horses were good swimmers, and in normal circumstances the high wheels of the machine would still have sufficient purchase on the sand to ensure a safe crossing.

Whether the young horse sensed the imminent danger or not we shall never know, but from the start of the journey the machine was difficult to control, and with the wind rising and the tide coming in, it was a frightening situation. The coachman saw that it was too late to turn back. Behind him the tide had turned, so on he went. As the water got deeper, the old horse showed no fear and simply launched itself smoothly into a swimming motion. The young horse, however, went completely crazy and tried to climb into the machine. The passengers faced certain death as the water got deeper and the rising wind carried their cries for help out to the Atlantic. On the Benbecula side one of the MacAulays from Creagorry Hotel was tying up a gate which had broken loose in the high wind and he heard what he thought was a play on the wireless coming from inside the hotel. When he went in and saw that the guests were eating and just talking quietly to each other, he realised that the faint sounds of mortal fear came from the South Ford. He quickly organised a rescue party, and it was just in time. The coachman and passengers were lucky: they survived, but the young horse drowned. In his panic he caught his hind legs in the harness and the tide did the rest. The other horse was cut loose and swam to safety. From that day my mother had the greatest fear of water going over her head, and when she washed her hair we could hear her making little whimpering noises.

In 1942 a causeway was built linking the two islands, and twenty-seven years later the completion of the North Ford Causeway joined the island of North Uist to its neighbours. As the Outer Hebrides had been erroneously called 'The Long Island' since the days when the receding Ice Age left the inlets between them still frozen, now at least the Uists and Benbecula fitted that description.

Money, in my young days, came from the sale of cattle and a few Government subsidies. Of course, there was also a workforce in paid employment including those who supplemented their income by gathering seaweed as their ancestors had done. My father and his peers sold it on at a fair rate to a factory, where it was burnt. The fine alkaline ash was then shipped out to manufacturers of such diverse goods as soap, glass, table jelly and orangeade. Their ancestors, MacDonald of Clanranald's crofters, had cut it for nothing as part payment for the lease of their bit of land. They also burned it in bothies and had to collect twenty to thirty tons of kelp to produce one ton of ash. This was sold by Clanranald for around twenty pounds per ton. My father told me about this and said that much of the ash went to France and that the Napoleonic Wars put an end to the trade; so in his day it was only done on a much smaller scale.

The island was a place where you worked hard and brought your family up to do likewise. We all want our children to have a better life than we had, and in this respect my parents were no different to any town dweller; they wanted us all to have the chances they themselves had missed.

For my parent's generation, education had been a hit-or-miss affair. All the schools were run by English-speaking masters who did not even acknowledge the existence of the Gaelic language, despite introducing the brighter children to Latin and Greek. One of our neighbours once saw my brother doing his Latin homework and said, 'I know all about mensa . . . mensae . . . feminine . . . a table.' This man could not read or write a word of Gaelic but knew the Latin declension for 'table'. The children were taught in a tongue which they did not understand, for much of the time. Pupil teachers and a few Gaelic-speaking assistants had the task of teaching little island children a foreign language so that they could understand their lessons. With such a system, coupled with frequent absences when the children had to help with the croft work, only the brightest and most ambitious pupils stood a chance. Despite this situation, many fine scholars emerged to make their mark in various fields. Far from being the idle, witless, drunken lot they were described as being by A.A. MacGregor in his book *The Western Isles*, the islanders have always been tough, resourceful and intelligent. Without their quick wits they would not have survived exploitation through many generations. It's a pity that certain authors did not take

11

the time or trouble to get to know this before rushing into print.

Although they worked hard at it, neither my mother nor my father were natural crofters. She was a good-looking young woman who had left the island to work on the mainland, first as a lady's-maid to a Lady Patten-McDougal in Oban, and then on to Oban Cottage Hospital, where she got bitten by the nursing bug and went on to Hawkhead Asylum in Glasgow to work with the mentally ill. She loved life away from the island and was in the throes of a romance with a young doctor when the summons came to come back home and look after her mother, who had broken her hip. My mother was reluctant to return, but things were desperate at home and her sister Catherine, a teacher, bought her a piano as a sort of consolation gift. She was very musical and used to sing at Mods (Gaelic Festivals) and ceilidhs, and that helped her to cope with her changed life. The romance with the doctor did not survive the parting, and some years later she met a young man called Tormod Ruadh (Red-haired Norman) MacMillan, when they were both singing at a ceilidh in his native Benbecula, and subsequently married him.

As a younger son in a family of boys, my father probably had little knowledge of croft work when he married her. (By tradition the older boys would shoulder most of the work in the knowledge that they were going to inherit their father's land and the land of unmarried or childless uncles.) Tenure of the crofts was handed down from father to son. If the son happened to have ten sisters older than he was, then that was their hard luck. When there were no sons, the land usually went to the first son-in-law in the line of succession.

My maternal grandfather had lost his eldest son in a tragic case of medical misdiagnosis. He was being treated for a stomach ulcer and his appendix, which was the real problem, burst. That same year had seen the worst epidemic of flu the island had ever known. It hit my grandparents hard, as they lost one of their daughters and the baby of the family, a little boy. My grandmother was so ill that her children were dead and buried before she could be told about her loss. The death of the last male heir meant that when my grandfather died, my father, the only son-in-law and an incomer from Benbecula, became a South Uist crofter.

From an early age we children were urged to study hard and get qualifications which would open doors to a better life. By then, education on the island had much improved, and even now, after a lifetime of teaching all over the world, I think that Uist schools were up there with the best.

The idea of 'getting on' and 'doing well' meant passing exams and leaving the island to go to senior school and then on to university. So, sadly, many gifted islanders left, never to return. In my own family, all six of us joined the exodus, leaving my parents with an empty nest for many years. They had always encouraged us to do well and get on, and in so doing lost us to the outside world. Fortunately, the call of the island is strong and one returned to live on the croft, while the rest of us maintained the link and have spent much time on the island over the years.

The first step towards achieving this exile was taken for me at the age of four and a half. My mother and father literally gave me away. They figured that my chances of getting on would be much enhanced if my two maiden aunts (my mother's sisters) brought me up, away from the rough and tumble of croft life in a very small cottage with an ever-increasing population. I was not given a choice. It was presented to me as a privilege and I was told to be very well-behaved so as to be deserving of such good fortune, and I felt very important.

One aunt, Catherine, was headmistress of a school in Benbecula, and the other, Christina, acted as her housekeeper. In their youth they may have been lovers of the bright lights, like my mother, but if so, by the time I joined them the impulses had long gone. They were good women in the full sense of the word. They lived blameless lives and spent a lot of it on their knees saying the rosary. All my educational and material needs were well met. They worried about me and often told me that they must be mad to take on 'someone else's property'; my place in Heaven was constantly sought, but it was a lonely time.

The schoolhouse where my aunts lived in Kyles Flodda was a large house with very high ceilings, and after the cosy crofthouse it was a bit frightening. There was a big spare room which housed all sorts of junk left there by the previous occupant, and I used to play among the boxes. I remember finding a big fox fur with glass eyes, and that was my dog, Scot. I hugged it and talked to it until one day its head fell off, and I gave it a lovely funeral, playing the part of priest, choir and congregation till Auntie Chirsty caught me and told me to stop being blasphemous or the Devil would come and get me. School was the only life I knew, so I played 'schools'. The teacher aunt told me stories of her days at college and read messages that her student friends had written in a little red book. I could picture scenes of great companion-ship: happy girls being taught to be teachers by kindly nuns. So a new game evolved: 'Packing my bag for the Convent.'

The highlight of the week was a trip to the shop. By now the war was well under way and many items were no longer available. On the way to the shop my aunt would tell me about fruit and sweets which were nothing more than a fond memory for her and a complete mystery to me. She described a banana. 'It is a long yellow thing and you open it by pulling a strip down on one side.'

'Ah,' I thought. 'It has a zip.'

'The inside is sweet and creamy,' said she.

'Filled with cake,' thought I.

Big disappointment in the banana department is my abiding memory of peace being declared.

The shop was on Island Flodda, which was a tidal island. Now it too has a little causeway, but then we had to be careful not to take too long over the shopping or we would have to stay overnight with the owners. This happened one night and I really enjoyed staying with the kindly Currie family. After a lovely meal of fried *sgadan ùr* (fresh herring) they settled down to share the local news with auntie and didn't mind if I asked questions, as children do. There was much excitement, as a young man from Roshinish was well on the way to being ordained as a priest, and if he actually finished the course, he would be the first priest to come from Benbecula in living memory. They all knew why this would be such an auspicious occasion, but I didn't, so they told me about the 'Curse of Nunton'.

Nunton, situated at the south end of Culla Bay, between Aird and Griminish, used to be the traditional seat of MacDonald of Clanranald. Gaelic folklore has it that many centuries ago a convent stood there, hence the name Nun-town. Ripples of anti-Papist feeling, following the Reformation, spread as far as the islands, and the convent was destroyed. The nuns suffered deaths too awful to contemplate: some were burned, some buried alive, and the Abbess and her main helpers were staked out at the waters edge to drown by degrees under the incoming tide. With her dying breath the Abbess cursed the island and decreed that no priest would ever come from Benbecula.

According to the Curries the story was true: the nuns had existed; folklore said so. The curse had been effective until that time and now it looked as if it was about to be lifted. It would be nice if I could say that they got their wish. However, some time later, shortly before his ordination, the young man from Roshinish suffered a nervous breakdown and left the seminary. Who knows if the stories about the nuns are fact or fiction, but there was one very nervous child sleeping in a strange bed on Island Flodda that night.

On the way home auntie sat down and rested once we crossed the ford, and I played in the rock pools where *partain* (little crabs) scurried. I thought about being staked out waiting for the tide to engulf me and decided that I would probably have been too frightened to curse anybody.

My parents came to visit now and then, and once they left my brothers with us for a week. It was a time like no other for me. I'm sure my poor aunts never forgot it either. The boys were high-spirited, and as just about everything was forbidden, they spent all their time there finding ways to outwit the minders. We sneaked out and played on the shore and the boys came back with pockets full of *partain*. That night when we were all kneeling down in our nightwear saying the rosary, in the middle of the third Sorrowful Mystery the crabs were released. They headed, as if programmed, towards the aunties' bare feet. I went into fits of hysterical laughter and the aunties leapt around, screeching, while the boys tried to capture the invaders. We had to re-start the rosary several times and each time one of us laughed, auntie intoned, 'The first Sorrowful Mystery, The Agony in the Garden,' again. We had sore knees in the morning and the boys were sent home.

War brought many changes to island life. A military base was established in Balivanich and the school there was requisitioned for use by the personnel. We children hoped that they would ask for our school too, but no luck. There was talk of huge planes called Flying Fortresses frightening the cows, but the tales of enemy U-boats being sunk by the brave young fliers and the awful losses of so many of their own numbers swung island opinion in their favour. Besides which, the NAAFI and other establishments in Balivanich provided employ-ment and excitement for the locals. The 'airmen', as they were known, embraced island life and I believe, although this is only hearsay, that many of the local girls embraced the airmen. Well, there was a war on, so who could blame them. Not I. Many years later I met, married and have had a great life with a handsome young soldier who was serving on the self-same base.

A bartering system between the service personnel and the locals meant that many goods in short supply were exchanged for eggs, chickens, butter, potatoes, cream etc., and that's how I first tasted chocolate. The aunties had contacts and managed to get a packet of Swiss chocolates. I was given one after dinner every night and to this day they are my favourite sweet.

It was the age of expediency, and, as the camp had a well-equipped hospital, the local doctor organised a mass tonsilectomy for all children who had tonsils. Well, that's what it looked like as I lay in a Nissen hut with what seemed like the entire child population of the planet. The noise was horrendous as they all cried for their mammies. I could hardly remember my mammy and I certainly wasn't going to cry for the aunties, but it seemed the right thing to do. So I cried too.

A voice from the next bed said, 'Hey, you! Come and see what I've found.' I stopped crying and followed this older girl into the bathroom at the end of the hut. Neither of us had seen a bathroom with porcelain fittings before ,but we just knew that all was not as it should be. There, in the washbasin, was a large turd. Obviously some parent had not told their child which appliance was which. There was a very stern lecture on disgusting behaviour that night. That incident and being given ice-cream for my sore throat are my only memories of the airmen.

School holidays meant a return to the family. At Gramsdale I was put on *Bus a' Mhuilich* (the Mull Man's Bus), a rickety conveyance, with much wood in the bodywork, which creaked its way from one end of the island to the other, delivering goods and people, very slowly, to various destinations. The journey was long and the talk among the adult passengers was mostly about the war. Much merriment was caused by the news that some crofts close to Balivanich airfield now had red lights on their roofs. The driver's insistence that it was a safety precaution for landing aircraft only gave rise to more ribald speculation, and there was shock at the news that a Benbecula girl had 'gone and married one'. The old men talked longingly of the exciting lives the young airmen led and how brave they were to fly a plane even without 'Jerry' trying to shoot them out of the sky. This sobering thought usually turned the conversation to the news from their own young men who were in various branches of the services, and I lost interest as I counted off the landmarks between me and home. Creagorry, where there were parcels and sacks of mail for the hotel. The 'New Bridge' over the South Ford, unexciting if the tide was in, but spanning sands full of cockle-pickers if it was out. Carnan, where the driver got out for a cup of tea. Then across Loch Bee, where the waters were flung over the bus if the day was stormy and anglers stood waist-high in the loch if the day was fine. Beinn na Coraraidh, where the road took a hairpin bend and plunged downwards with much shrieking from the passengers. Then Askernish and Daliburgh, where I started to look for the smoke from our chimney, till we stopped at Kilpheder crossroads and my brothers got up from the verge where they had been sitting against the post-box waiting for the bus to arrive. As we walked the half mile or so home we caught up on our respective lives. Their stories were always so much more interesting than mine, and at the age of six they taught me to smoke.

Chapter Two

MANY OF THE YOUNG men from the villages were on active service, and sadly many were lost. My father, after a short time with the Lovat Scouts, was given an exemption. The Department of Agriculture provided him with a tractor so that he could help other families who were short of labour on their crofts. He was also a member of the Home Guard. As in the series *Dad's Army*, they were often out on exercise, and our little windows in the crofthouse were faithfully blacked out every night; but thankfully they didn't actually make contact with the enemy. Once or twice my father's paratrooper brothers called in to see us when on leave, looking very handsome in their uniforms, but very tired and strained, and he would seem sad for a long time after they left. I don't know whether he wished that he was going with them, but I think he was anxious for their safety.

The spirit of community was high, and peat-cutting and harvesting of crops were all done on a basis of 'We'll do yours today and you'll come and help with mine tomorrow.' Thus everybody managed to complete their tasks without feeling beholden to anyone. Island sense of pride and dignity prevailed.

Peat-cutting day was very festive. Sometimes my father would do a bit of cutting by himself, but the bulk of the hard, black peat which was burned in the shiny black Enchantress stove which kept us warm, boiled water and provided heat for cooking was cut by a team of friends operating on the terms which I have just mentioned. They would have breakfast and their evening meal at our house, but at mid-day we took food out to them. One or more of the men's wives would come to help my mother prepare a substantial pile of sandwiches, hard-boiled eggs and freshly made scones and pancakes, spread with crowdie and cream over butter from our own churn. This was loaded into the wicker washing basket and we all set off over the heather to the workers. I can still recall the squishing of water between my toes and the prickling of heather on the soles of my bare feet as we played our way out to the bogs.

We could hear the men talking, singing and laughing long before we got there, and this added to the sense of occasion. They'd stop their work and build a fire on the bank to brew tea in a three-legged pot, before sitting round the crisp white sheet which we had spread on the ground and covered with food. Peaty hands were merely wiped on the grass and the food was consumed. Extravagant compliments were paid to my mother for producing such regal fare, and many amusing anecdotes would be exchanged about the morning's work. We children admired the large slabs of peat and found new games to play, well away from the deep watery trench of the bog. After they finished eating, the 'table' was cleared and everything wrapped in the cloth and put back in the basket. The menfolk smoked a cigarette or a pipe and got back to their work, and the children got rides home in the basket.

Some time later, once the black slabs of peat had dried on one side, we children were called into service. Each slab had to be carefully turned, so that the other side could harden. Then came the gathering into table-like piles of three, with two slabs leaning towards each other and one placed on top, to let the wind blow through and complete the drying process. This was known as *togail na mònadh* (lifting the peat), then came *cruinneachadh* (gathering) into small cone-shaped piles, still out on the bog, ready for the great day when it was brought home and stacked. You had to choose the right kind of weather for making your peat stack. If any rain got into the centre of your stack, it could soon spread throughout the whole structure and make the peat damp and difficult to light. You chose large slabs of peat for the base and tried to grade it according to size as the stack grew. Building a peatstack was an art in itself, and the better the brick-like construction of the outside, the better your peat would be protected from the elements and the brighter your fire would burn through the dark Hebridean winter.

Each crofter had a piece of land on the machair, sandy fertile soil where they grew grain crops and Kerr's Pink potatoes to die for. Nowadays, when I find some really outstanding potatoes I think of the machair crop. The sandy soil of the machair was fertilised by the seaweed, which lay along the shoreline in plentiful abundance. This was a messy, smelly job, but all it cost the crofter was his labour. At one time the powers-that-be came up with the idea of paying the islanders a subsidy for using guano and other fertilisers instead of the traditional seaweed, and this seemed to give good results, until the machair started to blow away in the wind. The kelp had bound the sandy soil particles together in a way that man's invention simply did not. A subsidy was then paid to the crofters to collect seaweed and spread it on their land. So they ended up being paid for a task which, for centuries, they had performed for nothing.

The corn and rye were cut by hand with a scythe, a task for men only. The children helped to tie the sheaves and prop them up into stooks which were gathered together to form small stacks. Then the stacks were brought home, either by horse and cart or by tractor, and made into *cruachan* (big stacks) in the stackyard. Many years into the future, my own little boys and their father helped with the machair harvest whilst home on holiday, and I heard them telling their friends what a great time they'd had. A lobster boat had come in while they were playing in the dunes and they had been given a sack of crab claws to roast over an open fire which my husband lit for them, and then they rode home on the tractor. They're men now and their grandfather and the lobster fisherman are long gone; but that day still lives in their memories.

Hay in the fields round the croft was given similar treatment to the corn, only it was a much more delicate operation and the weather played a vital role. After it was cut into long swathes and the rough shaws taken out, you prayed for fine weather. If it rained before it was dried, turned, dried, shaken and dried again, it would rot in the stack. It was a busy time and for me a golden time. I was back with my family and my father made me a small fork so that I could shake hay with the rest of them.

The hay was also destined for the stackyard, where it was made into a large loaf-shaped thing called a *dais*. While this was being built, we were hoisted up into the stack to stamp the hay down so that the finished product was compact enough to prevent pockets of gas being generated. This could make the hay hot and unsuitable for feed. Cows could be very ill if they ate it. This was my father's explanation for the procedure. I have no idea whether it is true or not, but the stamping was fun.

When the stackyard was full there was a great feeling of security, much the same as I still get now before visitors are due and I know that all their meals are planned and the shopping done. No matter what the coming winter could throw at us, the cows, sheep and horses would eat, and therefore so would the family. We children treated the giant stacks as an adventure playground. Great games were invented, and as long as we did no climbing or in any way interfered with the lofty structures, we could play our own version of 'pirates' and 'hide-and-seek' to our hearts' content.

Another annual event was the blanket wash. The canal, a wide channel of water which ran from Strome to Kilpheder machair and was regularly cleaned, provided the softest water you could wish for, and this was the venue. Usually two or three wives got together and with their children carried a zinc bath containing the family's supply of soft white Highland blankets down to the canal. A fire was made and canal water heated in the bath. Soap flakes were added to the water as it reached the required temperature and the bath was removed from the fire. Then, one by one, the blankets were put in the bath and relays of willing children lifted in to dance the dirt out. The process was repeated with clean soapy water, and then three rinses of warm clear water.

The women spent most of the time talking and filling and emptying and wringing and folding, but we just danced all day. The clean, fluffy blankets were then spread out on the rocks to dry, and once again we prayed for good weather. It is so much easier to wash your duvet cover in your washer/drier, but communal blanket washing by the canal was such a grand social occasion.

Speaking of social occasions, have you ever heard of the 'Polly'? If you've seen the film *Whisky Galore* or read the book, you can be forgiven for thinking that the people of Uist had little to do with the contents of the *Politician*. Well, think again. A whole lot of whisky and other goods found its way to Uist and Eriskay. Unfortunately, the Customs man lived in Lochboisdale, so the South Uist people had a great deal of his attention. The writer Sir Compton Mackenzie lived on Barra at the time and wrote a novel about a wrecked ship called *The Cabinet Minister* which was the subject of the film, shot on the beautiful island of Barra. There were some who would say that it was a bit unfair: the Barra people were not troubled by the attention of the Customs man, as he had his hands full in Uist, and they also got the film.

The 'Polly', for the uninitiated, was the good ship SS *Politician*, which sailed out of Mersey harbour on February 3rd, 1941 bound for Jamaica and the USA. Her cargo ranged from whisky to bicycles. There was also a large amount of Jamaican money on board, but it was of little value to the islanders by comparison with the 264,000 bottles of the finest whisky, distilled in the country which gave whisky to the world. Instead of sailing round Barra Head, the 'Polly' ran aground in the Sound of Eriskay, far west of her plotted course. Many theories exist as to why this happened, and the one which makes most sense to me is that the whisky knew where it would be most appreciated.

The money: what was it for and where did it go? A

question which has been asked many times. Naturally, the purpose of shipping vast amounts of money out of the country at such a time generated many rumours on the island. Some even said that King George was feathering his nest abroad in case we lost the war. Much of it was recovered legitimately and returned to the Treasury, and as for the islanders, they were much more interested in the cases of whisky, and any notes they found were given to their children, who used them to play 'shops'. Rumour, of course, tells a different story, and sudden unexplained affluence in an island family's lifestyle can still provoke whispers of 'Polly money'.

My father and his friends sailed out to the wreck many times, favouring the darkest nights, as the Customs and Excise man on the island was anxious that the ship with all its cargo would remain intact until it could be salvaged. When this proved impossible they towed it to Lochboisdale and blew it up. A wicked waste. Well, that was how the islanders saw it, as they congratulated themselves on having rescued as much of the cargo as possible. The 'rescuers' came from near and far in their little boats, and, working side by side on the oily decks of a heaving ship lit only by Tilley lamps and candles, they 'liberated' as much of the cargo as their little boats could carry. Sometimes they got a bit too ambitious and piled the boat so high that they had to throw some of their spoils overboard to make room for the crew. But, as my father said, 'We knew that there was plenty more there for the taking.' Plenty there was: his average night's share was 120 bottles of whisky, the odd bolt of fine cloth, shirts, and enough bicycle parts to service the Tour de France. When the Customs men stopped their searching and it was safe, he managed to make at least two good bikes out of the bits.

The raids were fraught with danger, as the most precious cargo was submerged in a hold full of oily sea water and had to be speared from above. As the wreck heaved around with the swell and the deck was covered in oil, one slip could be one too many, so one night my father thought that his time had come when he overbalanced and fell into the the hold. He was up to his shoulders in water and his legs were firmly jammed inside a bolt of cloth, too far down in the sloping hold for the men on deck to reach him with spears or rope. The boats carried only the minimum of equipment, as space was precious and the rope had only to be long enough for looping around a speared case and hoisting it on to the deck. As he struggled to save himself, my father heard someone say, '*Chaill sinn Tormod bochd!*' ('We've lost poor Norman'), and the nearest I can come to translating his response is 'Not bloody likely!' Somehow he found finger-holds, and, using the strength of his shoulders, clawed his way to safety with the unfurling cloth still wrapped around his legs. When he made it to the deck, the entire raiding party were on their knees praying, the Protestants reciting a psalm and the Catholics chanting the prayer for the dying, '*Dia nochd, athair nam bochd . . .*' ('Lord, father of the poor, be here tonight . . .'). 'When they saw me appear,' he told us, 'they got off their knees and got on with their thieving.' It's a wonder that none of the islanders came to grief on their expeditions, because, apart from anything else, no more than a handful of them could swim.

As the years have gone by, interest in the 'Polly' has dimmed, but it takes little to rekindle it and I'm sure that the latest book, Roger Hutchinson's *Polly* (1990), won't be the last one we'll see. Throughout his life, my father regaled Francis Collinson of the School of Scottish

Studies and Fred Macaulay of the BBC, and many other broadcasters and authors, with anecdotes of the period. To this day one room in the family bungalow, in Kilpheder, is called No. 5. That was the hold full of oily water in which the whisky was found buried beneath a jumble of assorted cargo – in other words, a mess.

I was a very small child when it all happened but was aware that something rather special was going on. One minute it was all sighs and people talking in hushed tones about the war. We had one of the few radios in the village and always had people in, 'listening to the wireless'. We children had to be very quiet, except when the traitorous William Joyce, the Irish-American hanged for treason in 1946, whom we knew as 'Lord Haw-Haw', spoke in praise of Fascism and called for British surrender: then we were encouraged to see who could produce a good fart.

Suddenly the visitors were all happy and full of suppressed excitement. My father was always getting ready to go somewhere secret at night. If any English-speaking stranger came to the door, we were coached to say, in English, 'My father is out on the hill herding sheep and my mother is not in.' Fortunately, our skills as decoys were never put to the test, as we often got it wrong in rehearsal and said 'My father is on the hill looking for ships.' Our closest shave came one day when I was playing outside and I saw the Customs man approaching on his bike. I called out the usual warning and my mother snatched me indoors, saying, 'For the love of God, girl, your pinny is made from "Polly" cloth.'

Whisky was always around at that time and my younger brother was delivered by a midwife so drunk that my father had to cut the cord. Funnily enough, I can't remember anyone getting nasty or any brawls resulting from the sudden deluge of 'the Water of Life', the literal translation of *uisge-beatha*, the Gaelic phrase that gives us the word 'whisky', although I can recall a group of sane but sozzled men digging for the Stone of Destiny in Clach Ghlas, the field opposite our house. All I know is that in the midst of the gloom of war, the entire population of a bleak and remote island always seemed to be excited and happy. But, as I said, I was very young.

We made our own entertainment and didn't feel the days passing. One of the many bicycle wheels to bowl along with a stick kept me happy for hours, I'm told. One day my little brother got into terrible trouble for sitting on a flat rock and smashing something to bits with a stone. At the time I couldn't see what the trouble was about, but I have since discovered that the something was my mother's gold watch. He literally wanted to find the tick. As it happens, his life-long hobby has been tinkering with watches.

Little brother was named Donald, the third boy in the family to bear that name, a phenomenon not uncommon among island families. In those days you always named your children after your parents and other members of the family. Mother and father took it in turns to name the children, and as my mother's father was Angus and her brother Donald, she named her first son Donald Angus. My father's father was Donald John, so he named the second son Donald John. I was named Christina Ann, after my mother's mother and St Ann. I think they felt that I needed someone with an established track record to guide me through life. Then the next son was Donald, after my father's brother. Later, when the twins arrived, my mother named them Mary Flora after her sister and Alick Iain after her brother. She was given the chance to choose both names as she wanted to honour her sister and brother, who had died, aged eighteen and two, in the year of the flu epidemic. As Donald was a popular family name on the island from the days of the Clans, you often found a family with a Dòmhnall Mòr (Big Donald) and a Dòmhnall Beag (Little Donald), a Donald Joseph and a Donald Patrick and so on. The second names were always used, so it was not as confusing as it seems.

Donald was the fourth child, and as I was born between him and the two older boys, they considered him a baby. When the twins joined us they were a self-contained unit from the day they could toddle, talking and playing as one and always watching each other's backs, so young Donald ploughed his own furrow and consequently became a very independent individual. He was always plinking out odd little rhythms on the piano instead of following a recognisable tune, but we were not to know that he was actually composing. Many years and many good tunes later, when his older brother, the late Donald John, wrote the popular Gaelic song *Tioram air Tìr*, it was young Donald who composed the swinging tune which made it a hit. His name did not appear on any credits or record labels due to an unintentional oversight, so now they know, little brother. His favourite playmates were the dog or the current pet lamb (one who had been rejected by its mother and had to be bottle-fed). In our society the animals were there for a purpose and one day at the dinner table he asked, 'Where's Tommy – I've been looking for him all day?' My father replied, 'You're eating him.' Donald is over fifty years of age now and since that day has never eaten lamb.

Home, in my childhood, always meant the periods of time which I spent on the croft, and going back to the aunties at the start of each new term was only made bearable by the thought that there was a school holiday to spend with my family at the end of it. The aunties questioned me avidly about the holiday activities and I tried to satisfy their curiosity, whilst instinctively watching my tongue, in case I told them anything which might show my parents to be less than perfect. Although I got to know Benbecula very well later on in life, my time there with the aunties produced a six-year-old who loved to read the works of Robert Louis Stevenson, but I might as well have lived on the moon for all I can remember of the place and its people. I wasn't miserable – just waiting for the time when I could go home. When a transfer to Barra came through for the teacher auntie, I thought that was it. I'd done my time. I'd been good, well, good – enough – so I'd be going home now, forever.

Chapter Three

HELLO, BARRA! ONCE AGAIN I said a tearful farewell to the croft and its occupants and sailed across the sea with the aunties to their new home. I stayed there until my primary education was completed and I came home at last at the age of ten and a half. The island of Barra is the southernmost of the large islands of the Outer Hebrides. If you see the string of islands as a clawless lobster, as I do, then Barra forms the tail. In the early 1900s it was the herring 'cash and carry' of the West Coast of Scotland and Castlebay was a thriving port. There the fishing vessels brought their catch and sold it to the curers, and girls from all over the Hebrides found work on the gutting, salting and packing crews. By the time I first saw Barra, the herring industry was only a memory, but there was a sense of bustle and optimism about the island that even a child could not miss. The people seemed warm and full of good humour. They are renowned for their excellent singing voices, and I have memories of many a good ceilidh in the church halls.

The schoolhouse, on the borders of Grean and Cleat, was not as isolated as the one at Kyles Flodda. By the door grew a bush which was almost a tree, with the sweetest-smelling white flowers. We have one in our garden now and every time I pass it, especially in the evening when the flowers are at their most fragrant, I'm back in Barra. One day I might find out what it is called. Coming from a virtually treeless island, I was fascinated by it.

I was also captivated by the island itself. To me, just having read The *Coral Island* this was a real island-shaped island, and it seemed so much lighter and more colourful than Uist. The grass appeared to be a brighter green, the sky a lighter blue, and the hills, dotted with sheep, looked smaller and more friendly than the stark majesty of Ben Mòr, with its browns and greys and rocky outcrops.

Perhaps the impression was heightened by the fact that, along with most of the island children, my face had been furnished with my first pair of glasses. I really needed them, unlike most of the children who got them, threw them away and have lived their lives with perfect vision. I don't know if it was a feature of the time, or whether it was an island thing, but it seemed that you had syrup of figs and worm syrup on a Friday, tonsils out when you started school, closely followed by the arrival of glasses, and you got false teeth at the first sign of toothache – it didn't seem to have too much to do with your actual physical condition. At least I managed to hang on to my teeth.

Although Barra covers a large area, the centre of the island is rugged and mountainous, so most of the island's core is unpopulated. All the main villages are coastal and the *taobh an iar* (west coast), the subject of many songs and poems, is a serene landscape of bays and sand dunes. Unlike Uist, where the main road system comes straight down the middle of the island, Barra is encircled by its thirteen or so miles of road. With or without spectacles, it is a lovely island, and much though I love Uist, it has a harshness to the landscape which is probably due to the fact that it is long and narrow and has so much water and volcanic rock in its formation.

Housekeeping auntie and I went shopping to Alasdale and we found distant cousins living there, whom we visited now and then. Their daughter was at our school and the same age as me. She was much taller than I was and fair-haired and very pretty. As if this wasn't enough, she had a kilt. At this stage in my life I discovered envy. Despite all this, we became good friends – only during school hours, of course. The landscape might have changed, but the aunties hadn't. They took me to church at Craigstone, and if my memory serves me right there were more relatives there, so more cups of tea after church. Then there was the biggest treat of all: a trip on the bus which went round the island, when auntie had to go to the bank at Castlebay.

Castlebay was unlike any place I had seen before. There was a real castle out in the bay, Kissimul Castle, the seat of the MacNeils of Barra, and it looked as if it had seen better days. Over the years I have learned that the island and the castle had been lost to the clan for some time and that when Robert MacNeil bought it back in 1937 it was in very poor condition indeed. Not only was the structure itself crumbling, but bits of the castle had mysteriously disappeared, and the original gate was found under a peatstack in Sponish on the island of North Uist. Robert, however, was an architect and a very determined man, and he lived to see his castle restored and lived in. It is now a place of interest and attracts visitors from all over the world, especially members of the clan. Its condition did not trouble me too much: I had never seen a castle before and in my eyes it was Camelot.

The beautiful church, Our Lady Star of the Sea, was up on the hill overlooking the commercial centre of Castlebay, with its few shops and pier offices on the road named 'The Street'. I was impressed. We used to walk past a large, stone-built house, perched above the others, on a flower-filled, rocky site. It was called Craigard Guesthouse. I vowed that, one day, I would live in a house with that name, without the Guesthouse bit. Well, having had many homes in many countries, I now have one called Dùnàrd (High Mound). 'Craig' is derived from the Gaelic word for rock and we don't have one in sight, but we are on top of a hill, so it was the closest I could get. After more than fifty years, I'm nearly there.

The bus wound its way round the other side of the island on the way home, past Northbay, which we also visited from time to time. The people on the bus laughed and chatted, and the Barra accent, slightly different to the Uist way of talking, was much in evidence. It was a cheerful, sociable kind of bus. This was the bus which I caught on the day that I ran away.

One of our relatives in Benbecula was getting married. He had seen me once or twice when he visited the aunties at Kyles Flodda, and when their wedding invitation arrived in the post there was a separate card made out just for me. Although the regime in the aunties' household was as strict as ever, I was beginning to develop a mind of my own and occasionally stood up to them.

The strap (the teacher auntie's tawse) was always brought in after school to keep me in line. Don't get me wrong: I wasn't a battered child or anything like that, and I have no hang-ups whatever about the quite considerable amount of corporal punishment I received during my school life. No doubt I deserved all of it and more. All I have to say on the subject is that it was great fun earning it! They say that the abused becomes the abuser. Well, neither during my long teaching career nor while bringing up three children have I gone down that particular road.

The aunties, as I have said, were good women, but I was not their natural child. They were fond of me, and I was a headstrong brat. They proved their devotion to our family in many ways over the years, but never demonstrated any affection openly. To say that they were prudish would be an understatement. Kissing or cuddling or anything of that ilk was just foreign to their nature. It was a cold environment.

I really wanted to go to that wedding. It would mean a chance to see the family again, and I had never been to a wedding and I had my own special, personal invitation. I really, really wanted to go. The aunties, however, had other ideas. It was winter and the crossing between Castlebay and Lochboisdale would be rough. Anyway, the school term was in full swing and only one auntie was free to go. This was not strictly true, as there were a number of perfectly capable relief teachers who could have stepped in for the couple of days. However, they had decided and that was that. With hindsight I can see that their reasons were perfectly valid, but, as I've already said, I was a headstrong brat. I waited until they were both outside doing something, then used the tin-opener on my money box, put my best dress into a bag, took my invitation and hot-footed it down the hill to catch the bus to Castlebay.

Once I got there it was simple. I got on the *Lochearn*, bought my ticket and waited for the boat to chug its way to Lochboisdale. I threw up several times, standing at the rail, clutching my bag in one hand and one of the horizontal bars in the other. I was only nine years old and pretty short for my age, so I had to stand on tiptoe when it was time to 'Call Hughie'. The boat was very busy, with several children on board, and nobody seemed to notice that I was travelling alone.

Inexperienced traveller though I was, I knew that a journey on the *Lochearn* was, for me at least, the worst possible means of getting from A to B in the history of travel. I got to know the dreadful tub even better as I grew older and frequently used it to get to school on the mainland, so I know that my initial diagnosis was spot-on.

I wandered about a bit, as it was very cold at the rails and people kept being sick on my shoes. One room I went into was called the Smoke Room and the other the Third Class Lounge. They were equally uninviting. The Lounge, known as the Steerage, was down below deck, in the bowels of the ship, and believe me, the smell down there left you in no doubt about being in the bowels. If you were a drunken sailor coming home from deep sea or a hardy drover on your way to a cattle sale, or had simply lost the will to live, this was the place for you. Added to the other smells was an overpowering odour of frying fish from a dining saloon which I never had any urge to locate.

The Steerage was quite well furnished, with padded couches round the walls and heavy tables bolted to the floor. As I prayed for death many times during my seasick school journeys, when surroundings and smells seemed immaterial, the same couches offered a comfortable place to suffer.

The Smoke Room was on the main deck and not quite as claustrophobic as the Steerage. It was a smaller room but had wide windows looking out on to the deck and was dominated by a large table which ran the length of the room and took up most of the floor space. There were leather-covered benches against three of the walls and a leather-seated, wooden-armed chair at the other end. I remember this chair because it used to clatter around the room when the crossing got really rough. The smell in there was different. It was a heavy, smoky smell, overlaid with the whiff of beer, as people bought drinks from the bar and drank them in there, and again there was the smell of fish frying in old oil.

On later journeys I found a Non-Smoking Lounge. This was a little bit more inviting, but always full of braying tourists, smoking, with their feet up on chairs to keep the riff-raff out. I can't remember ever using that room.

The journey from Castlebay to Lochboisdale took about three hours on the evening of my escapade, and when I wasn't being sick or poking around various rooms, I had time to wonder about the wisdom of my actions. The initial rush of defiant excitement had worn off and I had much to worry about. I knew that there was a bus service for boat passengers and I could use it to get from Lochboisdale to Kilpheder, even though I had only a few pennies left. The bus driver wouldn't leave me stranded, on the pier, in the dark, just because I had no money – or would he? And what of my reception at home? I had no doubt that my mother would throw the book and other objects at me when I turned up, having disgraced her with the aunties. I felt that I had been a bit rash, and I had a sinking feeling which had nothing to do with being at sea. Something to do with being nine years old and belonging to nobody.

As the boat came round Gob na Beinne and the twinkling lights of Lochboisdale came into view, I stood on the deck wishing that I was safe in bed, in Barra. Ben Kenneth gave us shelter and the wind was not as cold as before. Deckhands busied themselves with mops and buckets, and families gathered on the deck with their suitcases, peering into the dark for signs of relatives meeting the boat. I didn't bother. Nobody was expecting me.

The voice of the purser came over the Tannoy: 'Will passengers who are disembarking at Lochboisdale and have not yet purchased a ticket please make their way to the purser's office?' A clanging of bells, a whistle or two, and we were there. Soon the boat was tied up and the gangway was put in place. I felt a bit wobbly in the knees as I gave up my ticket, and clinging to the side of the gangway, clutching my bag, staggered down the steep incline, straight into my father.

He gave me a great big hug and it felt so warm. All recriminations were left until later. He just laughed and said, 'You're a wee devil, you know! Your mother and these two old relics in Barra have been wearing out the telephone wires since this afternoon. Thank God you're safe! They'll never make a *cailleach-dhubh* (nun) out of you,' and he laughed again.

My father never really got on with the aunties. He tried very hard, because he was a nice person, but they always viewed him as an interloper who had come from Benbecula and had gained possession of our croft by foul means. I think he was a little in awe of them to begin with and would agree with my mother and them for peace-keeping purposes. However, he told me, later on in life, that he had never been happy about my being farmed off to the aunties at an early age. 'They cooked it up between themselves,' he said, and I believed him. We were very alike, my father and I, and although we had many rows in our day, we loved each other dearly and none of them really counted for much.

When I arrived home I didn't get too big a lecture after all. There was much tutting and shaking of heads from the parents but my father still had a twinkle in his eye. The other children thought I was a bit of a heroine and it was just so good to be home. There were eight of us in the little house now, including my parents, with toddler twins completing the numbers, and the place was fairly bursting at the seams.

I went to the wedding, although I was left in no doubt that I was not being rewarded for my irresponsible actions. My mother painted a very vivid word-picture of the awful things which could have happened to me, and I took it all to heart. My father said, 'If you ever do it again, I'll meet you at Lochboisdale and throw you off the end of the pier.' I didn't believe him. Anyway my mother was going to the wedding, and my father said that I could go and keep an eye on her, in case she ran away to Barra. He couldn't go, as one of the cows was sick and the boys were at an age when they wouldn't be seen dead at a wedding. Young though I was, I realised that my father was looking after a sick cow and five children in addition to his usual chores so that my mother and I could go to a wedding, and that didn't seem fair. But, after all, it was none of my business, as I didn't live there. The boys asked me to be sure to tell them if I saw any good fights, and I, never having been to an island wedding before, wondered what they could mean by that.

The wedding was the traditional three-day event of the times. The wedding eve was *Latha nan Cearc* (The Day of the Chickens). Then there was the wedding day itself. The marriage ceremony usually took place about three o'clock. My father always said that it had something to do with the timing of the Crucifixion. In truth it gave the catering helpers time to ensure that everything was ready for the evening celebrations. On the following day there was the 'house wedding'. That's the direct translation from Gaelic (*banais-taighe*), and as it took place in a house, it will do.

Wedding arrangements up there were fraught with social minefields. First of all, you had to invite all relatives, no matter how far-flung. Everyone in your village was invited, as well as everyone in the world who had ever invited you to their wedding. The invitations were for the whole family, and as both sets of parents issued them separately, the list was immense. Fortunately, croft work and baby-minding meant that many families attended in relays, and this eased the crowd-control situation a little.

Catering was a miracle. Basically, the guests supplied most of the food. Although the invitation did not read 'Bring a bottle' or anything so crass, it could have said, 'Bring a chicken or sheep, and sugar, tea, bread, butter, and a present or money.' So, having a large guest list was not half as daunting as you might think. Your guests turned up on the previous day bearing a good share of the catering requirements between them. When I got married on the island, my English mother-in-law to be thought that all the packets of tea and bags of sugar being passed over were to start off our store cupboard. She just couldn't figure out how we were going to keep all the chickens fresh.

Everything to do with the organisation of the wedding reception had its own protocol. Some special people were invited to fulfil a specific function, and it was considered an honour. So, if you had been a waitress, cook, barman or MC at someone's wedding, you left them off your list of helpers at your peril.

Latha nan Cearc was the day when teams of helpers prepared and cooked the chickens. Sheep would have been slaughtered and prepared for roasting. Domestic refrigerators were a thing of the future, so everything had to be cooked as close to serving time as possible.

This particular wedding was being held at Torlum school in Benbecula, and my mother and I stayed for two days at the home of one of my mother's friends in the neighbourhood. As we took our chickens and other goodies to the bride's house, the two old friends giggled like schoolgirls over anecdotes from their carefree days in the living world before they became crofters' wives, or that's what it sounded like. As I listened, that's when I first saw my mother as a person who once had another life. One she now missed.

The scene at the bride's house was one of intense activity. Chickens were being plucked beside a vast mountain of feathers and all the outhouses were being used as temporary kitchens. I remember thinking that the feathers would probably be handy for stuffing pillows or something, and the smell of lamb roasting and chickens boiling made my mouth water. Among the feverish activity, men walked around offering tots of whisky to the workers, and judging by the merriment, they'd already had a few sips. Barrels of beer and cases of whisky had been laid in for the occasion, and when we handed over our bags we were given a chance to toast the forthcoming marriage. You were given a glass (no age discrimination – I was treated the same as my companions). You toasted the bride and groom-to-be, *Slàinte Bean 's*

Fear na Bainnse (Good health to the bride and groom), and, having taken a sip, returned the glass. You were then told to 'have another', meaning another sip, and only the least discerning of the womenfolk would accept, as this could cause 'talk'. We islanders lived in constant terror of causing 'talk'.

A sip from a communal glass was the usual way of serving spirits even among the menfolk. Most households only had one whisky glass, or tot, as they were called. Beer was drunk in the normal fashion, by men only, but although the island had its share of drunks and there were times when a good binge seemed appropriate, I think that the amount of whisky actually consumed by the ordinary people, on a day-to-day basis, was much less than tales of the islands would have you believe. We waited for our turn to eat a 'high tea', with sandwiches, cakes and scones at a table which was constantly being cleared and re-stocked to feed the never-ending stream of laden visitors.

To be truthful, I enjoyed the first day more than the actual wedding day. The high point was the display of presents. A bedroom had been specially set aside for this purpose and the bride's dress hung there surrounded by piles of tablecloths, bed linen, china and all sorts of new household equipment, including innumerable pots and pans. There was no such thing as wedding lists. Even to give a hint that you expected presents would be considered the height of vulgarity, so you kept what you needed, and I suspect unwanted and duplicated presents were often recycled and used as gifts for other weddings.

We went back to the friend's house and the grown-ups decided that, in the morning, we would not attend the marriage service at Griminish church, which was a fair distance away, as we had no transport. It would be too much walking for me, they said. I think I was being used as an excuse to get out of listening to a long sermon on the joys of procreation, as both my companions had had enough of that.

The wedding itself was a bit of a disappointment. The school was so packed with people that a person as small as I was had a good view of flannel covered knees for most of the evening. There was a lot of noise, with people shouting, trying to make themselves heard above the bagpipes, playing for some brave souls who tried to dance in the spaces left by the crowd. When the time came for the wedding reel to be performed by the bridal party, my mother lifted me on to a chair, so that I could see the amazing spectacle of the bride being whirled off her feet, first by the groom, then by the best man and finally, it seemed to me, by any man in the room. It started off as a Scots Reel but was not recognisable for long.

The food was being served in another building, and as we went across there we met the bride and groom coming over to join the main party. He had a puffy eye and she had blood on her nice white dress. Apparently some old boyfriend had decided to mark the bridegroom's card and, in giving him a thump, had caught the bride on the nose and made it bleed.

Of course, fights were always a feature of a good wedding in those days. I think it was taken to mean that you had provided enough whisky; but they didn't, as a rule, involve the bride and groom. We took our leave shortly after that, as my mother and her friend agreed that things could only get worse.

We were not involved in the 'house wedding', as that was usually a smaller function for the helpers, who, having been kept so busy on the previous two days, richly deserved their own special party. As honeymoons were not an island thing, the bride and groom would serve the helpers on this occasion, and would have to endure many ribald comments and innuendo relating to their new sleeping arrangements.

So that is how Highland weddings are often reported, as mine was, years later, in the *Daily Express*, as lasting for three days. I did not have to wear my wedding dress and sit there smiling for that length of time. One thing had not changed, however. There was a fight, but honeymoons had by then reached the islands, and the groom and I were on our way to Norway, so I didn't get blood on my dress. Now things are different. Some young couples have followed the trend of dispensing with all formalities and living together. Others go to the mainland and get married there. For people who wish to have an island wedding the local hotels and restuarants do the catering and there's no such thing as *Latha nan Cearc*. I'm so glad that I was there, so early in my life, to see it done in the old way.

Chapter Four

HAVING GIVEN ALL AND sundry assurances that I would be a model child for the rest of my time with them, I went back to Barra and the aunties. I think they were feeling a bit guilty about their lack of supervision which had made my escape possible in the first place, and therefore they didn't say too much about it. I was sent back on the boat, like a parcel, in the care of the purser, and I had to sit where he could see me for the entire trip.

I passed the time by listening to some tourists talking about the history of Barra and how that great philanthropist, Gordon of Cluny, had bought it from Roderick MacNeil, the clan Chieftain, who had got himself into debt. After he bought it the poor man couldn't work out what to do with it. Colonel Gordon's solution was to offer the beautiful island, home to every species of bird and plant found on all the different islands of the Hebrides, not to mention an indigenous human population, to the Government for use as a penal colony. That man was all heart. I didn't know the exact meaning of the term 'penal', but knew that it was something to do with prisons, and I was glad to hear that the offer had been turned down. That was before I found out about 'Colonel Gordon Nurtures his Purchased People' . . . Part 2, The Highland Clearances.' One of the tourists bought me a glass of lemonade from the bar and was very surprised when I thanked her in English. They probably knew that I was eavesdropping, as they moved away from me.

Nothing of much importance happened during my last stretch at the schoolhouse, apart from a fringe involvement as an extra on the film *Whisky Galore*, together with bus-loads of other Barra children. I have always believed that I was in the film, but a few years ago I tried several times, unsuccessfully, to see myself in the old black-and-white movie, in order to show my children; but I think that what I remember as filming may only have been an audition, or perhaps my elbow makes a guest appearance.

As I had never even seen a film at that stage in my life, I had no particular interest in the stars who converged on the island and had only seen Compton Mackenzie, an imposing bearded figure, a few times from a distance. I knew that he was an important mainlander who loved the islands so much that he bought the Shiant Isles and then an acre of Barra, near Tràigh Mhòr, the long stretch of white sand used as an aircraft runway, where he had built a house in 1935. As all this had happened before I was born my interest was minimal: I had heard of so many people buying and selling what I thought of as our islands. Compton, however, was spoken of as a good man who had done much for the people and had written a funny book about the 'Polly'. Now it was being put on film and he was going to play a character called Captain

Bunce, but we didn't see him on the set.

Joan Greenwood was there, and also Gordon Jackson, and a huge bearded man whom I later identified as James Robertson Justice. The pseudo-Barra accents caused us great amusement and the playground at school next day rang with 'Feenishh offf your composeetions, cheeldren.' The ladies all wore enormous amounts of make-up and so, to my amusement, did the men, while the whole filming business was not half as interesting as a trip to the visiting dentist who came to Barra every six months or so.

Mr Louth, the dentist, must have been quite surprised to find the same two little girls in his chair every time he consulted in Northbay. My friend and I had worked out a foolproof way of getting me away from the aunties for the day, by pretending to have toothache. We caught the bus to Northbay and had to present ourselves to the dentist, as an appointment had been made for us. He would pronounce our teeth perfect yet again, and would give us some leaflets and charcoal toothpowder samples. Then we would browse in the Post Office shop, have tea in the tearooms and catch the bus back, munching sweets. Eventually the aunties rumbled us and I was forbidden ever to see that friend out of school hours again.

My devious strategies for spending time with children of my own age were born of desperation. School finished at four o'clock and all the other children went home to talk about their school day and complain about the teacher. I went home with the teacher. They soon got to know that if they called at the schoolhouse door and asked if I could come out to play, they were told to go home. No child was ever allowed to go in there. Twice a week I collected milk from our neighbour and was allowed ten minutes for the walk there and back, and fifteen minutes playtime with their daughter, my companion in dental deceit. I was timed and sent straight to bed if I was a few minutes late, even if it was only half past six in the evening.

On one occasion, as well as milk, the kind neighbour sent the aunties a sack of potatoes and instructed Maria, his daughter, to help me with carrying it home. As it weighed half a hundredweight our progress across the field which separated their croft from the schoolhouse was slow. We speeded up considerably when we saw that a smooth red-haired shorthorn bull had detached itself from its harem of cows and was coming after us at a lumbering trot. No matter how fast we ran, mind you, we were still carrying the potatoes. It gained on us and we'd just managed to climb over a fence, having finally dropped the bag, when it caught up with us. To our astonishment, he didn't make any attempt to get over the fence and kill us; he just opened the bag with his stumpy little horns and started to eat the potatoes. We left him to it. The aunties were horrified by our story and forgot to send me to bed for being late. But I was grounded for most of my final year there, after I rebelled again and caught pneumonia.

Blackberries were the first soft fruit I had ever seen, and a fair distance from the schoolhouse they grew in magnificent abundance. All the local children used to bring me some and asked me to go with them to pick some for myself. I was not allowed to do this. I don't know the reason. I think it had something to do with the locals seeing me and thinking that I wasn't being properly fed. No fear on that score: I was a very chubby child and my brothers used to call me 'Plum Mac Duff'. However, once again I let bravado overcome caution, and I sneaked out to meet my berry-picking classmates. I figured that the game would be well worth the candle.

It was a great experience to pick handfuls of ripe juicy blackberries for the first time and eat them straight from the *dris* (bush). The others, having done this many times, soon drifted off home, and I was left there wandering around from bush to bush, until I noticed that it was getting dark and I had no idea where home was. I had the beginnings of a cold and I felt pretty miserable when it started to rain. 'I'll just shelter under this bush for a minute,' I thought; but the next thing I knew it was the middle of the night. I had fallen fast asleep. The rain was now a downpour and I was absolutely drenched.

I staggered out of my shelter and saw some torches in the distance. The aunties had grilled all my known associates and two of the fathers were on their way round the moor, for the second time, searching for me. I can't remember much of the next week or two. My foolishness had cost me dear. I had double pneumonia and have had a weak chest all my life for the sake of a few blackberries.

I can only imagine how frantic the aunties must have been. They took turns sitting up with me night after night, and every time I opened my eyes there was a figure in a chair next to the bed saying the rosary or reading a prayer book. I drifted in and out of consciousness, but apart from feeling as though the *Lochearn* was sitting on my chest and having a terrible wracking cough, I wasn't in pain – just very confused. Sometimes, in my delirium, I was back home and a toddler again. It was a Sunday, bathed in sunshine, and we had been to church and had eaten our dinner. My mother said, 'Let's all go down to the shore and take a picnic with us to eat later.' (The 'shore' was the term we used for the beach.) We walked along the wet white sands and I stopped to look at my footprints, tiny indentations with toes. As I compared them to the larger prints left by my two brothers and the long deep impressions left by my parents' shoes, I dropped behind the others. Just then I noticed a rabbit hopping along the edge of the sands, and I ran after it. It hopped a bit and stopped a bit, always just out of my reach. By this time we were halfway up *Bruthach 'Ic Ceileig* (MacKellaig's Dune), which to my small puffing body seemed like a mountain made of sand. I felt the tufts of prickly grass scratching my knees as the rabbit disappeared down into a burrow. I followed and was intent on doing an 'Alice in Wonderland' when my father, who had been keeping an eye on me, spotted my fast-disappearing red knickers and dragged me out by the feet.

I experienced that entire afternoon as I hovered between life and death, and it was as clear as day in my fevered mind. As was the other hot summer's day, again in my toddler days, when my father was haymaking on the piece of land behind the house and my brothers and I were looking for bees' nests. (There was a small hillock on that part of the croft where the wild bees sometimes gathered to use its little hollows as hives. When the haymaking began they flew away and left combs of tasty heather honey behind.) As we searched, I could see my mother coming down the croft, from the house, towards us. She walked slowly, and as she crossed the wooden bridge over the stream we could see that she was holding something, very gently, in her apron, and that she was crying. In her apron were three little ducklings. They had found a small puddle of tar which my father had dropped when treating some stirks for ringworm, and as it melted and shone in the sun, they mistook it for water and had played in it. Stuck together, but still alive, their frightened little voices sounded so sad. After talking to my father and deciding what to do, my mother took them back home and dabbed them with butter to remove the tar, or at least enough to separate them, and she put them in a rag-lined shoe-box by our big black stove for the night. By morning two of them had died, but the third survived to become a large drake and chase us round the haystacks.

Strange things happen to your mind when you are very ill and I wondered if the episodes had been a dream, as I had no recollection of the events actually happening. However, I checked with my parents, and the description I gave of the two days which I had relived were correct in every detail. They said that I couldn't possibly remember them, as they had happened too early in my life.

Strangest of all was the night when I was approaching crisis point. Tossing and turning, I looked up to check that auntie was still there, just as she crept through the door with a cup in her hand. As she walked towards me, I noticed that her chair was occupied by an old woman who looked straight into my eyes and smiled. She was dressed in black and her head was covered by a fine black wool shawl which crossed over on her chest. The shawl fell open and brushed my cheek as she leaned over and stroked my forehead, and I saw a wedding ring on the middle finger of her hand. The palm felt rough and papery, and the fingers were twisted, but her touch was gentle and cool on my face as I fell asleep.

I thought that someone had come to help auntie with her vigil and did not even mention the old lady to anyone at the time. Years later, after I was married, auntie was visiting us one day and she gave me a little package wrapped in tissue paper. It was my grandmother's ring, and as I saw it I knew that I had seen it before. Auntie told me that in the days when her mother got married only the rich could afford a ring of their own, so the priest kept a ring in the vestry which he used for the ceremony and was the bride's only for the day. When the teacher auntie got her first pay-packet she had bought her mother a wedding ring, but by then Grannie's fingers were so twisted with rheumatism that she could only wear it on the middle finger of her right hand. I couldn't wait to ask about the woman by my bedside. There had been no visitors to my bedroom on that night or any other night. My grandmother, another Christina, whom I could barely remember, had never recovered from her broken hip. She was bedridden when I was born and had died shortly afterwards. Auntie was not at all surprised when I told her what I had seen. She said, 'I felt her there, many a night.' I wore that ring on the middle finger of my right hand until recently and have now passed it on to my little American grand-daughter to pass on to hers one day.

When I was slightly better I got the row, but nothing like my just deserts. The housekeeping auntie still sat with me as I recovered. She told me tales of her young days and I got to know her a little better during my convalescence. Poor auntie hadn't been a very bright child at school, or so she maintained, but I think that was due to her frequent absences when croft work demanded it. She had taken her dead brother's place and had worked by my grandfather's side during harvest time. She had a permanent backache which she put down to the rigours of carrying heavy bundles of kelp and bags of peat before her back was strong enough. In a way, I now understand her attitude to my father, as she had kept the croft going, but as a woman she had no rights of tenure.

When she had tried to work on the mainland the only job offered to her was a place on a herring-gutting crew in Lerwick. I can imagine that it was a pretty grim experience for someone as modest and God-centred as she was. Standing on a freezing cold pier with the other fishwives, whose humour was not renowned for its sanctity, must have been a trial for her. The job itself, taking the guts out of box after box of herring, must have been just about as bad as it gets. As she was one of the shorter girls in the team of three, her job consisted of beheading, slitting and gutting the herring. The tallest girl could reach the bottom of the barrel, so she got the slightly better job of packing. Auntie was not a very fast gutter, but she told me that it was astonishing how fast some of them worked. Some teams could process thousands of barrels per day, while keeping up a non-stop stream of jokes and banter with the fishermen. She had a deep gouge on the knuckle of one of her forefingers where the *cutag*, a short razor-sharp knife used to slit the herring, had missed its mark. At the end of the first season she had come home, and as her sister, Catherine, had been appointed head teacher at Kyles Flodda school, she had joined her as housekeeper.

Auntie Chirsty had a great memory and could recite pages of facts about Nova Scotia, British Columbia, Cape Town and other places remembered from her school books – facts which came back to me as I visited the places which she knew so well, but had never seen. She told me about the Gulf Stream Drift and its warming influence on our island waters, and as for the life of every Saint who had ever breathed, well, she was word-perfect! In her funny squeaky, singing voice, she sang me songs of her own composing, which I'm sure were very deep and meaningful, but her voice was so bad that I couldn't keep my mind on the words; I kept wanting to laugh. In that short period she showed me much love, in her own way.

It was Hallowe'en while I was still an invalid, and the children of Barra were celebrating, knocking on doors and daring people to identify them in their disguises. If they were not given a few sweets or a kindly welcome, they would take their revenge. Crofters could wake up in the morning and think that it was the middle of the night because their windows had been blacked from the outside. Gates could be removed from their posts and swapped with those from other crofts. (I wondered if that was what happened to the gate from Kissimul Castle.) If you were really nasty to the *Gillean Samhna* (Hallowe'en Boys), they would put a *sgrath* (turf) on top of your chimney pot and your morning fire would fill the house with smoke. The schoolhouse was off limits and we never saw *Gillean Samhna* there, but I heard the stories in school. The pneumonia year was different. Teacher auntie invited them all to come and show me their masks and funny clothes. So stunned by this departure from normal procedure were they that they all trooped in and stood by my bedside, in their strange disguises, in total silence. One of them whispered to me, 'We're sorry that you're dying.'

Well, I didn't die. I survived and sat my eleven-plus exam nearly a year early. Despite my extreme youth and absence from school due to illness, I passed, and the remaining few months in Barra were a great deal more pleasant. I think the aunties were so relieved that they had survived their task of seeing me through primary school alive that they were in a permanent daze.

Many years later I went back to Barra as a member of a South Uist Concert Party, and I was amazed by the number of people who came up to tell me that they remembered me from my days there with the aunties. The warm-hearted Barra folk, I will never forget them.

As a farewell treat, before I went back to live with my parents, the aunties decided to take me with them to Glasgow for their annual fortnight's holiday. It was a very exciting experience for me and the aunties did things which they had never done before in their efforts to see that I enjoyed myself. I think they had a good time too.

We stayed with a lady from Skye, whom the aunts had 'found' in the *Oban Times* a few years previously – a Mrs MacKinnon, who asked me to call her Mistress MacKinnon, and that's how I've always thought of her. She lived on Robson Street in Govanhill, on the second floor of a tenement building. The people in the street had children of my age and I played with them in the close and out the back, by the wash-house, a small brick building with an enormous washing tub, a mangle and a thick odour of boiling suds. The children just absorbed me into their little group as soon as I appeared and we wrote a play which we performed for the people of the street. All who wanted to see it paid a penny and leaned out of their kitchen windows at six o'clock to watch. I think it lasted for about fifteen minutes and all I had to do was shout, 'Scene One' etc. as my new friends said, 'Ony mair an' they wulnae unnerstaun' yer Teuchter accent!', 'Teuchter' being the derogatory term used by Lowlanders for Hebrideans. They were being kind, as they didn't want me to be ridiculed. One of them wrote to me for years and invited me to visit her to watch the Coronation on her parents' new television, but my life had moved on even further by then and I had other priorities.

Mistress Mackinnon was always coming up with new things that the aunties should do with me, and so we went to Calderpark Zoo and saw huge primates in tiny cages, and I couldn't sleep that night. They took me to the Glasgow Empire to see 'The Logans', and we laughed at the antics of Ma Logan and her son, Jimmy. The beautiful old theatre with its tiered seats and velvet drapes was a wonderland to me, and later on, in my Glasgow student days, I became a loyal patron, when funds allowed. I introduced my student friends to the voice of Calum Kennedy and the comedy of Andy Stewart, and saw Nigel Patrick in *Dial M for Murder*. All thanks to Mistress MacKinnon.

During that holiday, as we walked in the Botanic Gardens and looked at the exotic plants in the glasshouses, the aunties unveiled their plans for our final outing – a day at the Fun Fair on Glasgow Green. I strongly suspected the hand of Mistress MacKinnon in this, as she had heard the other children describe candy floss to me and had seen their incredulous reaction to the news that I had lived so long and had never even tasted it. She had previously suggested to the aunties that they take me to have my hair permed, and the next day I was hanging from wires in the hairdresser's until I was curly. The day after that, half the little girls in the group had theirs done too. 'Keeping up with the Joneses' was alive and well and living in Robson Street.

So, off to Glasgow Green we went and I had my candy floss. I didn't like it then and I don't like it now. We tried to win a coconut and failed, and I had my fortune told by an old woman with a crystal ball. She said that I would spend a lot of my life in buildings with many windows. Maybe she could smell the chalk dust even then. There was much debate about finding a safe ride for me to go on, and seeing the 'chairoplanes' hanging, harmlessly, just above the ground, waiting for customers, the aunties decided that this was about my level. They couldn't have been more wrong. That was a lethal ride, and as the speed increased and the flimsy swings were whizzing around horizontally, I thought, 'If I survive this I'll never go on a fun fair ride again', and I haven't.

At the end of the holiday the aunties and I took the train to Mallaig and stayed with yet more cousins for the weekend. Mallaig was not very exciting, certainly nothing like Robson Street. I had a girl cousin, a couple of years older than me, but we just didn't have much to say to each other, and she seemed to have a lot of things already planned for the weekend, so I went for walks along the pier with the aunties, smelling the kippery air and dodging the grey and white splots from passing seagulls, waiting for Monday and the boat home.

The journey from Mallaig to Lochboisdale was very, very boring as we watched the islands of Eigg and Rum and Canna fade into the distance behind us and set off across the Minch for the final lap of our journey to Lochboisdale. I don't think I have ever 'sat still' for so long in my life. I wonder if the aunties had any sad thoughts that their years of responsibility for me would end in a couple of hours? In my youthful selfishness I felt only relief. They kept their thoughts to themselves, and as we parted at Lochboisdale, they transferring to the Barra boat, and I, with my father, catching the bus for Kilpheder and home, we shook hands as usual. No hugs.

Chapter Five

Beannaich an taigh 's na bheil ann,
Eadar fiodh is clach is crann;
Mòran bìdh, pailteas aodaich,
Slàinte dhaoine gu robh ann.

Bless this house and all within,
Including wood and stone and beams;
Plenty of food, abundant clothing,
Good health to those who live therein.

M Y BROTHERS HAD LEARNT many verses of the ancient *Duan* (poem) for their part in the Hogmanay celebrations. I just picked it up from listening to them. One thing I had also picked up very quickly since coming back to live full-time in a mixed household was that, on Uist, male and female roles were carved in stone, especially at times of traditional celebration, such as Hogmanay.

That night, when darkness fell, my brothers and all the other schoolboys from the village would visit each house in our township, and standing outside the door, they'd chant a poem blessing the house, before being invited in and given bread, scones and cake, fruit of the land, to put in their clean white sacks. My little sister and I stayed at home and helped to prepare the *fuarag* which was to be shared with the *Gillean Cullaig* (Hogmanay Boys) when they came to us. *Fuarag* was a mixture of fine oatmeal and thick cream, sweetened slightly with honey. We all had a dip as we prepared it and watched my mother wash her wedding ring and drop it into the bowl. Whichever boy found the ring would be the first to marry. Christmas puddings were not part of our culture, but this was a similar thing.

On the island Christmas was not a particularly festive day – just Midnight Mass on Christmas Eve and our socks hung by the stove, to be filled with sweets and odd things that my mother had managed to make for us. War had left the mainland devoid of luxury goods, and the island shops stocked only the basics at the best of times. Sometimes, if she didn't have enough stuff to fill the sock, she'd carve a funny face on a potato and put that in as a joke to fill the gaps. No toys or anything like that. On a treeless island, the custom of having a Christmas Tree is a relatively recent one, and in our little thatched house we barely had room for the simplest of furniture, so perhaps it's just as well. Christmas was the the time when you walked down to St Peter's Church in the dark and heard the choir singing *Tàladh Chrìosda* (The Christ Child's Lullaby) as you knelt by the crib at the church door and saw the baby Jesus at midnight, and that was excitement enough.

This particular year, my first since coming back from Barra, was an exception, however. From a cousin on the mainland a parcel had arrived. My mother had sent her two dozen eggs, and she had returned the egg-box full of gifts, just before Christmas. Sultanas and spices for my mother (in response to a request), comics for the twins, a comb in a blue leather case for me, and a 'blow football' game to be shared by the three older boys. My father's present was a strange one, but more of that later.

During Christmas week we'd all taken turns, in pairs, playing with the football game, and the two older boys were becoming experts. They all agreed that it was a great thing altogether. With the hustle and bustle of a Hogmanay afternoon under way, our little kitchen was a hive of industry. In a big steamer on the Enchantress stove a large dumpling made with the sultanas and spices bubbled away. The *fuarag* had been made and put out in the cream shed to keep cool. Scones and loaves of bread were ready for the *Gillean Cullaig,* and for them my mother had also made a *strùdhan*, a caraway scone sandwiched between two sweet treacle scones . . . very intricate procedure involving much juggling with the griddle and burning of fingers. First-footers would come late in the evening, and for most of the night the table would be laid and cleared and laid again with the New Year fare. A very, very busy time for the women of the crofts.

The boys restlessly awaited the coming of darkness, when they could join their friends and get on with the business of going round the houses, chanting their *Duain*, collecting the goodies and dipping into the *fuaragan* to see who would be first to the altar. Thankfully, the sharing out would be done at another house when the collecting and chanting was finished.

At the sharing house the contents of all the sacks were laid out on a table. One representative of each family took the empty sack to the table and one of the remaining boys was sent outside. The man of the house divided the goods into equal piles, and, pointing to each pile at random, asked the boy outside to name a family. The boy whose family had been named put that pile into his sack, and so on, until each family represented had equal shares. Whatever else we were short of in the New Year, even the ducks had their fair share of home-baked goods. The boys loved the old tradition and we all enjoyed the excitement of hearing the chanting at the door and the laughter over the *fuarag* and the ring. For old people it was a chance to see the young boys of the village and marvel at how they'd grown and squabble about which side of their family they resembled most. It was a very popular custom and the bread was just a useful by-product.

The boys usually went out at about six in the evening and would be home by nine or shortly after. To pass the time, on this particular Hogmanay afternoon, they brought the football game out and started playing it on the large table which stood in the middle of the room. Up and down went the little white ball, propelled by gusty blows through the straws.

By this time my mother was getting fairly 'trachled'. The dumpling was nearly ready and, as anyone who has baked or cooked for a special occasion can testify, a recipe which produces a perfect sponge for a family tea can turn out a leather pancake if you bake it to impress mother-in-law. My busy mother was anxious, but hopeful. The dumpling was to be the crowning glory of the first-footers' table, and it would have to be just right or it would cause 'talk'. (As I have already said, causing 'talk' was greatly to be feared in our community.)

Several times during the afternoon my mother, irritated by the shouts of 'Goal!' and hearing us bickering and begging for turns, had told the lads to 'Put that game away, or go and play it somewhere else!'

'In a minute. I can't move now or it will spoil my aim' and excuses like that was the only effect on the boys. They knew that she was busy and pushed their luck.

The dumpling was beautiful. Large, brown and glisteningly perfect in shape. As my mother unwrapped it from its floured cloth and gently manoeuvred it on to her bigggest china plate, a wedding present from long ago, we could see the sultanas dotted around it and the air was filled with the scent of hot mixed spices. 'Well, that's that done anyway, said she, as she turned carefully round to put the heavy plate on the dresser and stepped on the little white ball.

Six pairs of eyes were transfixed as she stumbled and the plate crashed on to the stove. She managed to grab the table and steady herself as the dumpling shot up over her head and hit the ceiling, before distributing itself among the white sand on the stone floor in small steaming lumps.

Only my mother moved. She got the sweeping brush and a shovel and swept sand and dumpling off the floor and put it in a pail for the chickens. Then she picked up the 'blow football' game and the little white ball, lifted the lid on the Enchantress stove, dropped it in and, in a terrible voice, shouted 'Goal!'

Hogmanay was a time for goodwill, and thinking back I really admire my mother for just carrying on as if nothing had happened. If it had been me, I think the boys might well have found themselves breathing through six feet of earth; well, maybe not: they had lost the game that they loved. They walked on eggshells till the other boys came for them and went to bed very quietly when they came home. I think my mother's lenience stemmed from the feeling that the show had to go on and throwing a few slaps about would only hinder her.

Later, much later, that night, when the Hogmanay bread had been safely stored and when the first-footers were in full tale-telling flow, we children sleeping in the next room were occasionally woken by a shout of 'Goal!' and gales of laughter as the story was retold. The dumpling was still there 'in spirit'.

First-footing, as most mainlanders remember it, before TV made it a spectator sport, was the lump of coal and 'Here's tae us, wha's like us? Gey few and they're aa deid!', on the stroke of midnight. In Uist it was different. Our men didn't carry anything but their whisky bottle and some had problems with that. The greeting was *'Bliadhna Mhath Ùr dhuibh!'* (A Good New Year to you!) and the response *'Mar sin dhuibh fhèin, agus cus dhiubh!'* (The same to you, and many of them!). Again, only the males of the species left the house, while the females got on with the business of seeing that there was plenty of food available.

It wasn't a case of trudging round every part of the village, indiscriminately knocking on doors. Only friends and relatives were visited. You could start as early in the evening as you liked, usually after the schoolboys had had their bit of fun, and, with breaks off for appropriate reasons like Mass and sleep, it could go on for days. It wasn't considered inappropriate to find a relative from Benbecula visiting you with a bottle and wishing you 'Happy New Year' on January 5th. The 6th, being the Epiphany and another Mass day, seemed to be the cut-off date.

Botal na Bliadhn' Ùire (The New Year Bottle) was the special bottle of good whisky which was taken round the houses. There was usually another left at home, so that first-footers who came in my father's absence could be given a dram from the family. The drams given and received were sips from a communal glass, and much of the resulting jollification came from the warm atmosphere generated by good companions in festive mood, funny stories, singing and eating. True, some imbibed more than others and the voices got louder as the night wore on, but by then the sips had become gulps.

We had our regulars, my father's close friends who came to our house and seemed to go no farther, so they were always there at daybreak, hailing the dawn of a new year as the curtains were opened with 'Oh, God, now we've got to go to Mass!' My father made his rounds fairly early in the evening or left it till New Year's Day, preferring to spend Hogmanay at home with the visitors, at least while we were all small children. In those days he was the life and soul of the party. Sadly, much later on in life, after we'd all left home, he got to like the brew too much, and after a few mishaps, he went to the priest and took a vow of temperance. So for many years before his death he was teetotal.

The Mass on New Year's morning was always fairly dramatic and the poor priest tried to keep it short. Some of the men had done the croft work and then stayed up all night making merry, but had managed to stagger to church. The 'holy families' of the parish, as my father called certain members of the congregation, stood out like beacons. Their men were very spruce and looked well rested. Fortunately, they were also the type of people who 'processed' up the aisle to the front seats, genuflected deeply and crossed themselves and said a silent prayer, before gliding into their places. This gave the 'awkward squad' who had not spent the night resting a chance to shuffle into the back seats, trying to make themselves invisible and as comfortable as the hard pews would let them.

Often there was snoring and other noises which people make in their sleep. It was not uncommon to hear 'Move your feet' or 'Get me a cup of tea, Mary' being mumbled loudly, but my own favourite memory is of the year when one old man lit his pipe in the middle of the sermon and proceeded to smoke it until his neighbour woke him up.

After Mass there would be the greeting of friends outside the church and hearing the same thing over and over again: 'Thank God this only happens once a year!' But that was not strictly true. There was Games Night and the biggest binge of them all – Cattle Sale Day. This was the day when crofters took their herds to market, and the sorrow of seeing their beautiful beasts go under the hammer – at a fraction of their worth – to the syndicate of dealers with an island monopoly had to be drowned with some of the proceeds. The outcome was a kind of New Year without the Mass or any other blessing.

For us children, sale day began with the rounding up of the young cattle, which had been fed and watered since their birth with this day in mind. If any of the cows had outlived their usefulness or you needed extra money, they also went. In addition, the mare, Sally, produced a foal now and then, and that was an added bonus in many ways. I'll never forget seeing her foals being born and standing up, so fragile and graceful – miniature horses from the first moment of their lives. It certainly beat living with the aunties, who treated birth and anything connected with it as unmentionable. Recently my son was present at the premature birth of his own first-born and he described his initial reaction thus: 'I wanted to apologise to this little person for not realising that he'd been living inside that bump for eight and a half months.' That's how I felt about the foal.

To get to the sale, the assembled cattle had to be walked up to Kilpheder crossroads and turned south, along the main road to Carisheval. It wasn't an easy task, and for the first part of the trek, or at least until the cattle got the idea of plodding along the road and not wandering off into the heather, it was a case of 'All hands on deck.' We didn't stop to think about the final destination for our lovely animals and we were certainly not encouraged to do so; we just herded them along, occasionally flicking them on the rump with a stick if they looked like exploring. There weren't all that many cars on the island at the time and those who owned them were probably herding their own cattle, so traffic was not a problem.

Our beasts were pretty complacent as a rule, although my husband would beg to differ on that score. When we were first married he offered to help with the cattle drive on sale day, and my father accepted gratefully. Some of the younger stirks were tethered in a field behind the house to stop them wandering back down the croft to their usual grazing ground. As they seemed small and relatively gentle, more likely to be kind to an English soldier, he volunteered to bring one of them up to the road. My father said, 'Well, if you're sure, but whatever you do, don't let go of the rope or the stirk will be at the far end of the croft before you can blink.' I don't know if he had time to blink, but he remembered to hold on to the rope as the strong little stirk, with youth on its side, felt the smell of freedom in its nostrils and ran like the wind round the croft, jumping ditches and trying to get through fences, only slowing down now and again to aim a kick at his captor.

My poor husband, not wishing to let the side down, had lost his footing in the first few minutes and was dragged like a bundle of rags through clumps of wild iris and thistles, cowpats and puddles. Over rocks and rough ground and along barbed wire fences, with the blood pumping in his ears, he couldn't hear my father bellowing, 'For God's sake, man, let go of the rope!' Eventually the stirk ran himself out, and with the honour of the British Army intact (unlike his trousers), my husband was able to drive his exhausted stirk to the sale. The story, related by my father to all and sundry, resulted in their being treated to many drinks from half-bottles, and my husband came back from the sale convinced that he wanted to be a crofter.

In the old days the same hard core of my father's friends would come back home with him, all having had a few drinks. For us children it was quite exciting. The thought of having a bit more money, although less than expected, always lightened my mother's heart, and the visitors would stop off at the shop and buy sweets for us. If we put our money boxes in a place where they could see them, they would put their loose change in there. As we didn't get any regular pocket money, we had to seize the day whenever it came. The older children were allowed to stay up a little later and help my mother with the tea as a special favour, and that is how I heard the story of Hector's teeth.

One of my father's friends, who, on similar occasions, came into the house singing *Gruagach Òg an Fhuilt Bhàin* (The Fair-haired Maiden) and went from song, to joke, to song, when he'd had a drink, was unusually quiet all evening. At the table he ate little, dipping his sandwich in his tea and making slurping noises. We thought he was just being funny, but he was wincing, not smiling. 'What's up, Hector? Not hungry tonight?" asked my mother.

'Well,' said Angus, the other friend, 'I think you'll have to find him a bottle with a teat on it. Hector's teeth are sticking out of a bullock's backside!'

Poor Hector had been walking home from the sale and had accepted a lift from a drover. He sat in the back of the truck with four bullocks. The drover was unfamiliar with the island roads and was driving much too fast. At one dangerous bend he didn't get it right and went into the ditch, overturning the truck twice and coming close to killing himself and his cargo. One of the bullocks was killed outright; the others were dazed but unharmed. The driver himself had cuts and bruises, and Hector was knocked out for a few minutes. When he woke up, his bleeding mouth was full of coarse brown hair and bits of skin, and at the other end of the truck were his four front teeth embedded in the the rump of the dead bullock. Poor man, in addition to his pain he took a lot of teasing about his fondness for rare beef.

Chapter Six

I HAVE NEVER BEEN PARTICULARLY fond of round-shaped events. You know, flower shows, music festivals, ethnic fairs and such-like gatherings, held out in the open. You seem to cover much ground for very little enjoyment. I think my aversion may have something to do with memories of early Games Days, the big happening of the Uist summer, which was another round event.

For days beforehand we prayed that the weather would hold, if we were having a warm spell, or that it would change, if it was being its usual blustery self. Many of the exiled islanders earning their living on the mainland booked their holidays to coincide with this week, making accommodation on the ferries even more cramped than usual, as all the islanders who had married mainlanders and settled in Glasgow had the same idea. Mainland pipers and dancers and strong people and fast people, and people who wanted to watch the same doing what they did so well, all crammed on to the *Lochmor* and *Lochearn* and, later on, its slightly less awful successor the *Loch Ness*, on the last boat day before the Games.

As the pipers took advantage of the time to fine-tune their skills in preparation for the competitions, the journey was enjoyable for the Glasgow Highlanders but must have been a nightmare for English tourists, who are not over-fond of hearing a march, strathspey and reel and two different *Ceòl Mòr* pibrochs being skirled simultaneously. I am sure some of them thought that the crossing was always like this and vowed never to return.

Games morning, in the glow of memory, was always a sunny one. I think the reason for this could be cancellation in cases of bad weather – I don't know, or perhaps we just didn't go if the weather was bad. The venue was Askernish machair and a fair step from our house. We walked westward from Kilpheder, down what we called Rathad na h-Eaglais (The Church Road), to the wooden bridge over the canal and on past St Peter's Church until the gravel road became sandy and we were on Daliburgh machair.

There was quite a good sand road as far as Hallin cemetery, which we skirted after crossing ourselves and saying a silent prayer for dead relatives. My parents always looked sombre at this point and I felt just a little uneasy at the thought of all the dead people lying under the sandy soil, listening to the sigh of the sea close by. Nowadays, when I go there to visit the graves of my father and the aunties, lying closer in death than they ever were in life, I find more of my old friends around me, enclosed by the stout stone walls of Hallin, than in any other part of the island.

As we walked my parents reminisced about friends and family who had died and how the funeral ceremony had changed through the ages. In olden times the whole township closed down to mourn the dead on the day of the funeral and the day after. Not a stroke of unnecessary work would be done and even talk was subdued. This silent time was reserved for praying for the dead and reflecting on human mortality, and was not a result of a drunken debauch, as A.A. Macgregor would have his readers believe.

The remains of the dead were kept above ground for a minimum of three days, during which time *caithris* (night watch) took place. This was the custom of sitting in the same room as the dead person day and night, and praying or keeping watch. It was not like an Irish Wake, which is more a celebration of the person's life. Family and friends, and indeed the people of the township, would volunteer to take their turn, and having done it myself a few times, I can testify that sitting in a room with a corpse at three in the morning makes you very much aware of your own eventual destiny.

In even earlier times the funeral cortège left the house of the bereaved and moved southwards through the township of Kilpheder, then turned westward to Kilpheder machair and proceeded along the shore until they arrived at Hallin cemetery. My father referred to this as '*A' leantail cuairt na grèine*' (following the journey of the sun). The priest would conduct a service at the graveside, but the coffin was not actually taken into the church at all, as it always has been for as long as I can remember. *Cosgais* (refreshments) – the literal translation is 'expenses' – consisting of biscuits and cheese and a small dram were offered to the mourners outside the cemetery wall after the burial, and this dates back to the time when people came from as far away as Eriskay to bury their dead in Hallin. It was a custom born of necessity, as the funeral party would have crossed the Sound of Eriskay to Ludag by boat, and then would have walked for hours, taking it in turns to carry the coffin along the traditional route towards Hallin cemetery.

Beyond the cemetery and one of the best trout-fishing lochs in Uist, we walked on and on, the road becoming more of a track where it was used by crofters to drive their tractors and carts at harvest time. After what at that time seemed to me like three days, we could hear the skirl of the pipes and knew that we were nearly there.

The perimeter of the Games arena was defined by stout poles and rope barriers, and all around the circle were parked an assortment of vehicles: a couple of buses and lorries, some cars, vans and even the odd tractor. There were some large marquee-type tents for the judges and for the committee, and of course teas and beer. Several events were going on at the same time and I didn't have any interest in 'putting the shot', 'tossing the caber' or wrestling. Pibroch to this day leaves me cold, and even the jollier reels and jigs paled after a time.

I kept losing sight of my parents, and after a while, once I got used to the crowds and found some of my friends, that was fine. We wandered around and watched some of our more nimble schoolfriends dancing the Highland Fling and Sword Dance, kilts flying, on the wooden platform, until that got boring. Eventually we made our way past the clusters of men drinking and talking behind the vehicles down to the sand dunes, where we played sliding games and held our own dancing competition. We all knew the steps and agreed that we were as good as any of the competitors.

When we got back to the games the junior sports events were in full swing and they were just announcing the girls' flat race. Well, now, this was our chance to participate, and we all took our shoes and socks off and lined up. After a few false starts we heard the official shout: 'Ready, steady, GO!' and we were off. It was over one hundred yards and fairly early on I realised that I was out in front, as I could not see anyone running beside me, so I carried on running as fast as I could. Just ahead stretched the finishing line, so I thought, 'I'll just look to see where the others are' and slowed down to do this while the rest of the field shot past me. So ended my career as a promising athlete. My brothers, who had been watching in amazement, did not let me live that down for a long, long time.

The tea tent was presided over by Mrs Lindsay, a distant relative of ours, and was always doing good business. Long folding tables and planks of wood stood on trestles inside and a never-ending stream of people were served buttered scones and sandwiches, currant cake and biscuits, and tea poured from huge kettles wielded by perspiring helpers. If the day had turned chilly, as so often happened on the machair, so near the Atlantic, a hot cup of tea and somewhere warm to sit were very welcome indeed. Any of us who went in could depend on the ties of family to ensure that our portions were very generous.

Occasionally some of the younger children, escaping from the restraining clutches of their parents and becoming bored with the entertainment on offer, would get up to mischief, such as sticking pins through the canvas of the tea tent, to the consternation of the *cailleachs* (old ladies) who were seated next to the canvas. Joan, the proprietrix, would run out shouting and brandishing a tea towel, but the culprits would show a clean pair of heels, knowing that she could not desert her post.

As the presentations took place immediately after each event, the successful competitors were free to walk around showing off medals and cups, and in some cases spending prize money in the beer tent. One young piper, Donald Morrison, then a mainland policeman, always took time to seek my parents out and have a bit of banter with them. He loved to hear the satirical verses that my father composed about happenings on the island in his own absence and urged him to do more recording. At that time crofting and seaweed were as much as my father could fit into his life, and ceilidhs which passed the winter evenings were his only platform. To me Donald Morrison was the most gorgeous man I had ever seen. In his full Highland dress, carrying an armful of trophies, his tall blonde figure made me think that if Michael the Archangel ever fell to earth he'd look exactly like Donald Morrison. My adoration took the form of gaping at him open-mouthed while hanging on his every word and still trying to think of some way of catching his attention as he said his usual farewell to my father: 'One day, Norman, we will both be famous and I'll compose a pipe tune in your honour.' Donald went on to win most of the piping contests worldwide, becoming Pipe-Major of the Police Pipe Band, playing for Royalty and even having his picture on beer cans. I think the latter achievement more than any other impressed my father. Until one day a good twenty-five years after the Games of long ago, when he was listening to a piping programme on the radio and the announcer said, 'Now we have Pipe-Major Donald Morrison playing his latest composition, the march, *Norman MacMillan of Kilpheder*.' My Archangel had kept his promise to his old friend.

And so, Games Day would draw to a close, the last event usually being a tug o' war between the North End men and the South End men. As my father came from Benbecula in the far north and my mother from

Kilpheder in the south, I was never sure which side to shout for; but whichever team won, I could not lose.

As we walked home along the machair road, past the cemetery, now looking even more lonely and forlorn, we were often a much larger group, with friends and neighbours from the village all walking together, talking over the events of the day. Again the cemetery evoked talk of the dead and ghost stories. Someone mentioned that an elderly man from Daliburgh was talking of building a house on the machair near the cemetery, and we all agreed that he had more courage than any of us. One of the group joked that Calum would be able to fish Loch Hallin as often as he wished and his neighbours would not be able to report him to the bailiff. Although we all laughed, I can remember shivering at the thought of spending a night near the cemetery walls. The house was built, and the old man lived quite happily there for many years; if he ever saw any ghosts, he didn't tell us. Conversation became more general as we got back to the gravel road, and the length of the Hebridean summer's day being what it is, we arrived home long before dark.

I mentioned Games Night as one of the binge nights, but early in my life it was pretty quiet for our family. After walking the machair road twice in one day and all the activity in between, we were all very tired and knocked out by the fresh sea air. We children would be asleep before our heads touched the pillow. Our parents likewise. They had spent the day meeting old friends, some of whom they had not seen since last Games Day, enjoying the spectacle of the dancing and other activities in a way that we children had yet to learn, and they were pretty tired themselves.

Occasionally a passing reveller would knock at the door offering a dram, and however late the hour, he would be admitted, given a cup of tea and listened to until he could be persuaded to go home. It was not the done thing in Uist ever, ever to let a knock on your door go unanswered.

As we got older we discovered that Games Day did not end with a weary trudge back home on the machair road. There were dances to go to: dances that were considerably enlivened by the presence of all the young pipers, dancers and athletes who had come to the island to compete at the games.

The main venues for the dances were the Gym, in Benbecula, so called because it had originally been used as an RAF gymnasium in the days of 'the airmen', then used as a community hall; and also the Territorial Army drill hall in Daliburgh. There were also dances at some of the schools in other areas, Garrynamonie and Iochdar in particular; and much later, when the North Uist causeway was in place, we would venture as far afield as Carinish and Lochmaddy. But that was still in the future.

The accepted age for such a mature practice as going dancing was fifteen at the earliest. You could go to weddings with your parents and even join in the dancing there, and we used to have end of term parties at school where my eldest brother would play the piano for a bit of Scottish dancing. As for real dances, we were all too young for that for some time. Also in the future, on the day which I have just described, were two Games Nights which will live in my memory forever. They both began with a knock at the door, but there the similarity ends.

The first knock concerns someone coming with news of yet another Donald. He was the young son of our nearest neighbours, a very hard-working young man and not one to get drunk or cause any trouble. Well liked by all who knew him, he had a passion for vehicles and knew his way round any engine. On Games Night he was coming back home in his lorry when the driver of a jeep, whose vehicle had broken down, stopped him and asked for assistance. He was about to tow the vehicle to the nearest layby, off the narrow single-lane road of the time, and was tying the tow-rope under it when tragedy struck. The brake slipped and the jeep rolled on top of him, killing him instantly. It took a long time for many people to get over the horror of that night.

The second event concerns my husband (the English soldier of stirk-catching fame). We were stationed in Benbecula at the time, before taking off for far-flung places, and had come down to the Games with our toddler son. We combined the day with a visit to my parents and stayed the night at Kilpheder. My mother, the little one and I all went to bed fairly early. My father went out to the post-box at Kilpheder crossroads to post a family birthday card which had been forgotten due to Games excitement and preparations for the grandchild's visit. Only my husband was there by the fire, reading the usual day-old paper and finishing a cup of tea before going to bed, when he heard a loud knocking at the door.

Thinking that it was my father pretending to be a Games Night drunk, he opened the door with a suitable greeting at the ready. It was a Games Night drunk, Peter, a very short fellow from the village, who could be relied upon to get plastered on every special occasion, and others in between. He had a sorry tale to tell, and as he made himself comfortable he produced a half-bottle of whisky and proceeded to share it with my husband, whose first thought was, 'If we finish this bottle quickly, he'll go and I can get to bed.' It appeared that Peter and some others had been drinking at Polachar Inn at the far south end of the island. When closing time came they got a lift home in Willie Jordan's car. He lived in Kilpheder and it was all very convenient. However, when they got to the crossroads instead of turning left towards Kilpheder village, Willie had driven into the ditch.

This happened from time to time with Willie, so my husband was not unduly concerned, as Peter seemed to be in fine form. He was concerned, however, when Peter, having finished the first half-bottle, produced a second one from another pocket. Thinking that a hasty dispatching of the contents would also dislodge Peter, he was past caring when a third was produced. Halfway through the fourth, it crossed my husband's addled brain that he had not heard of this man as being a generous person. On the contrary, he was known to have short arms and long pockets and would cadge a drink off anyone if he could. 'All lies,' he thought as he eventually shut the door behind Peter and tried to find his way to bed.

Before he'd got very far my father came back. 'Sorry to leave you alone for so long,' he said. 'I was giving some people a hand. Their car had been ditched out by the post-box and they were in one hell of a state.'

'Were many of them hurt?' asked my husband, shocked into semi-sobriety.

'Not a scratch on them,' said my father, 'but when they got the car out of the ditch all their half-bottles had disappeared, and I've been helping the poor fools to comb the ditch for them, but no joy.'

One of the reasons I remember that night is that after he had been sick for the third time, my husband decided that he didn't want to be a crofter. I don't know if justice ever caught up with Peter, but if it did I'm sure that he had a very plausible alibi, ready to cover his back.

Chapter Seven

COMING HOME FOR GOOD had been a dream for such an eternity that when it eventually happened it seemed like an extended holiday for a long time. Paradoxically, what I liked best and disliked most was being surrounded by the other children in the family. For years I had longed to be able to play and talk with children of my own age, and this I could now do at will. However, there was a downside – they just never went away.

I woke up in the morning and they were there; all day and until nightfall there they were, and when we got ready for bed I had to share a bed with my sister. We slept in the small room called the closet. That gives a good indication of its size. It also served as a bathroom on Friday nights when the zinc bath came out along with the worm syrup and the syrup of figs. The larger bedroom had three beds – one double for my parents and two singles, each with one boy at the head and one at the foot. Scathing comments have been made by present-day do-gooders about such sleeping arrangements leading to all sorts of incestuous behaviour among the peasants. Take it from me, it was all about fighting for control of the blankets and getting away from smelly feet.

Having lived in solitude for so long, I'd grown used to amusing myself and being quiet and studious for most of the time . . . I'd had no alternative. Now it seemed that there was no such thing as my own space. Our little house was seething with fast-growing bodies. Those who had lived there all their lives had not even noticed it, but sometimes it just closed in on me.

At the south end of the house stood my father's old cart, which, although he now had a tractor, was kept handy, as it was more suitable for hauling crops and peat from the less accessible parts of the croft. Its long wooden shafts lay along the ground, and the green and white wooden box resting at an angle against the wall of the house became my sanctuary. I'd go in there when I wanted to be alone, to read or just to think. Once I fell asleep there, dozing in the sun, until one of the other children was sent to look for me and saw the dog, another Scot, sitting by the cart. After that, they always knew where to find me.

The aunties, who had many times wished themselves free of 'other people's property', meaning me, must have felt the need for more good works to offer up to God. Either that or they felt lonely on their return to Barra, as they asked my mother to bring the twins over for a visit. They went over with my mother on a Friday. She returned on the Monday and the twins came back to the croft to stay three years later. We just accepted it, together with my mother's assurances that the little ones had insisted on staying as they were having such a good time. We just got on with sharing the extra space. The

81

aunties had mellowed somewhat and the twins were company for each other, but, as I found out recently, it was a lively household and not always a happy one. The task proved too much for the aunties and they sent Alick back six months before his twin, causing her much anguish, but that is not my story to tell. I missed my dainty little sister, with her will of iron, and the serious little boy who would fight dragons to protect her. As their return home coincided with my departure for six years of further education in Fort William and Glasgow, and they had left home by the time I came back to Uist as a teacher, we were all adults before we really got to know each other. I wonder about the wisdom of it all, but again I suppose it was all about survival.

School was about to start and I had much on my mind. Daliburgh School was on two sites at the time. The old corrugated-iron building by the loch, near Daliburgh crossroads, housed the academic section, composed of pupils like myself and my two older brothers, who had passed the eleven-plus examination. About a quarter of a mile further south, again by a loch, stood the technical school, where, if the examiner who had marked your paper had not had a good day and failed you by one point, you studied woodwork and domestic science instead of Latin and algebra.

We were indeed blessed by the quality of our teachers. Take that from the horse's mouth. I hated some of them, but they knew their subjects and could teach them, and at the end of the day that is what it's all about. Some of the teachers came from the island and a few were recruited from the mainland. The incomers lived with their families in the newly-built Swedish houses on the Daliburgh–Lochboisdale road.

I can't honestly, hand on heart, say that I enjoyed my time at Daliburgh School. I was a very small fish in a vastly wider pool than that to which I had been accustomed. Add to that the fact that my two older brothers had been spawns of the devil at school since joining the infant department. Although clever, even gifted, as later life revealed, they were involved in every prank played on the teachers throughout the school and had been belted so often that it no longer hurt. Donald John, a budding poet, specialised in composing stingingly accurate but uncomplimentary Gaelic verses about the mainland teachers and circulating them in class. He got away with it for a long time, as he told the teachers, who couldn't read Gaelic, that it was homework, but he wrote one about a local teacher once, got caught and that was the end of that, and nearly the end of him. He had trouble writing anything at all for a few days. Fortunately, it didn't extinguish his love of verse, and up to the time of his early death at the age of forty-eight he had songs recorded by well known Gaelic singers and poems well received at Mods, the Gaelic festivals.

Because of the closeness of our ages and my being almost a year ahead of my peer group, plus the fact that it was a rural school, we often shared the same classroom. To some of the teachers I was just going to be another problem, and they said so the first time they called the register, with such comments as 'Not another MacMillan! Well, I hope your brothers have told you that we stand for no nonsense here.' Later in life I shared a staffroom on equal terms with some of the people who had given me that rousing welcome to the most important part of my education, and I was tempted to tell them that they had done me a favour: they had taught me what I should never, never say to a new pupil, and I never did – I knew how much it could hurt. However, they were good colleagues, and I hope that by that time they had learned to judge me on my own merits. My brothers were certainly not unhappy about their notoriety. I was only one year behind them in educational terms, but many, many years adrift in terms of real life.

The school took pupils from all over the island, and also from Benbecula and Eriskay. If you'd passed your exam, transport was provided, and in the case of children from Benbecula and Eriskay, lodging expenses were covered. Benbecula had its own junior secondary schools, but if parents from that area wished to send their children to Daliburgh, they could do so. It meant that I was not the only new face on my first morning, and this helped me to settle in and make friends.

Despite the influx from feeder schools, classes were small and combined, to bring the numbers up. It was not easy for the teachers, as planning for a small mixed group is much more difficult than teaching a larger class, where the age and ability playing field is level. Despite this, we had a very good education, and although, or perhaps I should say because, the discipline was very strict and the belt always a reality, many of us went on to further academic studies from that little corrugated-iron school by the loch.

The headmaster, true to the tradition of the times, was a newly-appointed mainlander, and although he wasn't cast in the mould of some previous headmasters who made a name for themselves by consorting only with island aristocracy and throwing gifts to the natives, he had no knowledge of the language or the culture. Still, he liked the island, wore a cloth cap, and in time learned a little of our ways.

After a year at the school we had grown to respect him as a fair man and someone who knew his teaching subjects well. However, one thing which had obviously been preying on his mind since experiencing his first Hogmanay was the imminent arrival on his doorstep of a little gang of *Gillean Cullaig*, chanting and expecting something for their flour sacks. So he decided to do something about it, not recognising that this ritual had been in place for generations and that the *Duain* were a gem of Gaelic culture passed on by word of mouth throughout the years, which without annual usage would be lost. The *Gillean Cullaig* were as much a part of Uist tradition as Ben Mòr was part of our landscape.

Before the end of the autumn term the headmaster announced, 'There will be no Hogmanay begging this year.' He had summoned the whole school before him to deliver this announcement, and he followed it by inviting any boy who intended to defy his ruling to step forward. Naturally, my brother Donald Angus took it upon himself to put his hand up and say, 'Please sir, it isn't begging.'

'And will you stay at home?'

'No, sir!'

Donald John had become a bit more worldly-wise since his exposure over the the poetry incident and kept out of this little drama.

'Then step forward and hold out your crossed hands!'

And so the headmaster proceeded to administer a brutal punishment for something which was not in any way connected with school work and was going to take place during the school holidays. This illustrates the attitude of some of the mainlanders. They were there not just to teach us but to civilise us.

After six hefty strokes the question was repeated again, and again the same answer was given. Someone in my class told me that the total number of strokes was twenty-four. I didn't count them. I never could stomach blood sports and was silently crying my eyes out behind my hands. My brother would not change his answer, and so he was sent home, in disgrace, for the rest of the day.

It says much for the total trust that island people had in the infallibility of teachers, doctors and priests that the reaction my parents showed to that incident was to tell my brother, 'That'll teach you to be cheeky to your teachers. Shame on you!' Years later, when I was teaching at the school, I came across the personal files on the twins, who had left the school by then, and human nature being what it is, I had a peek. In the space for general comment it read: 'As with the rest of the family, no parental interest shown.' It made my blood boil! No parents could have been more interested in their family's welfare, but unlike some who were always beating a path to the school door, my parents trusted the teachers to know their jobs and, unless specifically asked to go to the school, they left them to get on with it.

The brother who had been punished was the pianist, and the Christmas party wasn't the same that year, as his hands were still so swollen that he couldn't play for the dancing. The *Gillean Cullaig* were, if anything, more in evidence than ever that year, but in Daliburgh they gave the schoolhouse a wide berth, and after New Year, when the new term started, the subject wasn't even mentioned. I wonder if one of the local teachers had had a quiet word with the headmaster. Someone had obviously straightened him out.

Some of the teachers and the headmaster taught in both the academic and technical school and spent a lot of time either walking or cycling between the two sites. Some of us pupils also had the opportunity to take this bit of exercise. If one of the female teachers had decided to belt anyone and they thought that their lighter, more lady-like straps were not fitted to the severity of the crime, the culprit would be told to walk to the other school and borrow the headmaster's strap, a quarter-inch thick 'Lochgelly'. Not a nice trip! You didn't mind the walk; it was the indignity of going into a classroom full of your peers and making the request, then walking back carrying the strap and meeting shoppers and other road users who knew exactly what was going to happen to you, that made it hatefully humiliating. Yes, I speak from experience. After receiving your punishment, you took the strap back. The good old days.

There was little in terms of organised after-school activities, especially for the girls. A boys' youth club was started once and my brothers really enjoyed that. They learned how to make plaques from plaster of Paris and how to play some new card games, but for some reason funding was withdrawn and the club closed. We had a very keen music teacher at the school. A mainlander, his main subject was science, and although all he taught us about music was the joy of memorising every song in *The Oxford School Song Book* and singing them in harmony, it gave us a lot of pleasure. I can still hear my brothers and their friends coming home from the youth club singing 'Swing Low, Sweet Chariot' and 'The Song of The Volga Boatmen', their young male voices carrying on the clear Hebridean air. We could hear them coming from over a mile away, as they walked home in the moonlight.

Once a year a teacher from Skye came to get us ready for the local Mod – a daunting task, as she had one school term to tour all the schools on the island, from Benbecula southwards. She taught choral harmonies, duets and solos for all different age-groups and tutored us up to competition performance standards for the big day. Although I enjoyed some success later in life, my own attempts at competitive singing at the Daliburgh Mod were pathetic. I had never sung in public before and was so nervous that all I wanted to do was finish the wretched song and get off that stage. My mother said that she had never heard a lament sung so fast in her life. As I was singing I could see Miss MacDonald, the teacher from Skye, at the back of the hall shaking her head in disbelief; when she covered her face with her hands I knew that the gold medal was not for me.

The household chores were still shared out and I had my own bits and pieces to do, but there was plenty of time allowed for homework and any other activity we wanted to become involved with. I joined the church choir along with some other young girls and that was nice. Singing and music of any kind was just always there in our family. My father was becoming established throughout the islands as a singer and comedian of some repute. He had people from the School of Scottish Studies coming regularly to record his enormous repertoire of traditional folk songs and Francis Collinson and later on Fred Macaulay of the BBC often invited him to Glasgow to take part in Gaelic programmes.

Born ahead of his time, as many people are, he received some recognition during his lifetime and that was enough for him. In the 1960s, when he helped Arthur Swinson with the research for his most enjoyable book *Scotch on the Rocks*, the author described him as 'possessing a voice full of fire and richness' and as 'one of the most straightforward and most reliable men I have ever met in my life'. That meant more to my father than money in the bank.

My mother also had a melodious voice and had once won a silver medal at the Mod, but she had grown to dislike performing in public. She loved her piano, which had been bought for her by the teacher auntie as a sweetener when she came home from the mainland, and it stood next to the dresser for as long as I can remember. She and Donald Angus would compete to see who could play the fastest, most note-perfect reel with their left hand, whilst covering their eyes with their right hand. Then young Donald started playing, and he was just as proficient but preferred the accordion. Donald John liked to write alternative, often unprintable, words for the songs, and I practised my listening skills and joined in the singing. Like many of the island folk, we were all born with music in the blood, so to speak, and one of the joys of going back to live with the family was having music of one kind or another around me all the time. On a Sunday night we would listen to the Top Twenty on Radio Luxembourg and try to scribble the words to *Tennessee Waltz* and other popular songs, so that we could sing them at playtime in the school shelter, much the way every little girl wants to be a Spice Girl nowadays: nothing changes all that much.

In the third year of secondary school we were all getting more fashion-conscious and I decided, in my spare time, to become an agent for a mail order catalogue, or 'club book' as we called them in those days. I risked ticking the over-18 box, and got away with it. It was a very rewarding venture in terms of meeting people and taking their orders, and I enjoyed the very simple accountancy involved, but really I needed much larger orders than my twenty members could afford in order to clothe myself from the proceeds.

Many of my clients were the people who had moved into the Swedish houses in Daliburgh. In fact, the wife of a mainland teacher at the school was a very good customer. I always timed my visits to her when I knew he'd still be at school, or on a Saturday morning when he had some extra classes. I thought he just might find it embarrassing to have a pupil collecting money from his wife. She must have been a very lonely person, as she always greeted me like a long-lost friend of her own age and gave me tea and cakes. We had long conversations about clothes and furniture and other more personal things. She asked my advice on many things and I found this extremely flattering. Some of my school friends lived near them and told me that Margaret was a very formidable lady and that she and her husband had rows which the whole neighbourhood could hear. I said that I had found no evidence of this and defended her stoutly.

One evening I was later than usual making my collection, and when I knocked on the teacher's door I heard the sound of something being thrown against the wall and glass breaking. The door flew open and my teacher rushed out, looking distinctly nervous. He pulled up short when he saw me on the step. From the kitchen came Margaret's voice, screeching in fury, 'Get out of my sight, you useless, bald-headed, skinny-legged bugger!' Need I add that he put his hand in his pocket, pulled out a wad of money, paid their account off, and told me that my services would no longer be required. I don't know which of us had the redder face. I think he had. I made no mention of the incident at school or at home. She had been nice to me and I owed her and him their dignity.

Another customer was a little, old local lady who lived by the canal. She was a little ball of a woman, who talked incessantly and could knit faster than anyone I've ever known. She often visited us, walking up the canal path and over the bridge, knitting a sock for one of her sailor sons as she went, and on many occasions leaving the ball of wool behind in her cottage. One of us had to follow the trail of wool back there and do battle with her current 'bad dog' to retrieve it.

She and my father were forever teasing each other. When we had the Christmas parcel containing the ill-fated 'blow football' set, my father's gift was a pair of joke spectacles with nose and moustache attached. This kind of thing was a complete novelty at the time, and right up his street. He'd put them on to tell the twins stories when they came over from Barra for the school holidays and have them laughing so much that they begged him to stop. One day, he happened to have the disguise in his pocket as he was passing Mary's house. As the door was open, he could see that she was doing something over at the dresser with her back to him. He quickly put the spectacles on and, with nose and moustache in place, knocked on the door frame to attract her attention. Mary greeted him politely with 'It's a fine day' in English and '*Cò an ainm Dhè, a tha seo?*' (Who in God's name is this?) in Gaelic. Like most elderly people who live alone, she talked to herself. My father explained in his poshest English that he was one of her daughter's friends from Oban, touring the Islands, and had called to see her, as her daughter had said that she made a very good cup of tea and was always glad of company.

Mary sat him down and continued to be very polite to him in English, while calling the wrath of God down on her daughter's head for sending mainland visitors to eat the little food she had in the house in Gaelic, and started brewing the tea. The light in the little cottage was always dim, as she used the sill of the small window as an extra shelf and had a very large geranium plant sitting there. When she poured the tea she asked, 'How much sugar do you take?' adding '*Tha mi' n dòchas gun tachd e thu*' ('I

91

hope you choke on it') in Gaelic. My father, who had whipped off the spectacles, answered in his own voice, '*Dà spàin, ma 's e ur toil, a Mhàiri*' (Two spoonfuls, please, Mary). She got the tea towel and started to beat him about the head with it till he had apologised to her satisfaction. Later she saw the funny side and they both had a good laugh.

When I started going round with the catalogue I took the canal path, as it was a good short-cut to the main Daliburgh–Kilpheder road. I had been passing Mary's door for a few days before she noticed me, and called me in for a glass of *Leann nam Biast* (Worm Beer), a drink which she brewed in a large glass sweet jar and kept on her dresser. It was made from beremeal – a kind of barley – treacle, sugar and water which fermented and produced a fizzy light brown drink not unlike a light ale. The grains at the bottom of the jar grew fat and flabby as they absorbed the liquid, and as they moved around during fermentation looked just like maggots – hence the name. The process of topping up with sugar and treacle to keep the supply going was known as 'feeding the worms'. While I sipped my drink Mary took a good look at the catalogue and exclaimed at the variety of goods on offer. She was very interested and decided to spend ten pounds on something. Now, she lived in a tiny cottage and had no mod cons whatsoever, so I expected her to order a new kettle or something really practical, but no: she turned to the fashion pages and ordered a very classy-looking blue crêpe de Chine dress with a cream silk shawl collar, for considerably more than ten pounds. As I had never seen Mary in anything other than a black or brown jumper and black skirt with a flowered overall covering most of it, I assumed that she was buying a present for one of her daughters.

A couple of weeks later I ran into her some distance from her cottage, stacking peat on the bog. As she had a bag filled ready to carry home, I offered to take it and leave it by her door. She accepted my offer, and as I was about to take my leave I asked her if the dress had arrived. 'Yes, indeed, and I am well pleased with it!' she said, taking off coat, cardigan and the overall to display the blue dress in all its glory. I'm sure it was the only model of its kind which had ever been worn to stack peat, but from that day on I knew that Mary, despite age and outward appearances, had the soul of a young girl. We became good friends and she taught me many things, including how to turn the heel of a sock. She was old enough to be my grandmother, but that didn't matter; and when, during my time at Fort William school, my parents wrote to tell me that she had died suddenly, I felt that someone very special had gone from my life.

Crofter's child and Barra cousin '. . . much taller than I was, fair haired and very pretty. As if that wasn't enough, she had a kilt.'

Twins at Barra School. Mary Flora, fourth from right, middle row. Alick Iain, first on left, front row.

My parents' Wedding Day. ' ... and so my father, the only son-in-law, an incomer from Benbecula, became a South Uist crofter.'

Convent Girls. 'we were 'Let Out' on Saturday and Sunday afternoons.'

The Ben Nevis Hike. ' ... we hiked up twice and it nearly finished me off.'

H.M. Queen Elizabeth talking to my father. ' ... the poor wee Queen looked half starved and her hand felt like a baby flounder.'

Daliburgh Academic School. 'The old corrugated iron building by the loch.' (now derelict)

Fort William School. ' ... on this site generations of children had been educated since the 18th century.'

Thatching the Croft House. ' ... it belongs to Donald MacDonald, a quiet dignified bard.'

Croft House Bench. ' ... the whole of the front wall was taken up by the bench... '
(Photo by kind permission, Uist Museum.)

Kyles Flodda Schoolhouse. 'A large house with high ceilings.'

A Field of Stooks. ' ... propped them up into stooks, which were gathered together to form small stacks.'

My Mother Stacking Hay. ' ... when the stack yard was full there was a great feeling of security.'

Chapter Eight

THE ISLAND WAS CHANGING, many new ventures were taking shape and the tourist industry was taking its first tentative steps. Due to the excellent fishing in all the lochs, South Uist had always enjoyed the patronage of the fishing and shooting set, mostly friends of the people who owned the island. We had grown up with the spectacle of tweed-knickerbockered, deerstalker-hatted strangers pulling up outside our house and creeping over our fields, shooting at flying things. The islanders worked their crofts, but at the end of the day the landlords owned crofts and tenants. Now, with the story of the 'Polly' immortalised on film and travel through the island becoming less arduous, we actually had people without guns and fishing rods visiting our island.

The hotels smartened themselves up and built cocktail bars, and although to go in there more than twice in a year could still 'cause talk' if you were a woman, liberation was on its way. The new Co-op in Daliburgh had fresh-baked bread delivered three times a week, so a lot of the wives baked their final scone.

My own favourite innovation was the coming to Uist of the tupenny-ha'penny bun. Again pioneered by the Co-op bakery, this was actually the name used to classify a selection of sweet iced buns with toppings of sticky icing and sprinkles of hundreds and thousands, little bakewell tarts, apple tarts and the unforgettable fly cemeteries, a pastry sandwich filled with a mixture of deliciously blended dates and currants which looked just as their name implied. We could walk up to the shop in the school lunch-hour and spend our pennies in style. Much time was lost dithering over choices, but it was always worth it. For those of us with a cash-flow problem there was the less appealing poor relation, the penny bun. This was an ordinary sweet unadorned currant bun and better than nothing. Unlike the present-day shopping magnates who are driving the small grocer to the wall, the improvements in the Co-op were immediately followed by marked improvements in the other shops, so we the customers were the winners, or at least so we thought at the time. Now on the island most of the milk, bread and coal comes from the shops, while acres of arable land lie fallow and cows are conspicuous by their rarity, as are peatstacks. Perhaps the advent of the tuppeny-ha'penny bun wasn't such a good thing for island culture after all.

In my schooldays, milking the cows was my mother's exclusive domain, and it always had been. I had tried it once or twice but they didn't want to stand still for me, and my father said that when they saw me coming, with my long nails, they ran screaming to the other end of the croft. In the winter, when the cows were in the byre, it was easy to get round them in a short time, but once the weather lightened my mother would walk down to the far end of the croft and milk them where they grazed.

They knew her well and always stood still, with no need for a *buarach* (tether), just chewing the cud, flicking at flies with their tails and nuzzling her shoulder from time to time. If she was ill or had to go out somewhere at milking time, my father would take her place, and the cows accepted him as a substitute, as he sang to them and he was the one who delivered their calves.

One evening both my parents were out and the task of milking was left to Donald Angus, as he had helped out from time to time. Off he went with the pails, and all went well until he approached Letty, a cow of some character who had been with us for a long time and was very attached to my mother. Letty took one look at him and decided that this person was not going to get a drop of milk from her. Every time he got near her she walked off. Eventually she stopped, and he hunkered down with the pail between his knees and got started. All went well until Lettty turned her head and nuzzled his shoulder. At once she remembered that this was not the usual milkmaid, and she was off again, taking the pail with her and leaving him lying on the ground covered with milk. Not one to give up easily, my brother came back home, camouflaged himself by putting on my mother's milking coat, covered his head with one of her scarves and off he went again. This time he had complete success. Letty thought that her own dear friend had returned and gave him a pailful of milk. He was coming back in, just walking round the end of the house with the pails, when Donald MacKellaig, one of his friends, passed by on his bike and called out, 'Hello, Kate!' Letty was not the only one who had been fooled. Donald Angus rushed in and, dumping the pails on the floor, announced, 'I'll kill any one of you who tells him that it was me!'

Donald Angus and Donald John missed the youth

club, but they were growing up now and in their final year at Daliburgh school. They were always full of schemes for making money. Fishing was not an option, as it was too slow a sport for their liking. Although they tried the canal occasionally, they soon got tired of waiting for a bite and started catching eels instead. This had no useful end-product, as eels have never formed any part of the island diet, and the whole thing was quite disgusting. They'd wait for an eel to slither through the mud at the shallow part of the canal, spear it with a fork and cut its head off with a knife. I think they discovered that I was a girl the day I ran screaming home to tell my mother what they were doing with her cutlery.

Rabbits also featured in their commercial enterprises. The machair was alive with plump rabbits and the crofters were always complaining about the havoc being wrought on their crops. So, together with some other young lads, my older brothers saw a window of opportunity. They went out on dark nights with a fast dog and a strong torch, and in the morning young Donald went round the township with the rabbits draped over the handlebars of the bike in pairs. He sold them, on behalf of his brothers, for one shilling and sixpence per pair. The other two paid him a commission of sixpence per pair sold, but they did not know until they were adults that he had been charging the housewives sixpence per rabbit for skinning and cleaning them, thus in fact earning more than they did. He was a very good salesman and never brought one back.

My mother had a strong aversion to rabbits, dating back to her time at Oban Cottage Hospital, where she said that the staff had been fed nothing else. She also said that the rabbits grew fat on the corpses in Hallin cemetery, and would not touch them. The rest of the family, however, could not resist the smell of rabbit meat stewing slowly in a pot with onions and a bit of turnip, and so someone had to cook them, usually me. I didn't mind the cooking, but sometimes I had to skin and clean them as well. The skinning wasn't too bad – I was quite glad when the skin came off like a glove and the carcass no longer looked like a fluffy bunny – but I had to clean them first, and the smell was just so awful that it made me feel sick. I'd rather gut ten barrels of herring than clean one rabbit. There was also a small amount of money to be made from the skins, as Willie Jordan bought them. I have no idea what happened to them next, but knowing Willie's acumen in matters of money, I'm sure he had some market for them. More of him later.

One day Donald Angus came home full of excitement, as he'd been talking to some of the other boys and they had told him about two men who had asked them to round up some helpers. They were digging up a large area of the machair. One man was a doctor by the name of Kissling and the other was called Tom. My parents wondered why a German would be digging on our machair and my father said, '"Polly" bottles.' Donald Angus was very keen to join the digging party, as the doctor was going to take them all to Askernish machair and show them how to play golf if they worked hard. He had also mentioned teaching them to swim. They were digging for unusual things like old bones and signs of people from long ago and had no interest in the 'Polly', my brother said. My parents were a bit worried about letting him go off with strangers and made their own enquiries before giving their permission.

It transpired that the men were archaeologists and that Dr Kissling, despite his German pedigree, had long been a lover of the islands. He had lived on Eriskay for many years and had been taking photographs and moving-pictures of the Eriskay people and their way of life. He had made his film, *Eriskay: A Poem Of Remote Lives*, and with the proceeds from it had provided a road for Eriskay. It also came out that he was so anti-Nazi that when Hitler came to power he had sent men to London to bring the doctor back to Germany for questioning. Dr Kissling had evaded capture by throwing his coat over their heads and running away. Someone also said that his brothers had been shot for conspiring to kill Hitler. True or not, he sounded pretty trustworthy, so Donald Angus was given permission to join the diggers.

Each day my brother would take some food and go down to the machair with my mother's words, 'Don't go near the sea', as a constant warning. The currents round the island are very treacherous and have taken many lives over the years. The islanders know this and respect the sea. My brother wasn't too happy about it, as the doctor liked nothing better than to cool off in the sea after a hard day's digging and could not understand the reluctance of his helpers to accept swimming lessons. However, Donald Angus was allowed to take advantage of the golf lessons, but he did not see much point in the game and soon abandoned it.

The digging went well and they uncovered what at first they thought was a 'beehive' dwelling, but as the work proceeded they found that it was a 'wheelhouse', the updated version of the 'Atlantic roundhouse' or 'beehive'. There were conflicting thoughts on its age but the date AD 2 was mentioned. It amazed the boys that people had lived in Kilpheder so long ago. At school they had learned that the islands had once belonged to Norway before they had been passed on to the clans as uncontrollable, but this find came from a past so distant that its place in time was difficult for the young helpers to grasp. They just knew that this little dwelling-place was very, very old. Also uncovered were traces of fire and some bone-needle type artifacts and pieces of a type of slate which is found only on one of the offshore group of islands – I think it was the Monachs – so the inhabitants must have been able to travel across the sea.

We all went down as a family to see the newly uncovered *Taigh Talamhanta* (earth dwelling), as we called it, and we were surprised to see that the walls were so low. There were four chambers enclosed by four-foot-high walls connected to each other by passages, the whole encircling a larger area, probably a communal fireplace or meeting-place which formed the hub of the wheel. The door apertures were also very low, three feet high at most, so we concluded that the inhabitants must have been very small people, or that this was just the base of the structure and that there had been other elevated sections of wall which had not survived. The archae-ologists disagreed with our theory and we were left to wonder just who these tiny people had been and what their lives had been like living in their little communes by the sea. As we walked home we trod a little bit more carefully on the machair soil and speculated on the possibility that more civilisations from prehistoric times lay beneath it.

We could have been right, as this year – a few months ago, in fact – student archaeologists from English and Welsh universities found another site under the sand right on the shoreline of Kilpheder machair. It was a grave with a female skeleton, and although no news of its origin has yet reached the island, it is believed, from the traces of rust in the tunnels round the burial place, to be Iron Age or later. Poor little Iron Maiden, lying diagonally across her rectangular grave with a large round stone clasped in her hands, I wonder what her life was like, or who, in future centuries, will uncover our graves and speculate about our civilisation.

The excitement of the digging died down as the artifacts were taken away for testing and the team left the island. Both my older brothers were coming up for their Junior Leaving Certificate examination, so career choices were high on the agenda and neither of them wanted to conform. The traditional path for the pupils who passed the exam was to follow the *air falbh* (going away) path and continue their education on the mainland, eventually becoming teachers, doctors or nurses. Other professional paths were just beginning to appear, but were viewed as 'not quite the thing' by island parents with their sights set on their children becoming members of the professions which then represented the elite of the island. So the question was: 'Are you going to be a teacher, doctor, nurse or priest, or are you going to sea?' These were the only choices open to us then, long before the advent of the Social Studies degree.

Priests and nuns had to have vocations, and most of the candidates were said to have manifested some sign of their calling since childhood. They left for the seminaries and convents in their early teens. One of Kilpheder's most celebrated priests was Father John Morrison. During his ministry on the island he came close to thwarting the Ministry of Defence's annexing of Iochdar machair for their Guided Weapons Range. He managed to win substantial concessions for the local crofters before the might of the Army defeated him. Father John had discovered his vocation in early childhood. He was a contemporary of my mother's, and she used to tell us how his father complained bitterly about his 'useless son'. During the haymaking season John would go missing and be found behind a haystack, praying for the poor people who had no hay or corn. His father would haul him to his feet, give him a shake and tell him that prayers would not fill the stackyard. Despite all the opposition, John persuaded his father that his life would be worthless unless he became a priest, and eventually permission was given. I have never known anyone more contented in their chosen field of work. Whether conducting his services or comforting the bereaved, talking to young people in their own language or fighting the islanders' corner, he was the right man in the right place.

There were many priests like him who had found their niche and gloried in it. Nuns, too, who from childhood had wanted no other life. However, there were also some little boys and girls sent off to seminaries far from their homes and committed to a life of celibacy and isolation, long before they knew whether they were 'Arthur or Martha'. Some just went along with it because they didn't want to bring shame on their families by leaving and 'causing talk'. I have never believed that wanting to have a priest in the family or 'giving a child back to God' was either humane or logical. The decision should be left until the person is old enough fully to understand the commitment. How can you know at an early age that you are doing the right thing unless you are very sure that God's call comes from your heart and not from your mother? I think that old Mr Morrison did the right thing, delaying Father John's decision until it became inevitable.

In our family the question never arose. It was pretty obvious that none of us was suited to a life in the cloth, and so, 'Are you going to be a teacher, doctor or nurse, or are you going to sea?' In my case I had no doubts. I was going to that nice place where nuns taught you to be teachers and you had lots of girls of your own age writing in your little red book, asking you to pray for them. Case closed. The boys were a bit more complicated. Donald Angus wanted to be a sailor, but not an ordinary sailor. He wanted to be a naval officer. Donald John wanted to be a policeman, but not an ordinary policeman – he wanted to be a detective and solve crimes by using his powers of deduction. I think he had just discovered Sherlock Holmes in the school library.

There was much discussion, and the results were that Donald Angus was enrolled for the Apprentice Navigation Officer's course at the Royal Technical College in Glasgow and Donald John agreed that completing his education in Fort William would be no hindrance to his ambitions. As it happened, he did become a detective and attained the rank of Detective Inspector, Special Branch, at Scotland Yard, spending much of his time in the Diplomatic Protection Unit, where he rubbed shoulders with Prime Ministers and Royalty. He died young and left a huge gap in all our lives; but I think that during his too short lifetime he had managed to achieve many of his ambitions, including solving crimes by using his powers of deduction. Returning to live in Uist was his eventual goal, as is illustrated in his song *Uibhist nam Beanntan* (Uist of Bens), but that was not to be.

Getting two boys ready for their lives as mainland students meant that many new clothes had to be bought, and this was a bit of a headache for my mother. She got most of our clothes from catalogues, but the delay between ordering and delivery was a nuisance and it was frustrating when the clothes did not fit. Fortunately, there was also a local supplier called Willie Jordan. An unforgettable person and one of my favourite characters of all time.

A legend in his lifetime and beyond, Willie made an impact on all who met him, and even now, when his name is mentioned in Uist, it is with affection and regret that such a larger-than-life personality is no longer around. An Irish packman, he came to our village as a comparatively young man, took up lodgings with a local family, and plied his trade there all his life till he died of old age. In his adopted family he was absolute ruler. Nobody dared to sit in Willie's chair. If you went in while he was eating, you addressed no words to him. 'Sure, if God meant you to eat and talk at the same time, she'd have given you two mouths.' He always spoke in a mixture of Irish and Scottish Gaelic, supplemented by bits of English, and confused his genders something awful.

The room which was his bedroom, shop and store was a veritable Aladdin's cave of garments wrapped in oilskin-covered bundles, and he always managed to unwrap a good three-quarters of them searching for the goods you wanted. Human nature being what it is, you bought twice as much as you intended.

During the day he'd fill his little Austin with as many packs as it would hold and, driving mostly in second gear, he would do his rounds, selling locknit knickers with elasticated legs and long johns to the *bodachs* (old men) and *cailleachs* (old women) in remote areas and picking up much local gossip as he went. In the evenings he was available for business in his room, where he passed on the day's news as he took your money, if you had it, and arranged payment on instalments, based solely on trust, if you were short.

Willie made a good living from the packs, but it was not through his commercial expertise that his name still lives on in South Uist. No, this fame came from his extravagant stories and his strange bursts of drinking. Any Irishman can spin a yarn, but Willie's had a flavour of their own. Totally improbable stories delivered in his own inimitable pidgin Highland Irish. His face was large and red and once described by a visitor as 'a cross between Alfred Hitchcock and a badly finished Toby jug'. I don't know if the visitor's words were his own but they surely fitted Willie. He really enjoyed telling whoppers. His eyes would twinkle and the punch-line was reached through a series of wheezy chuckles. Some of the older people he visited swallowed his tall stories hook, line and sinker, and as some of them had never gone very far from home, they took Willie's version of life in Ireland as gospel. My father's ambition was to catch him out and have the last word, but Willie always managed to stay one step ahead, most of the time.

One day my father was cutting peat in a part of our croft some distance from the house and my little brother and I were taking a flask of tea out to him. As we walked along the road, Willie's car came up behind us and he stopped to offer us a lift. When he heard where we were going he left his car by the side of the road and walked with us out to the peat bog to have a word with his friend and adversary.

'That's a good spade you've got there, man.'

'Aye, Willie, it'll do.'

'Begorrah, but you should see the one my father had, seven times the size of that one.'

'Aye, Willie?'

'My ould man, she was very big, eight feet tall and as strong as ten bulls.'

My father continued to cut the turf, rhythmically skimming off the grassy tussocks in squares and laying them on the bank upside-down in a neat patio to receive the wet peat. He knew that another tale of Irish valour was forthcoming, and his role was merely that of an admiring audience. My brother and I knew that something good was about to happen.

'Sure, and it's a warm job you're doing there, so it is. It reminds me of one day I was out with the packs in the ould country. Bejasus, it was hot. I was sweating so much I was walking in puddles.'

'Aye, Willie.'

'I was walking along sweating fit to disappear when I came to a river. I set the packs down and took off every last stitch of my clothes, even my semmit. Then, pure and naked as the day I was born, I jumped into the river. As I hit the water steam clouded my sight and the splashes made blisters rise up on the skin on my face. I swam at sixty miles an hour to get away from the hissing of the water, and after swimming for two miles or maybe ten I felt my blood come off the boil. Best get back to the packs in case the tinkers come and take them, I thought. So, round I turned, and there coming towards me with her eyes flashing like bicycle lamps and his great jaws wide open was the ugliest shark I ever saw . . .'

'Sharks in Ireland? In a river, Willie?'

'Damn you, man, I said the ould country, what I did not say was that it was my ould country. Now, where was I? . . . The ugly ould devil was coming straight for me with her mouth watering and I could see that this was no time for reasoning with him. So I thrust my hand in my pocket and took out my tobacco knife . . .'

'But you were naked, Willie.'

'Saints blast you, man, I come here to pass the time of day with you and all you do is argue with me!' Willie stamped off to his car and took off with much crashing of gears. My father chuckled contentedly as he finished his cutting and drank his tea.

106

'You got him! You got him!' we shouted. 'Aye,' replied my father, 'till next time.'

Months of hard work selling his stuff and counting his money, and then out of the blue Willie would change his routine completely and embark on the biggest binges the island has ever known.

Taking hundreds of pounds from his money box, he'd spend weeks drinking with all and sundry, treating everyone he met to bottles of the stuff. He would walk into the bar and take over. Everyone was his friend and the drinks kept coming until even the hardest-headed could take no more and the barman advised them to leave. Then a bulging Austin full of drunks and carry-outs would weave its way to the bar at the other end of the island, in and out of ditches, to repeat the process there.

Sometimes the entire contingent would keep going for the duration of the binge, but mostly it was a kind of relay. Some crawled home after a day or two, to be replaced by others. Willie himself was never seen to fall down or sleep, and although the driving was erratic there were never any casualties. He just kept drinking, singing, telling his dreadful stories, laughing his wheezy laugh, spending money and driving his little car backwards and forwards from bar to ditch to bar till he'd had enough. Then, as suddenly as it had started, it was over. Back home for twenty-four hours' sleep and back to normal again, sober as a judge for ages, or, as Willie himself would say, 'For two years or maybe ten.'

Eventually the boys were kitted out and they were off. Donald Angus left at the start of the summer holidays, as his course was about to begin. Donald John had a few more weeks at home and then he went on to Fort William. With my own Leaving Certificate exams looming at the end of the school year, tests which I did not intend to fail, I got my head down and wrestled with simultaneous equations and Latin vocabulary.

Chapter Nine

Mo *thruagh* mi 's mar tha mi 'n-diugh
Mo *thruaigh' mi 's gur muladach –*
'S e 'n gaol a thug mi 'n ghille dhubh
A rinn an-diugh mo leònadh.

Sadness fills my heart today,
My heart is sad and sorrowful –
The love I gave the dark-eyed boy
Today has left me mourning.

WE ALL REMEMBER WHERE we were and what we were doing on the day we heard some catastrophic news. Time stood still in the little crofthouse on September 25th, 1952. I will never forget the song my father sang softly to himself as he prepared to leave for Wallasey Hospital, where my brother Donald Angus had been taken for the amputation of his left hand. He had completed the first module of his course at the Royal Technical College and was embarking on the preliminary practical section on board his first ship, the *Kelvinbank*, sailing out of Liverpool. The accident happened as they were docking at Birkenhead, when a rope he was handling wrapped itself round his hand with tragic results. The rope was attached to a fender, the cushion-like device used on docking ships to avoid collision damage if the side of the vessel scraped against the structure of the dock. The *Kelvinbank* nudged the pier, the fender did its job, the swell caused the vessel to heave upwards and the rope suddenly played out, taking with it most of my brother's hand and all of his hopes of a career as a naval officer, a few weeks before his seventeenth birthday.

Each of us reacted in different ways to the message that the priest had brought us early that morning. My father, never one to hide his feelings, went outside and stood in Letty's empty stall in the byre thumping the wall and sobbing with great wracking tremors of grief coursing through his body as he railed against the God who had allowed this terrible thing to happen to his boy. Now and then he'd shout: 'Why did I listen to him? Why did I let him go away? He'd have been safe here.' There had been a time when my father had hoped that his eldest son would stay on the croft and work alongside him in the traditional manner but, sensing that Donald Angus had other ambitions, he had not put any pressure on him. It was quite frightening for the rest of us to see our normally stable father behaving in this fashion. Shouts of laughter we'd grown up with, shouts of anger too, when things displeased him, but these great shouts of grief shocked us all. Young Donald took the dog down to *Tobht' 'Ic Ille Chrìasda* (Gilchrist's Ruin), the knoll where we used to search for honey in the hayfield, and he sat there with the dog by his side, like two statues, staring down towards the machair for most of the day. My mother started to iron shirts, not the usual early morning task when cows were waiting to be milked. She had her back to me and I could hear sizzling noises as her tears hit the flat iron, but she herself made no sound apart from an occasional whisper of '*M' eudail bheag*' (My little darling) as she slowly walked over to the other side of the kitchen to replace the cold iron with the one heating up on the stove.

The little twins, over from Barra on what was to be their final visit before coming back home, were too young to realise the enormity of it all and were discussing the drawbacks of losing a hand. There was speculation about not being able to carry presents in a suitcase. I think they were frightened by their first glimpse of parents unable to contain their heartbreak and were drawing comfort from the sound of each other's voices. I kept seeing a vision of my brother's young hands, crossed to receive the strap for defiance at school. A photograph of him, tall and proud in his college blazer, stood on the piano. Never again would I see his left hand flying over the keyboard as he tried to outplay my mother's nimble fingers. I remember feeling astonished that birds were singing outside and that people on the neighbouring croft were going about their usual chores as if nothing had happened, while in my chest a great knot of tears built up waiting for the time when it could be released. Not a day to remember too often, although it will never go away. Donald John was at Fort William school and had to cope with the news of his brother's accident alone. I'm sure he wanted to be at home with his family, although none of us could have given him much comfort.

Tragedy always leaves its mark, and my parents took many years to get over their sorrow, but Donald Angus insists to this day that, although it has been an inconvenience at times, the loss of his hand has not had any adverse effect on his life. He has had the pleasure of seeing his son join the Navy and have a good career as a pilot with the Fleet Air Arm, another dark-eyed boy who wore his uniform with pride. As I watched the heads turn as my now silver-haired brother entered a London gathering recently, crossing the floor to greet his party with the confident stride so reminiscent of my father's walk, the thought crossed my mind that losing his hand had indeed not had much of an adverse effect on his life.

Our good friends and neighbours rallied round and, as life must go on, things eventually returned to normal in the family. Donald Angus did not return to the croft but wisely embarked on rehabilitation and training to help him cope with his changed circumstances, away from the sympathy and curiosity of the islanders, which though well-meant would have served him no useful purpose.

Donald John was doing well in Fort William, writing home regularly and enclosing the occasional funny poem in his letters, mostly irreverent descriptions of the teachers whom I would meet when my turn came. My father had become even more involved with the seaweed factory, or Alginate Industries as it was now called, and young Donald with the help of his friend the dog had taken on many of the crofting chores before and after school.

The dog who had been Donald's companion in grief was typical of the dogs found on any Hebridean croft: a Border Collie type, so easy to train and intensely loyal. We had a succession of them over the years, and although we had the odd Labrador and Spaniel as well, none could match the Collie Cross as an extra source of help on the croft. They seemed to have an in built sense of time and knew just which chore came next.

Our neighbour John had a dog which was quite

remarkable. John's cows did their summer grazing in a field which was separated from the main part of his croft by a distance of a mile or so across two main roads, and he would walk out there, with the dog, twice daily for the milking. When the autumn set in and the grazing was getting poor, he would bring them home for the evening milking and keep them in the byre overnight with full mangers to supplement their feed. Then he would walk them back out to the field again in the morning.

One day when they had reached the field, his dog jumped up, and with his nose he lifted the latch on the field-gate, causing it to swing open. As John stood by, the dog herded the cows on to the road and headed them homewards along the main road. When a car approached, the dog ran alongside the cows, and by barking and nipping at their heels he nagged them into an orderly file by the roadside, keeping them there until the vehicle had passed, and all John had to do was walk behind his herd. When they arrived at the main croft, the dog repeated the unlatching process with the gate in front of the byre, and peeling the cows off one by one, he sent them into the byre to find their stalls. Cows like their own stalls and their own manger, so in they went and stood waiting for John to come and milk them.

This went on for a few weeks, and as John was a creature of habit, he and his dog would walk past our house each evening at about five o'clock. Sometimes John would stop for a chat, usually about the dog, while it got on with taking the cows on homewards and into the byre as usual. Then one afternoon John wrenched his ankle badly and was hobbling around the house, dreading the long walk out to the grazing field in the evening. He kept putting it off and putting it off until he could no longer do so, and getting a jacket and a stick, hobbled outside and called the dog. He called and called but no dog came. As John cursed and fumed and hobbled about looking for his faithless hound, he happened to look out towards the grazing field. There in the distance he could see a long line of brown cows plodding towards Kilpheder cross-roads, being chivvied along by a busy black and white dog. His cows and his dog. From that day on John let the dog do the evening run by itself, and on the dot of five o'clock each evening we would see him loping past our croft on his way out to the grazing field to bring John's cows home for milking.

As the years went by, the dog and John, a bachelor who lived alone, kept each other company and worked the croft together. John was a diabetic, and from time to time had to go into the local hospital for treatment. When this happened the dog would sit outside the hospital, under the window of the men's ward, and stay there until John was discharged. The treatment often took days, but the dog stayed there day and night, refusing any efforts to feed it or move it until his master was ready to go home.

Our local hospital in those days was known as the Sacred Heart Hospital, staffed largely by a band of Sacred Heart nuns, and a much smaller building than the present large, well-equipped Daliburgh Hospital which has grown around it, as new wings have been added. It was originally called Bute Hospital and was given to the islanders by the Marchioness of Bute in 1894, when it was staffed by three women. That is the recorded account of its origin, but my Auntie Christina's version told to me during my post-pneumonia days was a little bit different. I stress that this is mere hearsay and apologise in advance to surviving family members of the good Marchioness, without whose generosity many of my ancestors would have been denied medical care.

Auntie's story had it that the islanders had asked many rich people for help in their struggle against illness and disease but no interest had been shown. Eventually the Marchioness of Bute told them to start building and that she would pay for all the materials if they managed to have the hospital built and roofed in a stated period of time. I forget the exact number of days, but according to Auntie it was a very precise time, from sunup on a specific date till sundown on another some time later. Now the period of time she had chosen was one where, for many years previously, without fail, the weather had been appalling. Gales and lashing rain had prevented outdoor work and the proposed site for the hospital had been reduced to a quagmire. In other words, the Marchioness had set the islanders an impossible task. However, as Auntie said, 'That year God was on their side. He sent the wind and rain to Bute and sent Uist a hard frost instead.' The builders worked day and night and the roof was in place on the day which the Marchioness had stipulated. She passed the money over and the island got its hospital.

As with the Nunton Convent story I tell later, I don't know how much of island folklore is based on fact, and Auntie had such a profound dislike of all landlords and so-called benefactors that it may have distorted her memory. According to her, MacDonald of Boisdale was so corrupt that eventually his body decomposed while he was still alive and he died screaming in agony. There was also a story about a Ferguson who lived in the big house in South Lochboisdale and who cheated the crofters so badly that on the night he died many people saw his evil soul being taken up into the sky in a black, flame-encircled chariot, driven by the Devil himself. A very bloodthirsty little person, my auntie.

The house was very quiet when the two older brothers had left. Alick came over from Barra, as the aunties were finding that looking after two children, however well behaved, was a bit too much for them; but Mary Flora stayed with them until the end of the school year. My parents were thinking of joining in the current trend of having a new house built and were always looking at plans and discussing sites. I could not imagine any home other than our little thatched house, but I thought that it would be nice to have running water and electricity and a roof which I could trust. The previous winter we had woken up in the middle of the night to find that the fierce wind which had gusted to gale force during the night had blown a large amount of thatch off the roof directly above the bedroom, and we could see the stars through the rafters. It was a frightening experience and one which has left me with a fear of night storms. Each crofter who wanted to replace his old house was given a loan to finance labour and materials, and if the building conformed to the required standards and specifications, he would then be given a grant which was deducted from the loan. There were only two types of house plans available at that time – a long rectangular single-storey type and the more conventional square bungalow with a bit sticking out at the front. They both had three bed-rooms, a living-room, a large kitchen and a bathroom.

By now we had graduated from sand on the floor to a square of linoleum, but otherwise the house had changed little over the years. The main bedroom still had an assortment of beds and our only wardrobe, with a full-length mirror set into the door. The *trannsa* (passage) which led to the kitchen had a tongued-and-grooved wall holding stout coat hooks groaning with outdoor coats and jackets. The kitchen, which was also the living-room and dining-room, still looked the same as it had done on the night my mother had dropped the dumpling. A square room, lit by two small deep windows during the day, and by a Tilley lamp suspended from the ceiling at night. Against the back wall was a large built-in dresser. The piano stood next to it, and a small table covered with song-books was tucked into a corner by the closet door. A table and four chairs stood against the inner wall with four more folding chairs (Army surplus) leaning against the bit of wall that was left. Opposite the table was the black stove with a high mantelpiece above it. A large pot full of bubbling water and a steaming kettle always stood on the stove. The mantel shelf was adorned with two brass candlesticks and some framed photos of relatives standing in stiff poses. A string, permanently full of drying socks or tea towels, was slung under it. Above the mantel hung a picture of the Pope with his hand raised in blessing. Shelves to one side of the stove held cooking pots and other odds and ends, and on the other side was a large box full of peat. To the side of the stove, in front of the dresser was the *sèithear mòr* (big chair), a Rexine-covered high-backed armchair. By the door stood a box-like structure supporting the water buckets, and next to that the whole length of the front wall was taken up by the bench, which had changed only in that it now also had a covering of linoleum, which made it even less comfortable.

Last summer the twins and I sat in a similar house, one of the few left on the island still used as a home and not a holiday 'let'. It belongs to Donald MacDonald, a quiet dignified bard who lives in South Lochboisdale. We all knew each other years ago and we spent a very pleasant hour sitting on the bench by his stove, with its peat fire, talking about old times and marvelling at how large island families had managed to fit into such a small room. As Donald said, 'We were always on the move, young and old, doing something on the croft, and when it got dark and the grown-ups sat down, the children went to bed.' Although he still lives in his lovely little thatched house, Donald has evidently moved with the times. When we were leaving he introduced the speckled hens who came up to inspect us as the 'Spice Girls'.

My parents had decided on the shape of their new house and had chosen the site. Negotiations were going ahead with one of the local builders. Unlike the present day 'kit houses' which are springing up all over the island, the new croft-houses of my father's time were built on site in the traditional way. It was boom time for anyone who knew how to build a house, and even a few who couldn't build a decent peatstack had jumped on the bandwagon. One new house in our village was condemned as being a hazard to its inhabitants within a couple of years of being erected. Still, we were fortunate with ours, as it is still in use over forty years later.

At school we soldiered on doing mock exams and generally getting ready for the big one at the end of the year. Our music teacher decided to try and involve the adult members of the community in a Gilbert and Sullivan production, but gave up, as the Hebridean accent made it sound so strange that he couldn't bear it. Also, the play on words, so typical of the operetta, went right over the cast's head. Gaelic humour, like that of the Irish and Welsh, is often sharp and caustic, unlike the gentle irony of the English tongue. His comments at school the next day were a bit unkind, as he had really wanted to produce something spectacular. I don't think the audience would have been too appreciative anyway, judging by the reaction to a concert arranged by the Scottish Co-operative Society in an effort to advertise its growing number of food stores on the islands. They enlisted the help of some local performers, like my father, and sent a woman singer and a magician as their contribution to the programme. The local artistes got the usual rapturous applause. The magician went down well, but the poor woman didn't stand a chance. She was obviously a trained opera singer well past her sell-by date, and as she screamed and trembled her way through 'Oh, My Beloved Father' the normally well-mannered and appreciative Hebridean audience convulsed with laughter and some wag from the back of the hall shouted 'For God's sake, send for the vet!' People still remember her, though, while the name of the magician has long been forgotten.

One bit of excitement in my final year at Daliburgh happened during the dinner-hour, which we spent ambling about the school playground waiting for the bell to ring, after walking up to the Co-op to spend our pennies on sticky buns to fill the gap left by the school dinner. Someone noticed that the Swedish houses were enveloped in smoke, and the cry 'Casimer Place is on fire!' went up. As the wind swirled the smoke around, we could see that two of the houses were indeed ablaze, and the smell of burning creosote drifted towards us. Fortunately, there were no casualties, although the houses burned to the ground. There was only one fire engine on the island at the time, and as it was based at Benbecula Airport, nearly twenty miles away, it took some time to get to the fire. All the crew could do was to spray the other houses and generally contain the blaze so that only two families lost their homes and belongings. We did very little school work that afternoon, as none of us had seen a fire on that scale before. Although quite frightening, it was an awesome spectacle.

When I went home that day, bursting to tell my mother all about the fire, I discovered that it was old news, as a tinker wife was sitting on the bench telling her all about it. Usually, if my mother saw tinkers approaching, she would lock the door and hide. Hebridean tinkers did not have the glamour of the colourful Romany tribes. They came out of nowhere every summer and camped in their strangely shaped tents on the common ground out at Carisheval, with their ramshackle carts, skinny horses, snappy dogs and ragged children; they were not a welcome band. They were suspected of stealing peat from the bogs and generally helping themselves to anything they could find around the houses as they travelled about, selling their pails and clothes pegs, and asking for handouts of milk and eggs. They also asked for rags or old clothes. Our cast-offs were usually of the collar and waistband held-together-by-a-hole variety, and as the tinkers wore most of their collection, they were a strangely dressed group. The islanders are generous people and they would always give to the tinkers, especially if they had a babe or two with them, but I think they feared them, and that, was why they were treated with suspicion. Tinkers, especially the women, were said to have supernatural powers and were pretty free with their curses if you didn't buy their wares. They were reputed to possess 'the evil eye', and if they looked at your beasts the wrong way they would bear dead calves or catch diseases and die.

So I was most amazed to find my mother apparently entertaining this tinker wife. She finished her cup of tea, sold my mother some clothes pegs and left after reading my mother's palm and telling her that generosity was her key to a happier life. Naturally, my mother embarked on this path straight away by putting some eggs in the woman's pail and filling an old whisky bottle with milk for her. The tinker wife left, blessing us all and promising to come back again next year – words which made her hostess go pale. It transpired that my mother had been out at the end of the house trying to work out where all the smoke was coming from and had been very worried in case the school was on fire. When she came indoors the tinker wife was at the stove making herself a pot of tea. Not wishing to be cursed, especially as her children might at that moment be in a blazing building, my mother had no option but to make the lady as welcome as possible.

The school year drew to a close, and the lucky children whose parents could afford the cost went off to the annual *Comunn na h-Oigridh* (Society of Youth) camp on the beautiful Isle of Skye. Donald John had gone once, the trip financed by the aunties as a reward for settling down and working hard at school, and he had enjoyed it immensely. On his return he had regaled us all with tales of the old castle at the head of Loch Dunvegan, the seat of the clan MacLeod. He told us tales about a *bean-shìdhe* (fairy woman) who had once given the clan chief a *bratach* (cloak) and a *sionnsair airgid* (silver chanter) with which the player could play any tune to perfection. Donald John had also learned to peel potatoes during that week, as he had been caught writing a poem about one of the less popular organisers. The camp was primarily a meeting-place for young Gaelic speakers from all over the Islands and was very well supported each summer.

The exams were over and we were all convinced that we had really blown it and that no bursary with which we could finance our further education would be forthcoming. However, one morning when we had all but forgotten about the tests, the headmaster came in to tell us that the results were the best ever at the school and that our entire class had passed. A summer at home, and then I'd be joining Donald John at Fort William. The sadness of the previous months was gradually fading.

Chapter Ten

THE CLANGING OF A bell fitted in perfectly with my dream. I was on the boat bound for Mallaig and it was a very rough crossing. The bell got louder and louder and someone in my dream shouted 'Abandon ship!' I leapt out of bed and climbed the rope ladder, which was in fact my cubicle curtain, shouting in Gaelic: 'Where are the lifeboats? How long have we got?' The nun in the doorway ignored the pantomime and chanted, 'Praised be the Lord Jesus Christ!' Sleepy voices answered: 'Praised for evermore, Amen.' Her footsteps moved on to the next dorm and a voice called out: 'You've got three years and the lifeboats have sunk!' My first morning at the Convent had dawned.

To start the senior secondary phase of your education in the Forties and Fifties you had to be a good sailor. The schools were located in Inverness, Portree and Fort William, and most of the Catholics went to Fort William or Inverness, while the sons of the more wealthy Catholic islanders paid to go to to the private school at Fort

Augustus Abbey. The non-Catholics favoured Portree school which was on the largely Protestant Isle of Skye and was thus avoided by Catholic parents when nominating preferences for their children. Neither Fort William nor the Royal Academy in Inverness were Catholic schools – just the usual inter-denominational mix – but that didn't seem to matter, and if you had passed the Junior Leaving Certificate examination, Inverness-shire Education Authority guaranteed the payment of your living expenses at the school of your choice for three years.

The Minch lay between you and your school, whichever one you chose, and you faced six crossings a year. The journeys alone would be enough to put many people off, but we took them in our stride, as indeed we had to – they were a necessary evil – and we were so proud of having joined the ranks of the chosen. As I packed all the newly name-tagged clothes into my new suitcase and prepared to go with Donald John to Fort William, I was filled with excitement. The dream which had originated in the junk room at Kyles Flodda after listening to Auntie's stories was about to come true.

Both parents went with us to Lochboisdale to see us off on the boat, and as the bus driver came out to help with the luggage he said, 'My goodness, you're sending two away this year.' They both looked very proud. Naturally, we travelled by boat – planes were for tourists and more wealthy islanders – and the journey was unfailingly awful. I have heard it said that many a local seaman who had sailed the Bay of Biscay without disgracing himself had cause to dread the trip between Oban or Mallaig and Lochboisdale. Something to do with tides and cross-currents, my father said; but with the enjoyable experience of travelling to South Africa by sea behind me, I think it had more to do with the boats. The crossing took anything from six to twelve hours, depending on the weather, and who can depend on weather in the Hebrides, where you can have a lovely sunny day in December and a howling gale in August? Between the ages of fourteen and twenty I spent a minimum of 216 hours on the water and fed the herring with monotonous regularity.

That night the boat carried a large number of potential doctors, teachers, nurses and at least one fledgling priest that I know of: students from Barra, Eriskay, Benbecula and South Uist, ranging in ages from about fifteen to eighteen. The Barra students had already crossed over from Castlebay on the *Lochearn* and were transferring to the Mallaig boat at Lochboisdale. Some preferred the Oban route and would wait for the *Lochearn* to make its return journey to Castlebay, then join it for the Tiree-Oban sailing; but most of them favoured the *Lochmor* and the Mallaig way.

Many of the older Uist students were greeting specific members of the Barra contingent with more than friendship, and after the boat sailed I was surprised to find my brother kissing a pretty young lady from Vatersay, by the name of Nancy, behind a lifeboat. Fort William, and indeed this next section of my education, were beginning to look more interesting by the minute.

The boat docked at Mallaig very early in the morning, and there was quite a delay before the train left, but there was one consolation. If the boat was delayed due to bad weather, the train departure would be put back for anything up to three hours, so that boat passengers could make the connection. Having deposited our belongings at the left luggage office and been given a receipt, we passed the time trying to find something to eat, and since most of us had experienced a seasick, sleepless night, we staggered around Mallaig trying to stay awake.

The train journey, along one of the most picturesque routes in the United Kingdom, was spent in a daze, as the rocking motion of the old steam train made one's eyes even heavier, and every time you nodded off someone would leap up to close the windows to keep the smoke and flakes of soot out as the train passed under bridges and viaducts. At last we arrived at Fort William, the capital of Lochaber, and hauled ourselves and our bags through the town to our new homes.

The town has had its name played with over the years since the days when it was settled by the followers of troops sent in to keep the unruly seventeenth-century Highlanders in their place. The names Maryburgh, Duncansburgh and Gordonsburgh failed to survive, and the name which reminds us of the town's primary purpose is the one by which it is known today – *An Gearasdan*, or 'the Fort'.

On digging a bit more deeply into the origins of one of my favourite towns, I had the good fortune to talk to the Curator of The West Highland Museum, Fiona Marwick, earlier this year. She told me that the growth of the town could be followed by tracing its industrial pattern. The workers on various industrial projects had come to work and had stayed to settle. The influx which had begun with the military continued with the people brought to the area by Thomas Telford's Caledonian Canal, the West Highland Railway, the British Aluminium Company, Hydro Electric Power, and the Pulp and Paper Mill. There has also been a distillery there, even since before the railway. Industries may close down and workers move on, but Fort William will always have the towering Ben Nevis behind it, the glittering Loch Linnhe in front of it and charming inhabitants like Miss Marwick to ensure that its year-round attraction for visitors remains. As Provost John Cameron put it so well in his 1954 address, 'Fort William is the one good turn which Cromwell did for Scotland' (*The Burgh of Fort William 1875–1975,* by Walter Cameron).

On our first bleary-eyed introduction to Fort William we were in no fit state to appreciate either its historic significance or its charms, but we were introduced to another of its features – the record rainfall figures with which the mighty Ben blesses it.

The boys in our group boarded at the boys' hostel, a fairly relaxed establishment with a nice friendly matron in charge. It was located next to the school, and from all reports was a great place to live. According to my brother, who had already spent a year there, nothing worth mentioning ever happened, and there were no tales to tell. On the other hand, the girls were housed in the Convent, and that's another story.

The Convent, formerly Invernevis House, was once the home of D.P. MacDonald of Invernevis Distillery, one of the original Comissioners of the Burgh, way back in 1875. In my day it was home to the Order of Notre Dame nuns and sundry female boarders. My own memories of Fort William are dominated by the Convent and events which took place there, as I had thought about it and dreamed of going there since early childhood. The building resembled a large country house, surrounded by high walls, and the gardens were immaculate green lawns bordered with roses and graceful willow trees. To someone coming from a treeless island where growing anything ornamental was a battle, it all looked so well-ordered and colourful.

The interior, all dark panelling and polished floors, was in two sections, as part of the house was for the exclusive use of 'other' nuns, the ones who took no part in the day-to-day running of the boarding enterprise and whom we only saw in the chapel. As always, a cousin of my mother's popped up, this time among the 'other' nuns, one who had been in the Order from her teenage years and was now pretty old. Although she sent for me once and came over to the visitor's sitting-room to talk to me, we could find little common ground. She spent most of the time asking me for Gaelic words which she had forgotten, and kept saying, 'You are so young to be away from your mother.' 'Amen to that,' I thought. 'Try four and a half.' She gave me some stale sweets and said that she would pray for my immortal soul, and I never saw her again.

Our part of the house was pretty functional: three floors and a little attic divided into dormitories, bathrooms, a study, recreation room, refectory, pharmacy, infirmary and a few offices. I visited the nuns some years after leaving and the impressions I left with were the smell of beeswax and incense, home-made lemonade and the most peaceful silence imaginable. I know it was holiday time and the boarders were not there, but it wasn't just that. Have you ever noticed the silence of an empty church? It has a totally different feel to that of an empty house, or any other building. It is a silence so complete that it wraps itself around you and a feeling of peace comes through. I felt that on my return visit, although I had never sensed it when I lived there. Now the Convent has gone, demolished in 1965 to make way for the large Belford Hospital, and only the imprint of the back gate, filled in with concrete, remains to evoke memories.

We Island girls were only part of the full complement of Convent boarders, as pupils from Mallaig, Morar,

Arisaig and other Highland areas too distant for them to be day-pupils at Fort William Senior Secondary school also spent the school term there. They could go home at weekends if they wished, but quite often they just stayed on, preferring to spend the weekend 'out times' with their contemporaries. We all got along very well together, and I had no shortage of friends. But I suspect that having a good-looking older brother at the school may have had something to do with my popularity. My cousin and friend from Barra days, now tall with long fair hair, was also there, as was the cousin from Mallaig, who was in an older group; but we all had different friends now, and although seeing them again gave my life a sense of continuity, we went our separate ways. It was great living with so many girls of my own age, mixing with new people from a different background, and I spent many enjoyable weekends in Arisaig and Morar with my new acquaintances and their hospitable families.

During my boarding days I didn't see much of the gardens, which had so impressed me on arrival. We always had to use the tradesmen's entrance at the back of the building, and only once did I sit under the willows and admire the roses. That was after I had suffered a bout of mumps and was put out there to get some fresh air. Come to think of it, I never saw anybody else using the garden either apart from the old gardener and the two nuns who helped him to cut the grass and trim the bushes.

We studied in the study and ate in the refectory and lived in the dorms in our little cubicles, which were furnished with a bed, a chair and a locker, with a jug and bowl on top. We were in groups of six to ten to a dorm, with a senior girl in charge. We prayed in the chapel, and we did an awful lot of that. Not even living with the aunties prepared me for the amount of attention the Almighty would require during my teenage years.

'Shivering in the grey dawn' is a much overworked phrase, but it describes exactly the condition of the girls scurrying between bathrooms and cubicles with jugs of lukewarm water for the morning wash before dressing in our navy-blue uniforms. Beds were made, hospital style – at least that's what they called it – but I can't remember seeing too many beds with a flat pleated counterpane folded into a knife-edge crease along the edge of the bed and drawn into perfect matching triangles at each corner in any hospital. Our dormitories were inspected after the beds were made and before we lined up for chapel just before seven o'clock in the morning, unless it was a Saturday, when we had a 'lie-in' until seven-thirty. The combined effects of running around like a demented housewife and kneeling upright for three-quarters of an hour speaking Latin before breakfast made me faint frequently, and in the end I was excused morning Mass except on Sundays and Holidays of Obligation. This happened only in my second year, and it surprises me how many times your head can hit a wooden floor and remain intact.

Breakfast was very frugal, as indeed were all the meals – just above starvation level – or at least that's what it seemed like to an island child brought up on the bounty of land and sea, and they appeared to be a month apart. After breakfast we all had household duties to perform. They were real sweeping, scrubbing, polishing, dish-washing duties, which left me thinking longingly of bed-time till I got used to it, and as we plodded off to school through the teeming Lochaber rain the day already seemed a week old.

The school which we attended was the old Fort William Senior Secondary. On this site generations of children had been educated since the eighteenth century, and there is a present-day primary school carrying on the tradition. However, in 1960 the secondary pupils were moved out of the Burgh across the river Lochy to the newly-built Lochaber High School, a large modern school better equipped to deal with the escalation in numbers brought about by the increase in population and the statutory raising of the school-leaving age.

From the Convent on the Lochy side of the town we walked past the Alexandra Hotel, through the Parade ,which was once a military parade-ground, and along the main street, pausing to admire the window display of tartan skirts and vegetable-dyed woollens in a shop called *Mairi Nic an t-Saoir* (Mary MacIntyre). The items on display were not priced, but we knew well that if we needed to ask the price we couldn't afford the goods, so we contented ourselves by dreaming a little before walking on past the Italian ice-cream cafe, the Town Hall, and on to the far end of the town where the school stood next to the boys' hostel and just past the West End Hotel.

The front windows of most classrooms looked out over Loch Linnhe towards the white houses of Caol, and the art students were often taken across the road to a shelter on the lochside where they sketched the loch in all its moods. Sometimes the teacher would have to evict a poor demented local woman whom we cruelly called 'Daft Sarah', who spent a lot of time round the shelter, occasionally enlivening our lessons by lifting her skirts and 'mooning' in the direction of the school windows from across the road.

The school offered a wide range of well taught subjects, and the faculty, led by an eccentric but kindly headmaster, had the usual mixture of characters. Gaelic was superbly taught in great depth by a Mr MacKinnon from Skye. I often wondered if he was related to my landlady in Robson Street, but could not summon up the courage to ask. In those days familiarity had no part in your dealings with teachers. Mr Murphy was our inspirational and fiery-tempered English teacher. There was always a rush to grab a back seat when you entered his classroom. We all knew that, if someone at the back offended him, he would spare himself the walk to the back of the class and slap someone at the front instead. Our art teacher was a lady who was rumoured to have obscure health problems and often arrived at school with bruises on various parts of her body, having fallen off her scooter. I have reason to remember her, as I failed the history part of my Higher Art examination because she had given the only other candidate and myself the wrong book-list to study. When exam time came I was word-perfect on the lives of artists whom nobody wanted to know about. The teacher only discovered her error only after the exams were over and was almost suicidal in her remorse; so we ended up comforting her. As it didn't blight my life in any way, I forgave her a long time ago. School lunches were served in the Garrison Canteen, a short distance away, and walking there and back took care of most of our mid-day break; so only at the end of the school day did we go back to the Convent.

Nuns at that time, not the trendy liberated sisters of the present day, were quite an intimidating sight at close quarters. The nuns at our convent wore it all: black hooded cloaks and stiff white wimples with faces and fingers attached, and rosary beads and bunches of keys rattled as they rustled and creaked along the highly polished wooden floors of the corridors. All except Sister

Rachel, who 'kerlumphed' along, as some of her toes had been amputated, and we really appreciated this early warning system.

At first glance the faces looked kindly and pious, but with some of them this was mere window-dressing. For instance, the one known to the girls as 'Baby Grace' was pious but definitely not kind. She was a cherubic little dumpling of a nun, and even in her austere habit looked cute and cuddly, but she took the most sadistic pleasure in humiliating girls in front of an audience, and would not have failed selection tests for the Gestapo. We all feared and hated her, and I'm sure she killed many a potential vocation stone dead.

Sister Rachel was in charge of our welfare in all departments during my first year and was a mixture of tolerance and bad temper. She was replaced by another nun, Paul Mary, and we all agreed that it was a change for the better. Although she could be as mean as a glove full of scorpions when crossed, she could be manipulated and was a real soft touch for a sob story. I had reason to be thankful for this, and remember her with great affection – but more of that later. A converted Anglican, she genuinely tried to understand and uphold the rules of her adopted faith. She had an almost pathological hatred of make-up, and we girls were her cross to bear; however, she was determined to mould us into nice young Catholic ladies despite our efforts to the contrary.

Then there was an Irish nun, Sister Rose, who was so immersed in her devotion that she was already halfway to heaven and gave little indication of inhabiting the same planet as the rest of us. Her duties included supervising our meals, which she did in the most absent-minded manner. One morning at breakfast a girl swallowed a mouthful of scalding tea and burned herself. She rushed up to the rostrum where Rose was immersed in some liturgical tome and gasped, 'Please, Sister, I've burnt my throat!' Sister Rose raised her eyes from her book and whispered, 'Hush, child, offer your pain to the Lord and rub the burn with soap.' She should have joined an enclosed order where her love affair with her Maker would not have to be interrupted so often by his more tiresome creations.

If I were to be asked which features of the Convent mattered most to me, I would answer the nuns, because they were all over the place, and the post-table, because it kept us going. All our mail was laid out there in the morning after breakfast, and, as you can imagine, letters were precious links with home. My parents were very good letter-writers and wrote every week without fail. One would write to my brother and the other to me, and we exchanged the letters at school. The aunties also wrote and sent the odd ten-bob note now and then, but my father's letters were the ones we both enjoyed the most, as he saved up little nuggets of island life and his own day-to-day activities to amuse us:

We had a great time yesterday at the sheep dipping. I know you are thinking that I have never said that before and you are right! I hate the stink of the dip and I always get the rotten job of catching the sheep as they come through the trough. At least three times out of ten they knock me over and I end up lying on the ground with a wet sheep running over my face. Yesterday was good though. Some of John's flock had gone missing and as there were more than enough men at the fank to send our sheep through, we left them there and went looking for the lost ewes. You know that John's dog is cleverer than anything in Kilpheder with half the number of legs so we let him do the tracking. We followed him along the way towards South Lochboisdale and over the back of the hill to Glendale and there they were, on their holidays.

We had never been to Glendale before and it is a great place. I had seen it from the sea at the time of the 'Polly', but only the lights as it was night time and we were always in a hurry. It is stuck away behind the hill and as there is no road the people have to carry all their food and anything else they need from the shops, over the hill, in sacks, on their backs. John was saying that they must be quite wild and different to the rest of us, living like that so isolated and lonely, but when one of them came out and called us in for a bite to eat he was willing enough to follow me into the house while the dog kept an eye on the sheep.

It was a stone-built house, a lot better than mine or John's, with a slate roof and skylights for the upstairs and a garden outside full of flowers which we could never grow here as they get the sun but not the wind. The old man and his wife were very pleasant and quite refined and they sat us down to a table all set up with a cloth and all the trimmings with a great variety of food in nice dishes. When we were leaving I thanked them and John added his bit, '*Chaidh sibh gu móran dragh, cha ruigeadh sibh a leas, tha sinne cho amh rib' fhéin*' ('You needn't have gone to so much trouble, we are just as uncivilised as yourselves'). He'd have done better to have let his dog do the talking . . .

Letters, parcels, and of course seeing my brother at school every day, soon took care of homesickness, but we all counted the days until the holidays. So we settled down to our new way of life – a busy one – and although the Convent regime was rather harsh, the strict rules gave us a feeling of security; but as with all young people, we were not too appreciative of that point at the time.

Chapter Eleven

IN MY CHILDHOOD DAYS bath night meant the old strip-wash routine. You went into the little room called the closet with an enamel basin or the tin bath full of warm water from the kettle and a bar of Lifebuoy soap. You stripped and sponged and washed and soaped yourself clean as far as the limited facilities and lack of privacy allowed. At Mistress MacKinnon's Glasgow residence there had been a bath in what she called the water closet, but the bath, a strange pear-shaped container on four clawed legs, was always full of folded sheets, so we didn't use it. So the first time that I was totally immersed in warm soapy water, at the Convent, was one of the most wonderful experiences of my life. It eclipses childbirth, seeing Table Mountain wrapped in its tablecloth in a pink dawn, and even the colours of a Vermont Fall.

Baths in the Convent, like everything else, were timetabled and timed. I still remember my place on the list. It was 6.45 p.m. till 7.15 p.m. every Wednesday. As the temperature was always pretty low around the building, bath times were the only times when I felt really warm. I have never forgotten the feeling of comfort and security I experienced when having that first bath. At various stages in my life when things have been been stressful and frayed around the edges, my first instinct is to head for the bath.

Naturally, a first time for anything is full of pitfalls, and the bath was no exception. Never would I admit to anyone else that it was my first time. A certain amount of heart-searching wasted some of the precious half-hour, as I stood there naked trying to work out whether I should jump in or insinuate myself gradually under the water. Having decided on the latter, I got in and found that I seemed to have over-filled the bath. It was a very large one and I was a bit of a shrimp. So I half-sat, half-floated around and tried sticking my big toe into the tap for safety, but that didn't work and I went under a few times. Eventually I found that the overflow slit provided a good toehold and the rest of the time was bliss. As the great unwashed became the squeaky clean, I was hooked on mod cons forever.

On my return to the study I still felt a warm glow, and as I wrestled with the translation of '*Quae cum Hannibal . . .*' I had the greatest difficulty concentrating. My eyes were heavy and I was almost asleep. Suddenly a cross voice in my ear hissed, 'You get up there and clean that bloody bath!' . . . Alas, nobody had prepared me for the etiquette of bathroom hygiene. I thought the bath cleaned itself as it emptied and had left it to do so. 'You can take the girl out of the heather, but you can't take the heather out of the girl.' To say that I was mortified is putting it mildly. A mainland dweller, the girl who berated me had no doubt been having baths from infancy and had no idea of my ignorance. She made darned sure that everyone in the study knew of my filthy habits and general lack of couth. I could have died of shame. To this day, when visitors arrive unexpectly, my first thought is 'Help! Is the bathroom clean?'

Sister Magdalene had shown me how to clean forks with a strange grey powder and had also given me some driving lessons on the 'bumper'. This was a heavy square pad with a very long wooden handle with which I had to polish the corridor every day. I have painful recollections of that handle embedding itself in my stomach on its return journey the first time I used it. I do wish that somebody had shown me how to clean a bath. It would have been a better preparation for real life and would have spared me much misery.

Happily, there was always something new happening to divert us, and so my notoriety soon died down. One week the town was full of young men in shorts and running shoes jogging along, and we admired them covertly as we stepped out of their way whilst walking to school in the morning. They were preparing for the gruelling marathon up to the top of Ben Nevis. Excitement among the locals was high and some local boys seemed to be in with a chance of winning. In fact, previous years had seen Fort William being well represented in the winners' list, with the names Kearney and Campbell jostling for top honours. The marathon had started off as a purely Lochaber event, with budding athletes who wanted to make their name challenging an established Ben runner to defend his honour. It had grown into a major mountain marathon with athletes, male and female, from all over the country taking part, but of course, due to its origins, there was always much joy when a local won. While I was at the Convent a local girl, Kathleen Connochie, gained the distinction of setting a new record.

We could not even contemplate the idea of running up Ben Nevis. We hiked up twice and it nearly finished us off. Personally I found it frustrating, as the weather was dull on both occasions, and although sitting in a cloud at the summit was a strange damp experience, the view was obscured by mists. We went up in a group with the more energetic members of our class at school, and as the town children no doubt had other weekend pursuits planned with their families, the group was composed almost entirely of Convent girls and hostel boys, led by a teacher or two.

We followed the Achintee trail, and although it required no ropes or pitons, it was definitely more of a climb than a walk. The descent was hair-raising, as the boys thought it amusing to give you a push just when the effort of making the soles of your boots grip the steeply sloping trail was playing havoc with your knee-joints. As you flew down the trail, frantically clawing at thin air, you tried to gain some braking control over your boots, which seemed to have acquired a personality of their own. The only way to do this was by flinging your body sideways and backwards at the same time. This manoeuvre stopped you, by throwing you backwards on to the ground as you prayed that you would land on grass and not on a rock. Amusing to watch but horrible to experience. The group leaders walked in front of us ready to act as a last-ditch safety barrier, and repeatedly tried to restore order; but there wasn't much they could do. Two years ago I hiked the trail to the summit of Mount Mansfield, the highest peak in Vermont, and on the way down I caught myself looking over my shoulder waiting for a push.

As we got caught up in the hurly-burly of teenage life, it would have been easy to forget that Uist ever existed:

everything was so different, and sometimes even my brother looked unfamiliar when I caught sight of him in the playground. Whether it was town living or merely the fact that he was growing up, he just seemed so much more self-assured. The letters from home helped to keep the link strong, and we also had the occasional brief few minutes spent at the station with my father when he went to Glasgow to do recordings. He didn't spend too much time away from home, just went there, did the recording and got straight back to the island. The croft, the seaweed factory and the building of the new house kept him busy, but like my mother he never forgot to sit down once a week and write to us.

I am going to Glasgow on Saturday week to record some more stuff. Come to the station to meet the Mallaig train and we can have a few minutes together. I expect your mother will want me to bring you half the Co-op and a barrel of salt herring, so would you write to her and ask for something small and easy to carry? Remember that the train does not stop for long so don't waste any time pretending to be shy. I know I'll be wearing my Sunday clothes and looking very *Gallta* [like a Lowlander] but it'll only be me without my dungarees. It will be great to see you both.

We are all well here. Your brothers and sister are working hard at school – at least that is what they tell me. Old Mary By The Canal was over yesterday and she was asking after you both. Her old 'Bad Dog' got into trouble last week. He was suspected of worrying Neil's sheep and Neil came over to Mary's with his gun ready to do the business. He had already spoken to Mary and she had agreed that the dog had to go. When he got to her house the 'Bad Dog' had just finished a bowl of porridge and was starting on a plate of bacon and eggs with a slice of black pudding and a sausage on the side. Mary was crying her eyes out and keening, 'Cò ris a bhruidhneas mise a nochd? Cò a bhios gam fheitheamh le fàilte mhór?' ('Who will I talk to tonight? Who will give me a big welcome when I come home?'). It was all too much for Neil. Nearly in tears himself, he said, 'Any dog who has a better breakfast than I do every day has no need to eat sheep. It must have been another dog. Just keep him tied up near the house for a few days till we catch the real killer.'

Well, I have my own thoughts about the whole affair and B.D. had better not look sideways at our sheep or Mary's wiles won't save him from a lead earplug . . .

The little packages my father gave us at the station, and also the larger parcels which sometimes appeared on the post-table, had one thing in common. They contained food. By trial and error our parents worked out which goods would survive the postal system, and if it arrived in one piece and could be eaten, they sent it. If we didn't like the contents ourselves, then someone else would be glad of them and nothing was ever wasted.

To appreciate a feast, one must first of all experience a fast. During my teaching days I frequently enjoyed being part of the school camp team and was often invited to join in 'midnight feasts' – sedate little gatherings where already overfed children crunched crisps and guzzled lemonade by torchlight. I've pretended to be terrified of intruders and agreed that 'we'll all be in terrible trouble if we're found out.' I would not dream of spoiling their fun by telling them that midnight feasts were timetabled as carefully as any other event during their week, and that midnight never occurred at nine-thirty.

Without fail as I crept back to my room to wash off the chocolate before easing my exhausted body into bed, my mind would turn to other feasts. Then the fear was real. The punishment for being caught out of bed after 'lights out' was bad enough, but to be caught three or four to a bed, eating, had you straight up before Mother Superior the following morning. She was small, but she was terrifying in anger and could verbally reduce you to a snivelling wreck before stopping large amounts of your precious 'out time'. We were never, never allowed to get into another girl's bed. I had no idea why this rule was upheld so strictly. Now I know, and I still think the nuns had nothing to fear but their own fears.

Food parcels, as I have already mentioned, were always received with whoops of delight, and we got very crafty. The rules read: 'All Food Parcels To Be Brought To The Refectory. No Food In The Dorms As This Encourages Mice.' Well, we brought the odd tin of condensed milk to spread on the bread and marge or perhaps a currant loaf to our table, and put the nuns off the scent by saying that the parcel had contained new underwear and suchlike. The best of the goodies were squirreled away in lockers all over the dorms of your friends. You waited for a few days to let the trail go cold and then hunger got the better of caution and the midnight feast took place.

At the agreed time, well after the nuns' lights, visible from Top Dorm's window, had gone out, a dozen or so girls would creep out of bed, and, carrying their 'stash', make their way through quiet dorms into your cubicle.

There the strange and varied menu would be enjoyed by ten to twelve girls, huddled for warmth in the same bed. How we talked! In whispers, naturally, about the nuns, the cold, boys, food, clothes, boys, fears, ambitions, school, boys, funny stories about nuns and, of course, home.

When all the food was gone and we were in danger of falling asleep in what was forbidden territory for all but one of us, it was over. Guests left as quietly as they had arrived. All wrappings, tins and jars went into our satchels to be dumped on the way to school. We were very tidy and I never saw a mouse in the Convent.

One night it all went wrong. On the floor above my dorm was a room called Blue Dorm. Directly above was Top Dorm, which had a safety rating of zero, as Baby Grace, the most hated nun ever, slept in a room a few yards down the corridor. Any midnight feasts involving food from top dorm were held in Blue Dorm, and as this was a very risky undertaking it didn't happen very often. On this particular night the food stockpile was very large. There were packets of jelly cubes, crisps, chocolates, packets of dates, bags of mixed fruit, cakes of all descriptions and a dumpling. Perhaps I should say the remains of a dumpling. It had survived its postal journey by being packed in a tin box; but the recipient had been eating bits of it on her way downstairs and there was a big hole in it. Nobody cared, however, as there was plenty left for all.

Happy girls lay there eating away and telling 'knock-knock' jokes when suddenly the air of suppressed festivity was shattered by a hissed 'N . . . u . . u . . nn!' from one of the other cubicles. All froze like statues for a second. Then there was a querulous, toothless 'Praised be the Lord Jesus Christ!' from the top of the stairs. From lights out to rising bell this was the only acceptable form of communication and you answered, 'Praised for ever more, Amen!' That is if you had just been to the toilet or had gone to get a drink of water etc., and happened upon a wandering nun, not if the nun was a toothless Baby Grace and you were sitting ten to a bed eating crisps. Like silent arrows from a bow, girls fled in all directions. Then there was an almighty crash and a black, squawking bundle landed on the floor. Baby Grace, trying to creep down the stairs, had trodden on a lump of dumpling and had taken half the flight in one screaming step.

None of the partying party offered first-aid, as getting back to bed undetected was first priority. One of the loyal non-participants picked the unharmed but dazed nun up and gave her a convincing explanation of nightmares and sleepwalking. Another made sure that her skirts remained over her face until order was restored. I think she was so glad to get out of it with what was left of her dignity that we heard no more about it. That was a midnight feast.

Apart from the letters from home and the gratefully received parcels, the post-table gave us another bit of excitement when we discovered pen-friends. Naturally, we were all very interested in boys, and most of our free time was spent talking about them. Locked up as much as we were, we could do little else about it. The school was co-ed, and sometimes innocent little romances flourished against all odds. Glen Nevis in all its glory was on our doorstep and we were 'let out' on Saturday and Sunday afternoons. A trip to the local cinema and a walk up the glen were always more exciting if you were holding hands with a boy, however pimply. That's as far as it went: holding hands and a chaste kiss or two; but we felt very decadent.

One of the Barra girls surprised us all one day by producing a letter with a German postmark. 'Look at this,' she said. 'It's from my pen-friend, Gunther.' This was really exciting. We all gathered round and practically grovelled at her feet until she showed us the letter. It was very formal and the greetings and salutations reduced us to tears of laughter. The information that 'I am two yards big' went down very well, and I am still trying to figure out what 'My father is gratitude a carved fish' was all about. Poor young German boy. He really made our day.

From then on we all had pen-friends. We wrote to boys who advertised in some magazine, and if the information they gave us about themselves was as fictitious as that which they received, who knows what they were really like? Naturally, we lied about age, vital statistics and looks in general. All our parents became Lairds overnight and those of us who didn't have cars had yachts. The Convent was explained away as a kind of finishing school, and we got many letters to pass around and giggle over. It got a bit complicated, the way lies do, and after a while the whole thing petered out.

Gunther, however, persevered. As his English improved, his ardour increased. Letters were not enough. A very large, very soggy parcel stood on the post-table and stank the place out one day. Gunther had sent his 'Beautiful Scottish Thistle' a half-pint bottle of 4711 perfume and it had not had a good journey. The nuns were a bit cross about it all and there was some explaining to do. Come to think of it, our time with the Sisters made many of us into pretty convincing liars. We thought of it as self-preservation.

Having prepared his ground, Gunther announced in his next letter that 'Your letters make me want to survey you . . .' that . . . 'I am coming to you expidentious' . . .

and 'You and I quite alone will roam around the countryside'. The letter caused a bit of a panic and she decided to stop writing in case he turned up at the Convent and got her expelled. The next thing that came was a telegram: 'Show signs of life! Love to you. Gunther.'

Then it all went quiet and no more was heard. After many months of silence she confessed to us that she had sent him a telegram, supposedly from her brother, informing poor German Gunther that she had died. We wondered if he would try to come to the funeral but we never heard any more about him.

Another important but extremely noisy event on the Fort William sporting calendar and beloved of the hostel boys was the six-day motorcycle trials. Legions of motor cycles roared through the town, having raced there from Edinburgh. For the next few days bikes and riders would be pushed to the limits of their strength in endurance trials over some very rough terrain. The traditional climax was the ascent of Town Hall Brae. The bikes roared past the school and boys and masters alike would discuss the merits of their favourite riders in the world of motor cycle trials and races. I can remember the name Geoff – or was it Jeff? – Duke being mentioned. We girls had no interest in the subject, but the boys, including my brother and, I suspect, the masters too, ran a book and stood to gain or lose money as the winners emerged.

In the summer, at the end of the school year the local Junior Mod was held. This event had been pioneered in the early 1900s, when a large percentage of the population were still Gaelic speakers. The numbers had somewhat dwindled by my time, so the fluent Gaelic-speaking children from the Islands were usually very successful. It was an event we all enjoyed, and the Winner's Concert on the last evening was not to be missed. One year the gold medallists from the Senior Mod, a stunning young couple, announced their engagement during the concert and the Convent girls swooned about the romance of the occasion for years.

There was little or no Mod coaching available to us at school, probably because the teachers were busy with the curriculum and the preparation of pupils for exams. The Gaelic speakers on the faculty were asked to judge some of the events, and this they did. A competition programme was circulated in school and you just found out what the category requirements were and entered your name against your chosen events.

Due to my accelerated race through primary school, I could enter a simpler section than most of my classmates, so, feeling confident, I put my name down for a few competitions. The day before the Mod I found out that my brother had entered me for everything else on the list. Touched by his confidence in my abilities, I spent the night before the Mod learning poems and practising Unseen Reading and generally being a nervous wreck. Towards the end of the next day and what had been a very successful Mod, knowing that I only had one more event to win and I'd have the Kilmallie Quaich, a large silver trophy, in my grasp, I felt very grateful to Donald John. I sat in a room with the last remaining competitor in the Proverbs Knockout Competition and I was touched to see him and his friends watching from the door. They hissed at me: '*Fad 's bhios slat sa choill bidh foill sa Chaimbeulach*,' the ancient saying of the Clan MacDonald after Glencoe ('While there's a tree in the woods there'll be treachery in a Campbell'). As the judge was a Mr Campbell, and a very strict teacher with whom most of us had crossed swords in class, I ignored their coaching from the sidelines and came up with a proverb of my own. My opponent dried up and I had won the event and the cup for my points overall. My treacherous brother and his friends were winners too. They had won a nice bit of money from the hostel book, on which I had featured as an outsider at 15 to 1. Apparently he had spread a rumour that I was useless. I forgave him, as always.

Life in Fort Willliam was not always laughter and midnight feasts. We had to work hard to keep up with the demands of school work, and as always, little petty disputes between friends could make you miserable. However, the school year was divided into three terms ,and each term had a wonderful thing called a holiday at the end of it. So we coped with our lives and waited for the time we could get on the Mallaig train and leave it all behind for a little while.

Chapter Twelve

AT THE END OF each term we Islanders were almost hysterical with excitement at the thought of going home again. We drooled at the thought of salt herring, lobster, scones with fresh butter and machair potatoes. We couldn't wait for the church hall dances and the bliss of not hearing a bell or seeing a wimple for a few weeks. We were a very merry band indeed as we joined the Mallaig train or took the bus to Oban. Then the sailings to the islands were not as frequent as those provided by today's car ferries, and the Skye bridge, which has been such a boon to non-sailors like myself, was not even a dot on a drawing board. So we found out from which port the next boat was leaving and planned our route accordingly.

The journey, at least initially, was almost as good as the holiday – that is, until the sea took its toll. It is said that travelling hopefully is often better than arrival, and many times in my life this has been proved true. For instance, some dire package holidays and rain-soaked summer breaks in tiny chalets with fractious toddlers, when I've counted the days remaining with dread, come to mind. When we went home from Fort William for school holidays, the buzz of anticipation in the company of our peers was great, and the holiday at the end of it always too short.

The rules of Highland hospitality were part of my family creed: 'Always repay a debt, and if it's a debt of kindness, pay it twice.' Many of the mainland girls had invited me home for the odd weekend and my parents encouraged me to return the invitation. They had fretted us into leaving, to better ourselves, and missed us all sorely. So they were always happy to welcome us back and were glad to meet any of our friends who had shown us kindness. Donald John never brought any of his friends home, as he tended to keep company with the Uist boys at school, and most of his non-Uist associates were girlfriends. He would not bring them home, even if it were permitted, as they would only cramp his style with the Uist girls.

The tiny thatched crofthouse with no running water and too many running feet had been vacated, and a nice roomy bungalow built next to it was now the family home. My mother had all the space which she had craved when bringing up a family in the old house. I know the numbers went down from time to time, courtesy of the aunties, but how she managed family and croft in such circumstances I'll never know.

The house had no plumbing whatsoever for cooking, washing or sanitation, nor was there any source of power other than the peatstack. I will not linger on the sanitation aspect. It involved a covered bucket in the corner of the bedroom at night and a grassy hollow with a spade in your hand during the day. Every drop of water we used for all domestic purposes was drawn from a well, five minutes' walk from the house, and carried very carefully in buckets by whichever children were water-carriers for the day. We were always sent in pairs, in case one fell in and had to be rescued. Mercifully, we never fell in, but on the way home we often fell out, and we ended up bickering on the doorstep with half-empty buckets. Back we went with swinging buckets and stinging bottoms. My mother had never read progressive books on child-rearing; she had no time. She always said that her training at Hawkhead Asylum was all she needed to help her cope with us and our father.

Even with the additional room in the new house, you had to be careful with your invitation. Holidays were precious, and if the girl didn't fit in, your own holiday and hers would be ruined. Happily, all the girls who came home with me were great fun and enjoyed themselves immensely. No thanks at all to the nuns, who kept trying to send their own favourites off on a free junket to the islands.

They were always imploring me to take one particular girl who was spoilt, spiteful and sulky. I'm sure she had many good points, but they were well masked. She was not too bright either. When asked in Home Economics what she would do if visitors came and she had only a loaf of bread, some butter and a tomato, she looked blank. 'Make a sandwich with the tomato,' said her teacher. 'Don't be daft,' was the reply, 'it would roll off.' I'm afraid that her chances of ever coming home with me had been reduced to nothing the evening she told the entire Convent study group that I hadn't cleaned the bath.

The girls threw themselves into croft work with the rest of us and loved listening to my father's stories of

152

events on the island during my absence. He loved an audience and no question was left unanswered: 'Who did the plumbing for your new house, Mr Mac?'

'Well, now, it was this man from the mainland called Jock. Am Plumair Mòr (the big plumber) we called him in Gaelic. He was a nice man and a good plumber too, but he had two faults. One was foul language and the other was that he read in the lavatory. We had always managed matters of nature in our own way before the building began, but knowing that some builders would be coming from the mainland we built a wee wooden house and put an Elsan chemical toilet in it, so that they could do their business in comfort and privacy. Jock found the wee house much to his liking and spent a lot of time in there reading magazines and books.

'I didn't mind. He always came to work early and carried on as long as the light lasted, and, as you've seen, days are long on South Uist. He didn't believe in God, so Sunday was just another working day to him. Yes, I was happy. Work was going well on the plumbing until the explosion.'

We had been drifting off a bit and wondering where the story was going, but now he had our full attention. 'Explosion?'

'Well, you see, it was like this. One day Jock was sitting on the throne, deep in Mickey Spillane, when your mother called, "Tea, Jock?" Now, Jock ran on tea the way a motor car runs on petrol, so he shouted back, "Be right there, missus!" and the very next minute there he was. There was an almighty bang and the wee house fell apart and there stood Jock, clutching his trousers, book still in his hand and, if you'll pardon the expression, covered in glory. He was so taken with the yarn he had been reading that he had quite forgotten where he was. When the call for tea came he just stood up and threw his fag in the the toilet. Bad mistake with a can full of chemicals. He just stood there and swore for ten minutes without repeating himself. My, but am Plumair Mòr had a fine command of the English language.'

As we laughed our heads off at the picture his words had painted, he added: 'So don't let me catch any of you smoking in my new bathroom.'

The one thing the mainland girls disliked intensely was the Sunday Mass at St Peter's Church. Although the main part was conducted in the familiar Latin, all the hymns and the long, long sermon were in Gaelic. Even after the local boys had been covertly assessed, there was always an interval of boredom. 'That awful sermon would make me an atheist if I lived up here,' they'd say. One Sunday, just as the sermon was getting to the painful stage and everyone wriggled and fidgeted, there was a loud 'clunk!' from the aisle at the end of our family pew. There, wagging his stumpy tail, standing over a large stone, was Sandy, our black dog. He had retriever blood in him and kept trying to prove this by presenting us with retrieved stones hours after they had been thrown for him. The sermon didn't seem half as long that day.

Now that we were older, the church provided us with more than a boring Sunday sermon. It was the social centre of the community. There were concerts and whist drives and, of course, dances in the hall across the road. The music was provided by some of the very accomplished accordionists on the island, and apart from the boy–girl thing and showing off your latest hairstyle, the dancing itself was sheer joy. We mainly danced the Scottish country-type dances but the quickstep was just coming into vogue and we followed the trend. My mainland friends always loved our dances and were never short of partners. Uist men are of course tall, good-looking and well-mannered, or perhaps I am biased; anyway, the girls were well pleased with the selection on offer.

My parents were liberal but not stupid, and we had to come straight home after the dance. If we had a boy in tow, we brought him in and gave him a cup of tea before sending him on his way with a quick goodnight kiss if he was lucky. Somehow my father was always around to check up on what he called 'camp followers'.

Drink was not sold at the dances and no one who looked drunk or carried a bottle was allowed in the hall, and this made our parents more comfortable about our moral safety. It worked, as a rule, but one night we met James, who was the exception.

At first sight James, whom I had not seen before, looked attractive and a cut above the usual. He was dressed very smartly in a fine navy-blue suit, and Maureen, my convent friend and I, agreed that he was 'with it'. Having worked for a few weeks in Glasgow, he spoke entirely in English, and although he danced with both of us I was obviously the object of his pursuit. I wasn't complaining, and after a couple of dances consented to his walking me home at the end of the evening. He didn't monopolise me and I carried on dancing with my usual partners, with an odd dance with James in between.

As the evening went on I began to regret my choice. The suit still looked good but the person inside it wasn't wearing half as well. James had obviously worked out a way of 'tanking up' away from the priest's watchful eyes and was getting more and more drunk. His English was peppered with 'sort of this' and 'sort of that', and now and then he'd look me straight in the eye and say, 'I've been in love with you for weeks but I've never seen you before.' Then he'd laugh like a donkey. The first time he said it I thought he was funny, but it wore off.

Maureen had no escort that evening, so we walked home after the dance in a threesome, giving James broad hints as to the desirability of his drowning himself in the canal. He was still there, however, when we arrived home, and although we said, 'Goodnight, then, we'll see you,' hoping that he would take the hint, he followed us into the house. My father took one look at him and whispered to me, 'Which one of you won the tailor's dummy in the raffle?' I dragged him into the kitchen and told him the story while Maureen settled James into a comfortable chair by the open peat fire. She was enjoying my discomfort and wondering how things would turn out. She didn't have to wait long. When my father and I came back from the kitchen with cups of tea, the gallant suitor was fast asleep. 'I thought so,' said my father, bending down to take a good look at James's face. 'I know him. He lives a good ten miles from here. Let him have his sleep. He has a long way to walk home and it's raining. I'll leave the front door unlocked and he can let himself out. Let's all get off to bed. You mind and lock your doors!' So we left 'Sort of . . . James', sort of . . . sleeping in the chair.

When my mother got up next morning James was still there. He was lying in the hearth, with his lovely navy-blue suit covered in fine grey ash from the now dead peat fire, sleeping like a baby. When he had been partially revived with a cup of tea, he focused his bleary gaze on the mantel clock and exclaimed, 'God Almighty! My sort of . . . grandmother is being sort of . . . buried today and

I am sort of . . . late!' With that he thrust the cup of tea at my mother and ran off through the fields towards the church. As he wasn't familiar with the geography of Kilpheder, he very nearly ended up in the canal and had to do a quick side-track up the soggy bank to the bridge. I would have liked to have seen the look on the other mourners' faces when James eventually lined up beside them in his muddy shoes and navy/ash suit.

Ceilidhs were the high point for winter visitors, the girls who were brave enough to brave the crossing for the Christmas break. The weather was always blustery, so many evenings were spent at home. The local 'talent', as we called the young people who came to have a look at the mainland girls, would join the usual friends who came to our house. We would spend the evening telling tales, singing songs or playing 'Catch the Ten', a whist-type card game which I have never seen played anywhere else.

By now the piano, which had been my mother's solace when she had unwillingly returned to the island so many years ago, had given up the ghost. My father had been going to bring it in from the old house when they moved, but he found that in addition to the damage caused to it by damp over the years, the back was full of woodworm holes. So the dear old instrument, which had provided us with much pleasure and had looked so out of place on the sanded floor, was not fit to be transferred to more suitable surroundings. It became two coffee tables and the rest was dumped. In its place we had a new radiogram and a good supply of large black 78-rpm records, mostly of Gaelic songs and Scottish dance-band music. In addition, young Donald was a good accordionist, so if there were enough of us, young and old, we'd have an impromptu dance right there in our living

157

room. Carpets were no problem. There was only lino with a few rugs which were easily rolled up.

On short winter days when the cows were snug in the byre, crofting chores were governed by the hours of daylight, so we made our own entertainment, stayed up late and slept till we woke up. A very welcome change from the regimented routine of the Convent. The ceilidh would often go on till well past midnight. When things began to flag, my father, who had to be up and ready for picking up by the factory lorry in the morning, would give the signal for dispersal. He did this by launching into the longest, dreariest song in his enormous repertoire, a 28-verse panegyric guaranteed to oust even the most determined hearth-hugger. 'Well, well,' he'd say, 'it's a strange thing. *Òran Mòr MhicLeòid* ('MacLeod's Lament') can clear the house faster than an air-raid warning. It's a pity I didn't think to offer my services in that line during the war. It would have suited me much better than the Home Guard.' As the people left he'd carry on singing, pausing only to nod in acknowledgement of farewells, and, following the last person to the door, would turn the key in the lock before delivering a final verse of his own composing, making pithy comment on events of the evening and the young hopefuls.

The shopping arrangements were another novelty. Of course they met Willie Jordan and heard his yarns and lined his pocket. He always had a soft spot for a young, pretty face, and he'd put a nice hankie or even a scarf in the parcel with their purchases. The nearest shop was small, but carried a vast stock of the needle-to-an-anchor variety. As the Co-op had been extended and stock upgraded, this shop had tried to keep pace, but being a family-run enterprise, they did not have the training or the space to ensure an efficient stock control system. The owner's motto was: 'No purchase too small and no hour too late.' At least, it seemed like that. He once sold us a packet of 'Kirbi grips' priced at two old pence at ten o'clock at night, dressed in his pyjamas and dressing gown, having spent a good fifteen minutes searching for them by torchlight in the store adjacent to the shop. The shop itself was no larger than one of today's single garages and had no refrigeration, yet he supplied meat and other perishable goods, sometimes a bit 'high', though I can't remember a single case of food poisoning being reported.

In even earlier times most merchants had owned their own primitive slaughterhouses. When I was little I once went into one of those places with my father, who was delivering a message to the shop owners, and I saw a sheep being killed. It was horrible. The large vein in the throat was cut and the sheep was just held by the horns and the feet until it bled to death. It did not struggle in any way as its blood gushed into a bucket, but I can see the poor beast's large hopeless eyes looking at me until they finally closed. I was told that it was a painless death and that the sheep merely thought that it was falling asleep, but I wondered, even at that early age, which sheep had come back to impart that information.

The merchants had a system of slaughtering on alternate weeks when the demand was low, and they shared the meat. Everything was seasonal, and if the islanders had been slaughtering their own sheep or there was a glut of herring, the demand for shop-bought meat went down. Sometimes the reverse would happen, and demand was high. At such a time, rumour has it, one shopkeeper would send the other a telegram saying, 'Send no meat. Killing myself tomorrow!' It makes perfect sense in Gaelic but assumes a more sinister sense in translation.

The girls were astonished by the size of the cod, ling and other white fish which my father brought home from Lochboisdale when the Eriskay boats came in. They had exactly the same reaction as I had to the enormous lobsters with which he delighted in terrifying them. We went cockling with iron rakes, but even when my mother minced the cockles and made them into tasty fishcakes with chopped eggs and mashed potatoes, they refused to eat them, declaring that it would be like eating snails.

So the visiting convent girls had a glimpse of a life totally unlike their own, and I'm sure that none of my young friends who came to Kilpheder ever forgot the experience. Judging by the number of pleas I had for second invitations, it was an interesting and enjoyable part of their education. My parents always loved the housefuls of young people who gathered around us during the holiday, and they too looked forward to the next time.

Chapter Thirteen

EVERYTHING BECOMES HUMDRUM AFTER a while, and so it happened with convent life. After two years, I was beginning to feel the constraints of having to be in at five each evening and seven o'clock at weekends. The Fort William schoolgirls who lived at home seemed to be evolving into young ladies with interesting lives outside of school. We convent girls, on the other hand, appeared to be caught in a time-warp of navy-blue uniforms and the dreaded beret. With hindsight I think it reminded me too much of the ever-present sense of being at school for twenty-four hours a day, seven days a week, which I felt during my time with the aunties. So when my age-group were given an option of moving out and boarding with local families, it seemed like a good idea to join the small exodus which took place. Donald John had finished his Fort William schooling. He had moved down South to Aldershot Barracks to do a compulsory term of National Service, prior to joining the Meropolitan Police Force. Suddenly he was grown up and out in the world, and I suppose that thought added to my discontent.

There had been changes at the school too. The previous Easter had seen the departure of a familiar and well-liked figure from the staff. 'The Boss', as we called him, Mr Charles Mitchell, who had been headmaster there since 1934, retired. He had always taken a special interest in the island children and knew most of us by name. During his summer holidays he'd tour the Hebrides and pass through Uist. He would call into our house for a few minutes, to drink a quick cup of tea and talk to my parents. I don't know if he called on the parents of all his island pupils, but I'm sure he tried. Afterwards, seeing his tall, slightly stooped figure walking around the town, often with a rolled-up umbrella in his hand, was a link with home. Many people missed him when he left. I know that I did.

We needed written permission from our parents to show the nuns that they were willing to let us spread our wings, so I had a bit of persuading to do. My friend Janet and I decided to stick together and try to find a place that would take us both. It was a very exciting prospect. We had been treated like little girls for too long. This was our chance to be grown up. So we decided to try and find lodgings in the neighbouring village of Inverlochy. Janet was older than me was by the best part of two years, and I was quite happy to let her do the hunting while I concentrated on selling the idea to my parents. She knew that, if my parents agreed, hers would follow suit. All we could think of was that never again would we have to be in for the night at five and that the weekends would be ours. The teenagers' dances at K.K. Cameron's loomed large in our plans.

Our families agreed without too much trouble, but they insisted that we find a place with a good Catholic family, preferably one with an island connection. This was difficult. Janet's search in Inverlochy had proved fruitless. Most Catholic families were too large to have any rooms to spare, and they quite rightly considered that the best place for teenaged Catholic girls was the very place which we were so anxious to leave. Pretty soon we were prepared to lie to our parents about the religion part and take anything going, at least on a temporary basis.

We found the perfect place with a young couple, who lived a stone's throw from the Convent, in Tweedale Place. Mr and Mrs Murtagh, Margaret and Bob. They had a baby daughter to whom they always referred as Baby, and a long-haired dog called Rupert. The advert read 'Young family offers accommodation to two girls sharing. Husband working away from home Mon.-Fri. Low rent, as company appreciated.'

We had no experience of looking behind the printed word in adverts and immediately paid our deposit and arranged to move in. A posse of hostel boys was organised to help with our flitting and I said goodbye to the nuns and the three green curtains which had served as my bedroom walls for two years.

Both Murtaghs were there to welcome us, and Bob told us how pleased he was that his wife would have company during the week: 'She's only a wee lassie hersel', ye ken.' She was much younger than he was and quite glamorous in a tarty sort of way. I kept wondering what Sister Paul Mary would have said about the eye make-up. The Devil would certainly have featured strongly in her comments. However, we were only looking for the positive in our new independent frame of mind.

It soon became quite clear that life with Margaret and Bob was not going to be much fun for us. Margaret only wanted us for baby-sitting. She had her fancy man for company during the week. The lonely little wife waiting patiently for her husband only existed in poor misguided Bob's imagination.

We got to know Baby very well, and a dear little thing she was too. We walked the floors with her many an evening while we tried to get her to sleep so that we could do our homework. As soon as Bob came home at the weekends, we were effectively locked out from early morning till late evening. 'Bob needs his rest, ye ken.' I think she wanted to keep us away from him in case we let anything slip about her weekday man. As for lunch or dinner, on weekdays we ate school lunches and had beans-on-toast or egg-on-toast for tea. At the weekends she told us: 'Yous can make your own arrangements for meals at the weekend. Didn't I tell yez? It's not included in yer rent.' We spent many a cold, wet, hungry, penniless weekend walking up and down the streets of Fort William and sitting on a bench on Alexandra Parade, literally all dressed up with nowhere to go. We managed to go to one or two teenagers' dances, but most of the time our money went on fish suppers from the chip shop down by the station.

I became very familiar with the statue of *An t-Uasal Urramach Domhnall Camshron* (The Honourable Gentleman Donald Cameron), twenty-fourth Chief of the Clan Cameron of Lochiel, as he gazed benevolently at us from his plinth. We read the names of the young men who had given their all in the service of their country. Sgt K.J. Cameron of the RAF, and the names McInnes, MacDonald, MacPherson, MacPhee and even McMillan were there, all *Dileas Gu Bàs* (Faithful Until Death). They all got a little prayer from us as we sat on the bench by the War Memorial. We were particularly in tune with the war dead, as our history teacher had taken a group of us to see the controversial new Commando memorial on the Inverness road. It had recently been unveiled by the Queen Mother, and, although not everyone liked Scott Sutherland's nine-foot high monument, we had found it very thought-provoking.

One faint gleam in the darkness of the memories surrounding that period concerns the time when Margaret had a bad dose of stomach cramps. She dosed herself liberally with tablets that Bob had kept in the medicine cabinet. No immediate effect, so she took a second and then a third dose. Soon she was well enough to get dressed ready to meet her weekday man. 'Off tae the Braxy an' not a word to Bob, min'. Ye'r only young while ye'r young!' The Braxy was a dance hall in Inverlochy. It was hard to dislike Margaret. In a way I think we secretly admired the fact that she had two men dancing attendance on her. We noticed that her long auburn hair looked particularly glossy that evening and it turned out that the tummy tablets were actually Rupert's mange tablets, and she'd taken six.

We kept in touch with our convent friends. In fact we were free to go in and have a chat and a cup of tea with them after school any day, and this was very welcome. As you can imagine, some nuns made comments about 'Paying in St Peter's and praying in St Paul's', but Paul Mary was always very pleasant to us and encouraged the visits. Naturally, we did not tell it like it really was. Loss of face was to be avoided at all costs. We regaled girls and nuns alike about life on the outside, and if we varnished the truth a little, then they were not to know.

Even letters from home didn't seem to have the same warming effect as before. I was aware that I was being economical with the truth in my replies, as I had not told them about the cold, hungry weekends. They, thinking that food parcels were no longer necessary and that our landlady would be offended if they sent any, unwittingly added to the problem. However, now and then my father's letters still had the power to lift my spirits, even while some of his news disturbed me:

> Your mother is in hospital for a few days. I hope you don't get all worried about her as it is nothing serious. She's been feeling giddy for some time and fell over the other morning when she got out of bed. She didn't hurt herself, but we thought that she'd better see the doctor and he said that a few days in the hospital while she found her sea legs again would be the best thing. They say that a lot of women of her age get like this and I'm sure they know the right treatment. I know of a few men round here who keep falling over, but it has nothing to do with their age and the hospital is the last place they want to be.
>
> We have cause to be grateful to the good Sacred Heart nuns, they are treating your mother like a queen and I'll have to mind my Ps and Qs when she comes home. The place is very quiet without her rushing around and although Donald and the twins don't say much I think they miss her too. We've got used to her strange manic ways. One day last week I came home from the factory and she was sittting down drinking a cup of tea with Peigi Mhór (Big Peggy) who was in no hurry to leave. After a while I got annoyed and asked if they knew of any other man in Kilpheder who came home from a day's work and found two gossips and an empty table waiting for him. Peigi took the hint and went off home very smartly and I got my dinner, but your

mother gave me the cold shoulder all evening. Next day I came home and what did I find but a plate of soup and a spoon on the gate post waiting for me. All the men on the lorry thought it was very funny but I think your mother had the last laugh. Mind and write a nice letter to her and send her a brooch or something pretty with the enclosed.

My mother's illness was short-lived and I think she quite enjoyed the only stay in hospital she had ever had. All the children, twins included, had been delivered by our neighbour's wife, the local midwife, in the big double bed in the crofthouse.

After struggling with the Murtagh situation for the best part of a term, we put out feelers for other lodgings. Winter was approaching and the weekends getting colder and colder. It was easier this time, as we had more scope for searching – all our weekends, in fact. We were very pleased when a friend of Janet's family who had married a Fort William man made contact with her and offered to take her in. Janet told her that she and I came as a package, so, reluctantly, she agreed to take us both.

For some reason, at various times throughout my life complete strangers have taken an instant dislike to me. They take one look and I know it has happened again. I can feel it happening and haven't the faintest idea why it should be. It happened the first time I met Mrs Hodges. I just knew that she wasn't going to be my best buddy. However, despite her obvious antipathy, she didn't withdraw her offer. I was relieved, because in the circumstances I didn't have much choice. We'd already told the Murtaghs that we were leaving and their next babysitters were being interviewed.

We went off on a preliminary visit. Mrs Hodges had invited us to Sunday tea so that we could meet the rest of the family. The house was small and grimy in a fairly large tenement block, close to the railway line. John Hodges worked in some department of the railways and I think the house came with the job. The evening started well, with a blazing fire promising winter warmth and a table laden with home-baked goodies – so far, so good.

Mary Ann, as Mrs Hodges asked us to call her, was charm itself, mainly to Janet, and even asked me to take my coat off. As the visit progressed, her four little girls draped themselves round me and I felt that this would be a nice place to live. Mary Ann asked for my mother's address so that she could assure her that her daughter would be in safe hands. All seemed well.

My mother showed me the letter on my next visit home. I didn't wish to disturb her by correcting a few falsehoods. 'Your daughter will be given every home comfort. I will treat her as my own. She will have the freedom of the larder and the pantry . . . etc.' A total distortion of the facts. Mary Ann was the kind of person one should not meet on a dark night without a pocket full of crucifixes and a clove of garlic or two. Not a nice lady.

From the very first day she treated me with a kind of sneering contempt and seemed unreasonably jealous of my friendship with Janet. She had a very strong personality and John and the girls scuttled around trying to keep out of her way. He was an inoffensive little man, and, come to think of it, his life must have been pretty grim. Occasionally he'd try to speak to me about the way I was being treated but broke off before he said much more than 'See her. Ach, ye puir wee lassie . . .' and he'd shake his head and sigh. I simply couldn't do anything right by her. She rarely spoke to me and if I tried to join in any conversation she'd treat me to an icy glare, look at Janet, nod her head towards me and go off into peals of laughter as if at some shared joke. My clothes, hair and even my brown eyes were ridiculed. 'Tell me, dear, did your mother know any Chinese airmen?' followed by the usual peals of laughter.

Going back to Mary Ann's letter to my mother: I was to have the freedom of the larder and the pantry. That was a bit misleading. Nobody had the freedom of the larder except Mary Ann, and the pantry was full of old sewing machine parts and wellies. I really don't know what made that woman tick. She even seemed to hate one of her own daughters and that poor child couldn't put a foot right. She was never physically abused but had to endure ridicule and name-calling and was generally made to feel ugly and stupid. Her and me both.

Once or twice things got mislaid, as they will in any household, however tidy. Mary Ann's brooch, which she claimed to have left in the bathroom, 'where anybody could have lifted it . . .' (glare in my direction), went missing one day. There was a great flurry of looking in corners amid bits of innuendo aimed at me. My side of the bedroom was thoroughly searched, pockets turned out in my clothes and even my mattress turned. I'd nothing to fear but felt so embarrassed. The beastliest thing of all was that she turned to Janet and said, 'Of course I know who your people are, Janet,' and she didn't search an inch of her space.

Fortunately the brooch turned up, pinned to the lapel of a jacket she'd worn the day before. There was no apology. I felt that Janet should have stuck up for me or at least not have been so firmly tucked in Mary Ann's pocket. Still, I suppose she felt flattered, as our landlady paid her compliments and gradually poisoned her mind against me. Soon the cameraderie of our strange but friendly fight for survival in the Murtagh household was replaced by an icy silence.

The coldnesss between us was exceeded by the refrigeration to which we were exposed in the tiny attic boxroom which was our bedroom. It looked out on the snowy Ben and was without any form of heat save our breath, which hung in icicles from the window sashes each morning. It's the only time in my life that I can remember wearing more clothes in bed than out of it. It shows how far apart Janet and I had drifted if you can picture us maintaining a stony silence whilst donning cardigans, socks, scarves, gloves and bobble hats on top of our pyjamas.

As I took it upon myself to meet the little girls and walk home from school with them each day, probably in a vain attempt to ingratiate myself with Mary Ann, she started to lay a place for me at the kitchen table with them. Janet shared the more substantial evening meal with her and John when he came home from work. I ate so many fish fingers in that time that it should have made me a better sailor.

The atmosphere was always very tense when I was around, so I took to spending more and more time studying in the bedroom, preferring its icy loneliness to the symptoms of leprosy which Mary Ann's presence aroused in me. Soon I was told that I was using up too much electricity. So I lay on my bed in the icy darkness, listening to the trains and imagining that they were taking me to some exotic country where I would be welcomed into a huge house full of roaring fires and pleasant company, like my family. As it was dark outside, I couldn't go for a walk. Anyway, I'm sure that my so doing would have given rise to more ambiguous comments.

I still visited the Convent, although no longer living within such an easy distance of the place. I had some good friends there and dear old Sister Paul Mary always greeted me affectionately, often expressing concern: 'You're not so bubbly, are you happy? You look smaller!' One Saturday I'd gone to the cinema with convent friends to see Bing Crosby in that lovely film *High Society*, and afterwards we sat around in the recreation room singing the songs, while a very mellow Paul Mary tried to improvise the accompaniment on the piano. The thought of going back to fish fingers and cold shoulder seemed to hit me like a physical blow. As Sister Paul Mary bid me farewell: 'Watch out for the Devil and walk with God, my child!', I astonished her by throwing my arms around her and wailing like a banshee into the comforting folds of voluminous black which at that moment seemed to represent all the security in the world.

'Come, now, you can't let Mother Superior see you looking like this,' she led me off, talking all the time: 'She'll know what to do. We can't have one of *our* girls looking so ill and worried all the time. Look at you, there's nothing left of you . . .' and other motherly mutterings. Just before we entered Mother Superior's sanctum she said, 'Not pregnant, are you? Of course not.' That made me giggle and she said, 'Humph! You're still in there somewhere!'

Mother Superior didn't have to be told anything. Over the weeks she and the other nuns had kept tabs on all the girls who had left. They had their informants. She took one look at me and said, 'Your place is ready for you. Do you want to come back?' I couldn't wait to say, 'Yes, please!' It was like coming home. A week's notice to the Hodges' ménage and I was back in and mighty glad of it.

My friendship with Janet suffered a setback, but not a terminal blow. She saw through Madame Hodges in time and went to live in other lodgings. We have met at various stages in our lives and renewed the ties of shared memories as only ex-convicts and ex-convent girls can.

My last term went by in a flurry of exams and fears about the future. Fortunately, being back in a stable, albeit strict, environment meant that I had nothing else to worry about except school work, and once the exams were over we all relaxed a little. The music teacher at school produced a very successful *Pirates of Penzance* which ran for three nights at the Town Hall Theatre. As I pranced and sang around the stage as one of Major-General Stanley's daughters, I remembered another music teacher who had wanted to produce Gilbert and Sullivan. It all seemed so long ago.

Even at this late stage, with only a few weeks to go at Fort William school, I fell foul of a new member of staff, a burly Highlander with a wicked temper. He was known to have a mean right hook and was what is known in the profession as a very physical teacher. One day he floored me by hitting me over the head with a thick dictionary for talking in class. As soon as I could see straight, I dashed off a Gaelic poem in his honour and circulated it. The title was 'Ode to a Caveman' and it began 'Hail to thee, O hulk of meat, I know full well you think you're *it*. Perhaps it's just as well you do, 'cause no one else thinks that but you.' It loses a lot in translation and it was never Rabbie Burns's style. It was very long and had cutting references to parts of his anatomy best left unmentioned. My friends loved it and it made my head feel much better. I managed to get away with it, although some members of class wanted to pin it on the school noticeboard. I managed to change their minds for them, as I already regretted my actions. At the leavers' dance I was very surprised to find my former adversary asking me to take the floor with him and being very nice. He asked about my plans for the future and holiday plans and such like pleasantries. When the music ended he wished me well and said, 'That was a very funny poem you wrote about me, but coming from a convent girl some of the language surprised me.' As my old friend 'Mary By The Canal' would say, 'I was very put about.'

My future depended on getting the requisite number of passes for teacher-training and I had my heart set on going back to teach at one of the island schools one day. My earlier ambition, to be an art teacher, had been squashed by my father: 'Art school is full of weirdos and queers.' God only knows who told him that, as I don't think he had ever even met an art student. I knew then and know now that his assessment was totally without merit. My poor old art teacher's slip-up with the syllabus meant that I couldn't even think of going to art college anyway, despite getting a very high mark for the drawing and painting module. I was quite happy to send my application to Notre Dame College of Education, my aunt's old college in Glasgow, and hope for the best. It was a residential college run by nuns, but after three years with them I felt that I had got their measure. Some good, some not so good, just like the rest of us.

The end of this term would be like no other that I had known. I would be saying farewell to my schooldays – well, not quite. As it happened, they continued until a few months ago. My teaching life followed the same pattern as my days on the other side of the desk, beginning in the Hebrides at a little school even more isolated than Kyles Flodda, where I boarded with the very people whom John and my father had visited. They were very civilised indeed! In fact, John's comment had caused them much merriment. Then I moved on to a larger school and then across the sea as I had done in childhood, but as we say in Uist, that's another story. For now all I knew was that the coming holidays would be exciting and, as always, enjoyable, as would all future visits to the island croft which had been my lodestone throughout my childhood.

I would see the young Queen and Prince Philip driving past our house on the newly tarred and newly named Queen's Road. (I never heard it called that again after the Royal visit.) The young Royals would visit the factory and my father would declare that 'The poor wee Queen looked half-starved and her hand felt like a baby flounder.' She would look at the mountains of tangles and ask, 'Do people enjoy gathering all this seaweed, Mr MacMillan?' The Rocket Range would be disputed and fought over and eventually become the Guided Weapons Range which would bring a certain English soldier to the island. Very nice man, but with no talent for catching stirks. All this was in the future, as were my examination results.

At last the great day came and we were called into the school office. Janet, the secretary, who had been much more than a secretary, more like a mother figure to most of us, despite her own youth, sat at her desk as we went in with ashen faces. When I came out, she put her arm round my shoulders and mopped my tears, saying, 'Calm down now, you have passed all your subjects, haven't you?' She had seen it all before. 'If they cry, they've passed. If they faint, they've failed.' I was upright and crying but I had failed my art exam, and although I had known in advance that it was going to happen, it still hurt. However, my tears were mostly tears of relief: I had indeed passed enough subjects to get into teacher-training, and despite all appearances to the contrary I was well pleased.

I joined the long queue at the Post Office telephone box and eventually got our neighbours to bring my mother to the phone. It was strange, hearing her voice from so far away. We didn't make phone calls lightly in those days. I told her my good news twice; she was so nervous that she couldn't hear me the first time. Her voice went all trembly as she said, 'I'm sending you a big, big postal order and you go to that Mairi Nic an t-Saoir shop that you are always looking at and buy yourself anything you want. Anything at all.' She didn't heap praise on my head, but I knew that she was pleased. I also knew that it would take at least three of my father's weekly pay packets to buy the kind of outfit she had in mind from the shop she had mentioned, so I didn't even go in there. As I spent the money on a lovely dress in a much less prestigious shop, I decided that I would not tell her where it came from. She deserved the pleasure of thinking that she had made my dream come true. At that moment I felt older and more worldly-wise than my little mother, and I knew that I had left the days of my childhood behind.

Twice Around the Bay

For Norman, Philip and Shona

Uibhist nam Beanntan	Uist of Mountains

Air an fhonn *An t-Eilean Dorcha*   Tune: *The Dark Island*

Nuair bhios mi leam fhìn	When I'm all on my own,
Agus m' inntinn fo leòn,	Feeling mournful in mind,
Bidh mi cuimhneachadh uair	Carefree days of my childhood
'S mi gun uallach 's gun bhròn,	In my memory I find:
'S mi a' ruith is a' ruaig	I run over the fields
Feadh nam bruachan 's nan lòn	Where the brown streams unwind
Gu làithean m' oig'	To my young days
Ann an Uibhist nam beanntan.	In Uist of mountains.

Fonn   *Chorus:*

'S ann gun strì rachainn sìos	Then with ease on the wings
Air dhà sgiathaidh mo smuain	Of my memory I soar,
Gu tràigh mhòr an taobh 'n iar,	The Atlantic before me
'G èisteachd fìor-ghlag a' chuain;	A welcoming roar;
A' ghainmheach gheal mhìn	Barefoot running through
'S i gu h-ìseal fom bhonn,	Silvery sands on the shore,
Is gach tonn a' seinn	As each wave sings out,
'Uibhist nam Beanntan'.	'Uist of Mountains.'

Anns a' mhadainn gum b' èibhinn	At the dawn to awake
Leam èirigh moch tràth	With the dew on the ground,
Is an driùchd air gach gèig –	When the cattle start moving,
Bidh an sprèidh len cuid àil,	Calves calling for cows
Is an uiseag bheag bhinn-ghuthach	High above me the skylark's
Dìreadh gu h-àrd	Sweet voice would pronounce
A' cur fàilte	Salutations for
Air Uibhist nam beanntan.	Uist of mountains.

Ged a tha mise 'n-dràst'	Though I'm far from the birthplace
Ann am baile na strì,	That nurtured my soul,
'S mi cho fada bhon àit'	And the strain of the city
Anns na dh'àraicheadh mi,	Is taking its toll,
Gu bheil sàsachadh àraidh	I'm sustained by the hope
Toirt blàths do mo chrìdh –	That one day I will go
'S e gun till mi	Back to my home
Gu Uibhist nam beanntan.	In Uist of mountains.

Donald John MacMillan   English version: Alick MacMillan
London, 1965   Glasgow 1999

Chapter One

'WAKE UP! WAKE UP! If you're not on the bus in ten minutes you're walking it!'

I was catapulted from my deep sleep, the kind of near-death stupor which follows a night spent dancing Highland reels and falling into bed at dawn with my fingers in my ears to block out the noise of birdsong. As I struggled to focus my eyes on the bedroom door, I could not believe the face I saw there.

'OK! Just go away, five minutes will do me . . . I promise!'

As the door closed I was already jumping into my clothes and gathering my school books. My father and brother had long gone to work and I could dimly remember my mother giving me a wake-up call before going down to the far end of the croft to milk the cows. Obviously it hadn't worked, and although my mind had gone through the motions of getting up and dressing, my body had stayed in bed. My second and final warning had come from Fergus the driver of the school bus, and the reason I found this so embarrassing was that I was not one of his pupil passengers – I was the teacher.

By the early 1960s the houses on the Hebridean island of South Uist were all much of a muchness; a few thatched houses remained but most of them had been replaced by two types of bungalow. Also scattered around were the strong, stone-built, two-storied houses which gave testimony to ancestral affluence and can still be seen on the island. The layout of living areas and bedrooms was the same in most of the new houses like ours and so, having waited outside the gate for some time, Fergus had come in and searched until he found me and delivered his ultimatum. It is the kind of awakening which only happened once in my lifetime and one I will never forget.

I was back! Back on the island where north is down and south is up, where the only reliable weather forecast comes from looking out of the window. South Uist, the place where I was born and where I had spent only seven and a half consecutive years in our little thatched house with my lovely if sometimes chaotic family throughout my whole childhood.

I had been raised on Benbecula and Barra by a teacher aunt and her housekeeping sister, and my school-holiday visits home had been precious and had kept me going throughout what was a fairly strict and lonely time. Then came the three years at Daliburgh School, when I found that being back with the family was something which took a bit of getting used to, and by the time I had settled in it was time to leave for Fort William and senior secondary school, followed by three more years in exile at Notre Dame College of Education in Glasgow, all to fulfil my ambition of becoming a teacher in an island school. Now, as they say in the Bible, it had come to pass.

South Uist lies due west of the Isle of Skye and is part of the long string of islands joined together by causeways and known as the Outer Hebrides. Today time has moved on and it is a place where progress and tradition live in harmony. The modernisation of the island and its inhabitants, which began at the end of the war, came slowly at first but soon gathered momentum, and when I returned I found that much had changed since I had left the island to complete my education. But there was still a long way to go to reach the islanders' present living conditions.

Ambition is not a characteristic with which writers over the years have credited Hebrideans. In fact, the inhabitants of my own island were once slanderously described as work-shy and unintelligent by a certain renowned author, not one of my favourite people. We may not be as forceful and brash about achieving our aims as your average Lowlander but, believe me, we know ambition. I had decided that I was going to be a teacher very early in life – well, perhaps not, it was more a case of deciding to be a student, and I had worked hard and endured much in order to achieve this and make it work.

My academic ability was a good average but nothing special; in the more relaxed atmosphere of a college campus I saw many students fall by the wayside, and it would have been so easy to do likewise. However, I managed to enjoy every minute of my free time and ensure that the coursework got done as necessary. No matter how much time I spent away from home, letters from my parents and the college holidays kept the island at the forefront of my mind, and it was a proud day indeed when I received a letter from J. A. MacLean, Director of Education for Inverness-shire, informing me that I had been appointed as Teacher-in-Charge of South Glendale Primary School, South Uist.

In those far-off days when a crofter's family was a tight unit and children were considered a valuable commodity to be nurtured by their parents, talked to and guided by their elders, there were often three generations of the same family in the village, if not still sharing a home. Television and computers had not yet taken the place of family conversation, and old people who were respected as having a valid place in island society passed much folklore and wisdom down the ladder of years.

This child-nurturing philosophy meant that no matter how isolated a community was, there was a primary school within walking distance from the child's home. Sometimes the entire roll would be in single figures, but the formal school building and the provision of books and teacher gave the children the same chance of an education as their peers in much larger communities, without their having to leave home at a very early hour and be transported to a large central school. Small rural primary schools abounded in the Highlands and Islands at that time; such a school was South Glendale.

Nowadays getting to South Glendale is easy – you get into your car and drive there. In the days when I was appointed as teacher it wasn't so simple, as the village was inaccessible by road. The bus driver who woke me up was doing me a great favour by transporting me part of the way. He was passing our house with an empty bus on his way to Ludag to pick up children from the south end of the island and bring them to Daliburgh Junior Secondary School.

Under strict instructions from his employers not to pick anyone else up, he was really risking his job by doing me this favour, but that's Uist folk for you: I never had to walk to Ludag, even if the noise of the bus's horn being leaned on, as Fergus got tired of waiting outside our house, sometimes frightened the cows.

Ludag was the end of the road. Literally. The spine road, which ran the whole length of the island, came to its southernmost conclusion at Polachar Inn and another long spur veered off eastwards towards Ludag jetty. I had never even seen South Glendale and was very excited at the thought of teaching there. I had visions of living at home and travelling to the school every day, but when I first went out to see the place I found that this was simply impossible. The only vehicle our household could boast, apart from a small tractor, was an equally small motorbike, and this was how I went to take my first look at the terrain, on the pillion of a little 'putt-putt' ridden by my father.

'The only way to climb that hill is by boat!' On Ludag jetty we had been joined by Neil Campbell, the ferryman, who had spent most of his adult life on the water, and despite the twinkle in his eye, which betrayed the fact that this was not the first time he had used that line, I had to agree with him. Between my first school and me rose a rugged expanse of heather-clad hill. There was a well-worn track meandering around the base, gradually increasing in gradient until it disappeared into the horizon about halfway up the hill. The sea lapped around the rocks and clumps of heather at the base of the hill and surged on around it and out of our field of vision, where it curved inwards to form a bay. Round this bay stood the tiny village of South Glendale with its little corrugated-iron school. Things did not look good and I could see my social life vanishing before my very eyes.

Sailing cost money and I had none. My monthly salary would be £36 clear, inclusive of Isolation Grant and Responsibility Allowance, and although this was higher than my father's monthly salary from Alginate Industries, I had to work for a month before receiving it: so the hill it had to be. With a sinking heart I contemplated my varnished toenails peeping out of fashionable sandals and remembered another fact of island life – the Wellington boot will become an essential part of your wardrobe regardless of your age, sex or professional status.

'How long will it take me to get there?' I asked Neil, anxiously.

'On a day like this with a moderate wind, I'd say the back of half an hour.' Then he added, 'If there's a gale behind you and you lift your feet, you could be there in ten minutes. On the other hand, if you couldn't stop running you could end up missing it altogether.'

Both he and my father thought that this was very funny and walked off chuckling.

Neil has often been mentioned in books about the island, in particular by writers who have used his services as ferryman over the years as a way of visiting other islands. Tall and well-built, with permanently tanned features, he had the quiet calm bearing of a man who knew exactly why he had been put on this earth. The sea was his workplace and before the arrival of the present day multi-million pound car ferry and causeway link to Eriskay he would transport people over there, or further on to Barra, in his boat.

No matter what the weather threw at him, and although the boat was open and powered only by a small engine, if you wanted to cross the *Caolas* (Sound), Neil was your man. He regarded the sea with a respect which held no trace of fear. He also regarded the Glendale teachers as beings who had been put on this earth to amaze and amuse him in fairly equal quantities, and who could blame him?

The teachers assigned to the little isolated school were always female and nearly always new to the profession. They were young, idealistic graduates of a college of education where teaching was regarded as a sacred vocation and the words 'I am a career teacher' would have earned them instant expulsion, if not excommunication.

True, they would have cut their teaching teeth on the children of Glasgow while at college. If my own personal experience is anything to go by, students doing teaching practice were often used as unpaid supply teachers and could be stuck in front of forty Gorbals street-war veterans for a week before they had time to say, 'I am only allowed to teach one unsupervised lesson.' It was a very valuable part of training but a million miles from the Glendale scenario. That thought crossed my mind as I looked across the Sound of Eriskay and knew that I would be seeing a lot more of it in days to come.

Although South Glendale and the hill were foreign territory to me, I was quite familiar with Ludag. I had been there many times before, as a young girl on my way to the island of Eriskay to spend the weekend with a friend from Daliburgh School, a girl called Margaret who boarded with relatives near my home. Her mother knew mine and Margaret came to our house from time to time. It was always a hospitable house and, though small, thatched and crowded with MacMillans, she always enjoyed visiting us. In return she would invite me to go with her at weekends to the tiny island which was her home.

We would go up to Ludag on the school bus on a Friday afternoon and Neil Campbell would ferry us across the Sound along with the other Eriskay people who had come over to Uist for a dental appointment or a shopping trip or whatever. We would come back on the Sunday evening, and as there was no bus service at the weekends, we would walk home. Distance seemed to matter not a bit. Feet were there for using. Having spent so many years under virtual house arrest living with my aunts, I can't begin to describe the joy of being able to go off to another island with a friend and my parents' blessing.

The little island of Eriskay has been immortalised in the hauntingly beautiful 'Eriskay Love Lilt' collected and made popular by Marjorie Kennedy Fraser. It is the subject of many books and photographic works: *Father Allan's Island, Eriskay, a Poem of Remote Lives,* and the recent *Eriskay Where I Was Born* by Angus Edward MacInnes, to mention but a few. It measures two and a half miles from north to south and is less than two miles wide. An old friend of my Glendale teaching days once told me, 'When the good Lord finished making Uist he found a bit of specially blessed earth under his nails. He scraped it out and flicked it into the Sound and the next day there was Eriskay.'

The truth is not quite as romantic. Gordon of Cluny acquired the island in 1838 and used it as a dumping-ground for the victims of his infamous Clearances. Although the soil was poor and rocky, the hardy islanders knew that they had two choices – survive by whatever means they could, or die. In unimaginable circumstances they made that barren, rocky, wind-lashed scrap of an island, and the sea around it, support themselves and future generations.

I recently read a book written by an American who had come to the Hebrides to trace his ancestors. Of the Clearances he writes: 'The crofters were given a choice of moving nearer the sea or emigrating. As most of them disliked the sea, they decided to take the softer option of assisted emigration.'

No comment. Who has not heard of people driven off their land to Badbea in Helmsdale to make room for sheep who had to tie their children and cattle to posts to prevent them being blown over the cliffs? When the harvest was poor and they could not pay the rent for their pitiful bits of land, the landowners burned their houses and drove them on to the emigration ships.

The Eriskay settlers had been 'cleared' at least twice before being sent to Eriskay. Then there were the Barra crofters of 1851. The 1500 crofters to whom I refer thought that they were going to a meeting to discuss rents. Instead they found themselves brutalised and bound between the stinking decks of wooden ships on their way to America – if, that is, they survived the cholera. Soft option? Assisted emigration? Yeah, right!

Despite the gruelling hardship which was the pattern of their daily lives, the people of Eriskay survived and at the time of my visits the population was about 200 people. This may seem tiny as head counts go, and it was not the least populated Hebridean island of the time. Berneray had even fewer people and the least populated was Vatersay, with less than 100 inhabitants.

Perhaps the most famous visitor Eriskay ever had was Bonnie Prince Charlie, who landed there on 23 July 1745, when he sailed over from France at the start of his attempt to reclaim Scotland for the Stuarts. He sheltered in a cove which is named Coilleag a' Phrionnsa (the Prince's Dell), and there he is reputed to have planted a species of convolvulus called Flùr a' Phrionnsa (the Prince's Flower). We saw the flowers, Margaret and I, and the little hollow in which they grew looked just the right shape for a weary traveller to rest: a splash of soft colour against the bleak landscape, as out of place as the pretty Prince must have felt, standing on the shores of

Eriskay. Had he been able to look into the future and see the terrible price his loyal followers would have to pay for rising to his cause, he might have heeded MacDonald of Boisdale's advice and gone straight back to France.

Margaret's family lived in a house with a thatched roof much like our own in our Daliburgh schooldays, and they were kind and welcoming. We talked a lot. Margaret's mother seemed to know everybody who lived in South Uist and we spent a lot of time bringing her up to date on births, marriages and deaths. In return she gave us nuggets of information which often surprised us about some of the more prominent islanders, always starting off by saying, 'I shouldn't tell you this, but . . .'

On Saturdays we went to the shop and helped around the croft. As there were no men in the house, I could find myself holding a fence post while Margaret's sister hammered it into the ground, and doing other jobs which were done at home by my father and brothers – it was not very exciting but it was different. Eriskay women were very self-reliant and equal to any chore, as they spent much time holding the croft together while the menfolk were at sea.

In the evenings Morag, Margaret's older sister, any visitors and Margaret and I played cards, while her mother knitted the most wonderfully intricate patterns into fishermen's jerseys for her husband and son. I have heard it said that in a seafaring community like Eriskay each wife had her own individual patterns, which she knitted into the hardwearing socks and jerseys that all the sailors wore. The patterns, handed down through the generations, were as individual as a signature or indeed a fingerprint.

The wool was oiled and could withstand both wind and salty sea spray, so that, in common with the jerseys worn by the Guernsey fishermen, the Eriskay patterns could serve as a means of identification when time spent in the sea rendered a drowned sailor's body unrecognisable.

Like a vast percentage of Eriskay men and men from other islands, Margaret's father and brother were both deep-sea sailors. This was the term used to distinguish men who went to the mainland ports and picked up berths on merchant navy vessels bound for destinations all over the world from others who only sailed in British waters. The island sailing men were always in demand, as they were hardworking and reliable, often working their way up to positions of authority. Other sailors went to South Georgia and lived there for six months, working either on the 'catcher' – the ship that chased and caught the whales – or on the factory ship where the dead mammals were processed.

The South Georgia men lived a fairly monastic life, as it was a work–eat–sleep environment, but they came home with huge amounts of money, having had no opportunity to spend it for six months. As my brother said in his song *Tioram air Tìr* ('The Whaler's Lament') '*an t-airgead ga chosnadh, 's gun dòigh air chur bhuainn, 's e sìor losgadh toll 'na mo phòcaid*' ('piled up money, with no place to spend it, setting my pocket on fire').

At the end of their long voyages the deep-sea sailors would come home with tales of wondrous things that they had seen on their travels and many souvenirs of foreign lands. Strange carved figures, paper-thin Japanese tea-sets with a Geisha girl's head hidden in the bases of the cups, trays inlaid with butterfly wings and suchlike exotica were often to be seen in the crofthouses of deep-sea sailors.

During the post-war rationing period the sailors'

double-ration entitlement enabled them to come home with huge tins of jam, big bags of sugar, large tins of Capstan and Senior Service cigarettes and many other luxury goods in short supply on the island. The money they brought back was a lifeline to their families and it meant that they themselves could spend a few months back on dry land before the call of the sailor's life beckoned them again.

They did not all return. Long periods of abstinence followed by mammoth binges when the ship was in a foreign port sometimes had heartbreaking consequences, and I know of one young man who went out celebrating the end of a long voyage, drinking the night away with his friends in some dockside bar on the other side of the world. Not too steady on his feet as he made his way up the steep gangplank, he stumbled and fell backwards on to the concrete dock. He never got up again.

At least one other contemporary of mine 'jumped ship', in Tasmania. It was almost impossible to come back to this country if you had done this, and he is still over there. I saw him on Gaelic TV recently and he has made a good life for himself, but I remember his mother talking to mine and crying her heart out more than once. The sailors were not the only ones who had a hard time.

As we sat in Margaret's house playing 'Catch The Ten' and 'Old Maid', by the hissing light of the Tilley lamp, we listened to the radio. Reception was crackly on the old battery and accumulator wireless, and no matter how many knobs you turned and tuned an Italian station kept breaking in. One night Margaret's mother got fed up with all the fiddling and changes of music and language and, getting up, threw her knitting to one side and tuned the radio straight into the middle of the Italian signal, shouting, '*Mura faigh sibh Radio Luxembourg, gabhaibh ur diol de Radio Mussolini! Tha mo cheann-sa gu sgàineadh!'* ('If you can't get Radio Luxembourg, you can have your fill of Radio Mussolini, my head is splitting').

So every time I visited we played cards to 'Radio Mussolini'. The voices of Italian tenors seemed to blend in quite well with the background sounds of wind and sea from outside.

I have great memories of that little house in Eriskay. To me its inhabitants epitomised many of the complex and fascinating mixture of qualities that made the first settlers on the island determined to survive against all odds. I can still picture Margaret's mother standing in her little kitchen in front of a big black stove making our dinner, a small rotund lady of late middle years, her face sweetly featured but deeply lined and burnt brown by sun and wind. Hanging to her waist was a thick plait of equally mixed brown and grey hair that she rolled into a bun when she went 'out on the town', as she called her shopping or church trips. In my memory she is wearing the flowered overall that in the days of my youth appeared to be the garment that you changed into when you took your wedding dress off. On her feet are the Wellington boots necessary for so many outside chores in an all-female household that taking them off was a waste of time.

'A Dhia Fhlathanais, cuiridh am buntàta uaine seo a' bhuinneach oirnn ach chan eil an còrr againn – fàgaidh e làn sinn airson greis' ('God in Heaven, these green potatoes will give us the runs, but they're all we have. They'll fill us for a while anyway').

As she scraped away at the blighted potatoes and fried them with *cudaigean* (young saithe or coalfish), she entertained us with such a tuneful and soulful version of

'O Sole Mio', picked up from Radio Mussolini that it would have put Pavarotti to shame.

I have seen very little of Margaret and even less of her family since our days at Daliburgh Junior Secondary School, but I have thought of her many a time. I remember her and her family and our days on Eriskay, before the car ferry made it easy for the tourists to visit it and the young folk to leave it. I thought of her as I walked over the hill and round the coast to my little school in South Glendale, on days when the early morning mist hung low over the Sound and Eriskay in the near distance appeared to be suspended in mid-air above a sea so glittery and blue that it hurt my eyes.

I walked the hill and sometimes ran it, as Neil had forecast, every Friday after school and Monday mornings to get back to my lodgings, the house where all the teachers over the years had been well looked after by the MacIntyre family. Often the lure of a dance, concert or a boyfriend would make the walk seem less arduous and I would go home mid-week as well. The best dances were always the furthest away, and sometimes I only got back home to bed at six in the morning. All things considered, despite the hill walking, I had reason to be grateful that my post was not as demanding as working in a city school and that the bus driver was a saint.

Chapter Two

I HAD ABANDONED the idea of living at home and had arranged to board in Glendale during the week, coming home at weekends, and when I went out to South Glendale to take up my lodgings my mother went with me. I had made a couple of half-day visits to the school to familiarise myself with the building and the children's records, as you do, and each time I seemed to lose the path on the return journey – no sense of direction, not then, not now.

My mother was worried about me and wanted to make sure that I was going to find the place and be all right out there. We had contacted my future landlady by phone and had agreed that my mother could stay with me for the night, and we travelled to Ludag on the mail-boat bus which ran from Lochboisdale three days a week. She arranged to get a lift back the next morning on the school bus. As the boat came in at about 7 p.m., and by the time the passengers had boarded the bus and it had travelled through the townships to Ludag, stopping here and there, we knew that it would be late before we arrived at our destination and set off across the hill. It was a dark lowering kind of evening, so we thought we'd better take a torch.

Things went well for part of the way, and although we were well burdened with my luggage, we would have made good time if we hadn't followed a sheep-track for about fifteen minutes until we realised that we were getting nowhere fast. By the time we got back on to the proper track it was really dark and we had to keep our eyes firmly on the ground, as we didn't want to be misled into taking another detour. I noticed that my mother kept looking over her shoulder, but as my mind was busy going over the things I would have to do on my first day and hadn't noticed anything out of the ordinary in our surroundings, I didn't say anything to her.

After a while, when I began to puff a little, I realised that she had stepped up the pace considerably and that we were practically running, so I asked her if anything was wrong. 'Listen,' she said, stopping and pointing in the direction from which we had come. I could hear ghostly voices and strange laughter carried on the now brisk wind, and the eerie sounds made the hairs on the back of my neck stand up. Fortunately, by this time we could see the lights from the Glendale houses and we walked very fast, keeping as close to each other as we could. The house we were aiming for was the first in the village and we nearly ran through the door when it was opened for us.

I noticed that my mother's hands were shaking and I didn't feel too steady myself, so, although our hosts were very pleasant while we got the introductions and formalities under way, I still felt uneasy about the voices in the wind. I even wondered if I should give up the idea of living out there and go back home with my mother in the morning, away from that place of ghosts.

Shortly afterwards the door opened and in came the daughter of the family and her young son. They had been out to Ludag getting some stores from a grocer who came out there in his van. Two other women from Glendale had been with them. We hadn't been aware of them but they had actually followed us all the way. Our detour up the sheep track had worried them, as they could see us in the distance, apparently stomping off into the wilds. They had seen us getting back on course and had tried hard to catch up with us in case we veered off again. Knowing the hill so well, they had no torches, and as we were walking so fast they eventually realised that they couldn't catch up with us and had dropped back; theirs had been the ghostly voices and laughter we had heard. We never told them how they had frightened us into breaking the speed record for hill walking, just smiled and nodded when young Allan said, 'I suppose you walk so fast because you come from the city.'

I felt a little apprehensive about moving in with a family of strangers, as teenage memories of freezing rooms, starvation and hostile landladies were still fresh in my mind, but I needn't have worried. My lodgings with the MacIntyre family were a sharp contrast to the dreadful humiliating experience I had had during my Fort William days. I was just a child then and two unscrupulous landladies had nearly destroyed my health, my self-esteem and my faith in my fellow human beings. If it hadn't been for the Notre Dame nuns I would have given up on further education completely.

Although my new family lived in a very isolated community, it was obvious from the first meeting that their standards in most things were a good deal higher than those of many a mainland dweller. Their house was comfortably furnished and scrupulously clean and the walled garden at the front was a riot of colour, with flowers of all descriptions. Not for them the common hardy marigold that was a favourite flower in most Hebridean gardens at the time. It could withstand all efforts of the gales to uproot it and indeed was very difficult to shift once it got a hold in your garden. My father hated them. Once he cleared a patch of marigolds, rotovated the bed and planted potatoes in it. The potatoes failed to thrive but he had the best show of marigolds in living memory.

No, the flowers in Macintyre's garden were of an infinitely more adventurous variety. I remember the name of one: Chincherinchee; it was a little white flower, not particularly striking, but the name stuck in my mind as we had trouble deciding how to pronounce it. There were dahlias, lilies, Michaelmas daisies, foliage plants and flowering shrubs and much more. At the far end of the garden was a large flourishing vegetable plot, and fruit bushes for jam-making were planted against the boundary walls. The wind coming off the bay could be fierce at times, but with a steep hill behind the house and a fairly high rise in front if it, the growing area was well protected.

The MacIntyre family had been a large one but only a widowed daughter, Kate Ann, and her youngest son lived with the parents in my time. The rest of the family were living on the mainland, and by the positions they had attained it was obvious that the isolation of their home had not hampered their natural abilities in any way. The parents, although old and showing the physical signs of having worked hard all their lives, were still active and of lively minds, and I remember evenings spent discussing many interesting subjects and never a hint of idle gossip. Come to think of it, they'd had so many young teachers boarding with them over the years that there must have been many stories to tell, but not a word was ever said about them. Total integrity.

The school was only a five-minute walk away and I could look out of my bedroom window and see it there silhouetted against the bay. In addition to the cream-painted school with its porch, there was a grassy playground, a small storage building, two outside lavatories and a coalhouse. Coal was provided by the County and was shipped out once a year. The one-roomed school had a little stove and in the winter Kate Ann lit a fire there first thing each morning and left a full box of coal so that I could keep it going for the duration of the school day. She also cleaned the school and made up the National Dried Milk, to which every child in the country was entitled as a mid-morning drink, even if cows with fat udders surrounded the school.

Tins of the powdered milk were stored in the stationery cupboard, as were supplies of books, chalk and other necessities. I thought that this was a strange arrangement, as the cupboard wasn't very big, but when I asked Kate Ann if it might not be better to put them in the storage building outside she laughed and said, 'Perhaps in ten years' time! Come. Let me show you.' When we opened the door I couldn't believe it. The whole shed was stuffed from floor to ceiling with large cardboard boxes each containing twelve dozen toilet rolls. There had been a clerical error some years previously and someone, either a teacher in Glendale or a dispatch clerk in Inverness, had ticked the wrong quantity on a form. The result was that Neil Campbell's boat had to make two trips across the bay to deliver the goods, and by the time I left the school my few little pupils had hardly made any impression on the contents of the shed.

At first it was strange teaching such a small group of children, but as they were all at different levels we certainly found more than enough work to fill the day, and they were a delight to teach. Although they were accustomed to seeing me out of school, once they came in through the door it was strictly business. They were totally formal in their approach to me and to each other in the classroom. If a brother stepped out of line his sister would have no scruples about drawing the matter to my attention: 'Michael John MacPhee is not doing his work, Miss.' Not 'My brother . . .' So they practised the etiquette that they would one day use in their workplace.

Wherever you find a teacher you will find stories about children, some funny and some just plain boring. I have no funny stories about the children in South Glendale School. It was a long time ago and the children were serious and well behaved, most unlike the tough cookies with whom I'd had dealings in Glasgow.

One child called Mary at St John's, Gorbals, comes to mind, a little six-year-old going on fifty. We had just finished a lesson on Good Manners and the class had been instructed to write a few lines on how they could be pleasant to people. Mary came out to me and said: 'Gie's a pencil!', to which I replied in a slightly reproving voice: 'Go back to your seat, Mary. Think about the lesson we've just had. Then ask me properly.'

Mary sat down for a few minutes and then came out to the desk and said in a louder voice: 'Ah ken what to say. It's gie's a pencil, MISS.'

Flushed with partial success, I patted her hand and said: 'Nearly there, Mary. Just take a few more minutes to think about it and ask me again.'

Soon she was back tugging my sleeve. 'Do you know what to say now?' I asked, confident that at least one of the forty would become a better person through my efforts.

'Yes!' said Mary. 'Keep yer bloody pencil!'

We had a long talk at playtime about that incident, but I doubt if Mary saw the point of it all.

Catherine, my teacher aunt, told me her favourite school story from the days when she was a pupil teacher at Garrynamonie School with Fred Rea, author of *A School in South Uist*. She was teaching a little girl her alphabet, using the old way, which has just been rediscovered by the education establishment. We called it 'Chalk and talk'; they call it 'Teaching phonics by rote'. She wrote the alphabet up on the blackboard and, pointing to the letter 'o', she asked one little girl to identify it. She was given the right answer but then she tried 'a' and the little girl said, '*Cearc*' (a hen). I suppose the letter does look like a little fat hen.

'No,' said auntie, 'it is an "a".'

Next day she tried again and the little girl said: '*Bha thu fhèin ag ràdha 'gur e "a" a th' ann, ach tha mise cinnteach gur e a th' ann ach cearc*' ('You were saying that it is an "a", but I'm still sure that it's a hen').

Strange the things you remember.

Over the years I have heard snippets of information about some of my ex-pupils and they have become a cross-section of society, with some rising to great heights and some others doing the best they can. Sadly, last year a young Bristol man whom I had taught briefly towards the end of my teaching days was convicted of a dreadful murder and put away for life. It doesn't do to imagine that as a teacher you are making a lasting impression on young lives. A child like Mary or a few turns on playground duty soon cures that illusion.

During my first year in Glendale we had some exciting news. At last, after years of waiting, the children of the Western Isles were to be allowed to learn how to read and write their own language in the primary schools instead of having to wait until they went to secondary school. There was one snag, however: the teachers already in service, myself included, had not been trained to teach it at primary level. At my own college we had had an old man called Nicky, who came in for one hour every week and rambled on at us about ancient Gaelic bards and stuff like that, but I'm afraid he lost me roughly five minutes after I first met him and I wrote all my letters during his session. As I recall, there was nothing in his lectures about the finer points of teaching a five-year-old who probably thinks an 'a' is a hen, that in Gaelic 'bh' is pronounced like 'v' in English or the concept of broad and slender vowels following each other selectively.

A young Adviser was appointed and he toured the schools, monitoring the Gaelic teaching programme and generally asking us which approach we thought would work. A bit like the blind leading the blind, really. He got very excited about the Glendale children. They had made a papier-mâché and raffia croft house with little plasticine animals and people, all labelled appropriately, in Gaelic. Every day the children moved the little characters around, creating story plots around them and using this time to learn the shapes of basic words from their own environment. The young Adviser was very impressed and spent a whole afternoon writing notes and making sketches of the project.

Most classrooms of the period had little in the way of

visual aids and the standard decoration was a large map of the world with the British Empire coloured pink and a plastic-coated poster depicting the Life Cycle of the Butterfly, courtesy of Shell Oil. Interactive education was still in its infancy and project work in the primary school was a very new idea, so at the next meeting of the EIS (the Educational Institute of Scotland) I was gratified to hear the Gaelic Adviser talk at length about the virtue of using a model croft as a teaching aid. He said that he'd got the idea from a little school 'at the back of beyond' and I thought it a pity that he could not even remember the name of the school. He certainly remembered the way to 'the back of beyond', and during the time I taught at Glendale he showed up many times in his brown corduroy suit and wellingtons. Noticing the frequency of his visits my landlady said: 'Why don't you ask Mr Corduroy if he would like to move into the shed with the toilet rolls?'

He always wrote screeds in his notebook, so I suppose that in a small way the children of Glendale played a part in the revival of Primary Gaelic. Either that or, as Kate Ann suspected, Mr Corduroy fancied the teacher.

For the first two years after graduation teachers were classed as probationers and had numerous unheralded visits from the Schools' Inspectorate. They would drop in unannounced, sit in a corner of your classroom and watch you teach for a morning or an afternoon. They would then look at the children's exercise books, the teacher's lesson forecast and record of work, attendance register, logbook, stationery ordering records and so on. They must have been trained to intimidate, as I have never met a teacher who enjoyed their visits. The inspectors were always male. They would speak to you as little as possible and give you no indication of their findings. When the inspection was over they would sweep out of the classroom with barely a nod towards the children, who by then would be thoroughly cowed and acting like little zombies. The teacher would be so light-headed with relief at having survived that she wouldn't be able to remember which part of 'good-bye' came first. I wished my first Inspector 'Bye-good'!

Fortunately for me, I had an angel on my shoulder: Neil Campbell. The inspectors never walked the hill; when they were ready to pounce they booked Neil's boat, usually a few days in advance, and approached the school by sea. Neil would either call MacIntyres' or, if the inspector was coming on a Monday morning and I had gone home for the weekend, he would phone me there and tell me at what time to expect the visitor, finishing the call by saying, 'If you are not ready for him, hang something on the school fence. I'll take him twice around the bay and blame it on the tide.'

I never had to send the boat on a circular tour, but the kindness behind the warning was well appreciated.

The only thing I found a bit strange when I first joined the MacIntyre household was being treated like a lady. In Gaelic we use the plural of '*thu*' (you) and say '*sibh*' (you plural) when addressing someone who by reason of age or status is our superior. At the age of twenty I found it difficult to have Flora and Calum MacIntyre and their daughter Kate Ann Alexander using the plural '*sibh*' when talking to me. They were all superior to me in age and wisdom. Although I tried to change this mode of address at first, it was a waste of time. This had always been their courteous way of speaking to their teacher lodgers and I just gave up. I insisted on trying to lend a hand around the place in the evenings, as I couldn't imagine just sitting there acting like a lady while they waited on me, but although I was allowed to set the table, washing the dishes was considered to be beneath my dignity.

One evening, Kate Ann was late home, so I volunteered to bring the cows home for milking, and after some argument off I went. The crofts at Glendale were all steep, as they were part of the hill behind the houses, but the cows were docile as I rounded them up and with Captain the dog delivered them to the byre. Calum stood there waiting, not too happy about my being seen doing menial work for him and I could hear him complaining to himself: '*Nach ann an seo a tha 'n gnothach, an tidsear a' toirt dhachaigh nam beathaichean.*' ('This is a strange business, the teacher bringing the cows home').

Then he saw us and slapping his thigh he bellowed with laughter: '*Càit 'eil sibh a' dol le crodh Alasdair*?!' ('Where are you going with Alasdair's cows?!').

I was sure I had the right beasts, but to a horn they all belonged to his neighbour. Things loosened up after that and, from time to time, with a twinkle in his eye, he'd say: '*Cuiribh an tidsear a dh'iarraidh nam beathaichean a-nochd. Tha mi searbh a' bleoghainn an aon fheadhainn.*' ('Send the teacher for the cows tonight. I'm bored with milking the same ones').

The fresh sea air blowing from the bay gave me a great appetite and Kate Ann was a very good cook and baker. If it hadn't been for all the walking and the dances, I'd have been enormous. Most of the produce in the pantry came from Finlay MacDonald's travelling shop and had to be carried over the hill from Ludag. (I never heard the women complain about the heavy weights they carried in sacks on their shoulders every week.) There was also a shop at South Lochboisdale, again accessible by a long walk over rough ground. However, Kate Ann's garden provided fruit, vegetables and potatoes, and there was always a variety of fish and shellfish to supplement the meat from the van and the occasional slaughtered sheep or chicken. When one of the young males in the family came home for a visit, the gun came out and we had game birds to add to the variety. We ate very well. I had my first taste of *sgarbh* (cormorant) and *naosg* (snipe). I don't know if either of these birds was a protected species at the time; all I know is that the villagers of South Glendale had to endure far more than anyone who makes laws and they richly deserved to take whatever nature offered.

It really annoyed me to see causeways being constructed and existing roads being resurfaced to take the weight of Army vehicles, while out in Glendale a short stretch of road running out from Ludag would change so many lives. The villagers told me that many letters and petitions had been sent to the County and nothing had happened. So I passed the winter evenings writing letters to all and sundry, some pleading, some angry and some downright rude, all with the same theme: the road. Sometimes I collected signatures and Flora would say, '*Mura leig sibh fois air na daoine, clìoraidh iad a-null a dh'Eirisgeigh sinn*' ('If you don't stop bothering them, they will clear us over to Eriskay').

She didn't really believe this, but like me she could see that the letters, like the many written before my time, were having no effect.

I wrote a particularly sarcastic letter to the Member of Parliament for the Western Isles, asking him how he would like to live like a tortoise carrying all his household supplies on his back over a hill his entire life, but again it brought no reply. However, a few months after I had finished my time at Glendale School, Kate Ann phoned to tell me that the Member of Parliament had just visited them and wanted to meet Mr MacMillan – I had just signed the letter with my initials and he had automatically assumed that I was male. Although I was only a few miles away at Daliburgh School, he didn't call in to see me, and from what I gathered, the villagers of Glendale had been given the same old story: the road was on the agenda, but a starting date for commencement of work had not yet been finalised.

Chapter Three

DECORATING THEY CALL IT now. Then we called it 'Doing up the room'. I had just spent a precious weekend giving our bathroom at home a face-lift: red marbled Fablon halfway up, a border and white paint round the rest of the walls. The builders had painted it pink in something called distemper, and every time you wiped a mark off the wall, the cloth was full of pink gooey stuff. After many years in a little thatched cottage without any kind of bathroom, my mother wasn't fussed about the decoration at first, but five years on it was getting on her nerves. My father did all the preparation, and when I'd finished doing my bit he declared himself so pleased with the results that from then on he was going to ignore the rest of the house and live in the bathroom.

I think that was the moment I realised that I really enjoyed 'doing up a room', and since then I have added to the profits of DIY stores in whichever part of the world I happened to be living. Only once have I volunteered to inflict my services on someone else, and to this day I'm not entirely sure how it all came about.

Shortly after the bathroom weekend I happened to be visiting the Steeles, in a house not far from our own, where we were always welcome to drop in and have a cup of tea, a gossip and perhaps a game of cards if we could make up the numbers for 'Catch The Ten'. Donald James Steele was an elderly man who had married a younger woman, Mary Ann, in middle age. His eldest child, Calum, was only a few months younger than I was, and so I always remember Donald James as an older man. Wives who married older men in that era often found that they had to do both inside and outside work on the croft in addition to bringing up a family and in Mary Ann's case there was an even older, bedridden sister of Donald James's and two Irish packmen lodgers to look after. By the time the children were into their teens the sister-in-law had died and one of the packmen, Peter Jordan, had moved on, leaving his brother Willie to become quite a dominant part of the family for the rest of his life. Mary Ann coped with it all and never seemed to lose her sense of humour in what could never have been an easy household.

On the night in question Willie was carrying Donald James, who was recovering from a bad stroke, up the stairs to his bedroom. His was the strongest back in the house and he didn't seem to mind helping out – in fact Mary Ann told me that he did this morning and night without even being asked. I must have said something along the lines of 'Why don't you let Donald James sleep downstairs in the closet? It would make getting him into the living room so much simpler for you.'

'The closet is a Glory Hole,' said Mary Ann. 'It hasn't been used since his sister Flora died some years ago. The whole place is so dark and horrible that I can hardly see to clean it any more.'

At that point I must have said, 'Why don't we do it up?

She took me in there and I could see what she meant. It was dark! There was a reasonably sized window and the room itself was a lot larger than the small room in the thatched croft house commonly known as the closet. Steeles' was a two-storied stone-built house, a sign of past prosperity, but the march of time had well and truly tramped all over the closet. However, I could not withdraw my offer, especially when Mary Ann said, 'I'll get the boys to wash the walls down and get some paint and paper in, and we can do it up the next time you're over from Glendale.'

So that's how I found myself up a ladder with a paintbrush in my hand and Willie Jordan standing at the foot, offering me a dram and telling me that I was a saint.

Willie, as I have mentioned, was a packman who travelled all over the island selling clothes. During his long tenure of one of the Steeles' rooms he had become accepted as part of their family, godfather to their children, and had assumed at least as much authority in the house as its owners. His legendary tall tales, mostly of Irish valour and the superhuman strength of his father, are still remembered by all who knew him. The mammoth drinking binges he enjoyed, although infrequent, were always memorable and made his name known to all. By now age had taken its toll and more often than not he preferred to drink at home when the urge came upon him. He would go to Polachar Inn, have a tot at the bar and bring a bag of bottles home with him. Then he would close the door of his room and disappear from the world for a week or so. Not as spectacular as his behaviour of previous years, when he and his chosen drinking companions could be on the razzle for days or even weeks non-stop, but a lot safer, as even when he was stone-cold sober his driving was becoming erratic. Nobody begrudged him his peculiar 'package holiday', and as he was never noisy, violent or in any way abusive, the Steeles simply turned a blind eye and waited for him to appear at the breakfast table again when it was over.

Somehow the 'doing up of the closet' and the thought that his services as hospital orderly would no longer be required prompted the desire for a celebration. He contacted my father, himself not averse to a drop at the time, and invited him to come along for the ride. For many years they had indulged in verbal sparring as Willie told his crazy stories and my father tried to disprove them, yet throughout that time they remained the best of friends. Off they went to Polachar Inn and I got on with the painting.

It was the first time I had ever used a roller and, having painted round the edges and corners with the brush first, I was amazed at the speed with which this new gadget transformed the khaki-coloured surfaces. The brilliant white ceiling lit up the whole room. While the first coat was drying I measured up the rose-sprigged paper that Mary Ann had chosen and together we matched and pasted and hung. She wiped the newly finished sections of wall to get rid of the air bubbles while I, having the stronger head for heights, took care of the lining up and all the rest of it. It didn't take long, and the light bright room that was gradually emerging spurred us on.

Now and then Mary Ann would go out of the room and come back in again just to see the effect; it must have pleased her as she kept saying 'Well, well!' in a happy tone.

This is a common Hebridean observation, and can be

used to convey all kinds of emotions, depending on which tone of voice is used. Towards evening, with the papering done and only the woodwork to paint and a second coating of the ceiling (which had dried to a slightly patchy finish due to my lack of expertise with the roller) to do, we decided to call it a day. Promising to come back on the next day to finish the job, I went home, had a bath and went to bed.

The next day being Sunday, we all went to church, and only after we got back home did I hear about the spectacular ending to the Polachar run. My father was saying, 'Never again!' in the time-honoured manner. I didn't pay much attention at first, but then I heard him telling my mother that Willie had been relatively abstemious at the pub – just a few halves of Bell's and a few half-pints of beer or, as the locals called this, a half and a half. Then he bought the usual dozen bottles of whisky to take out and they left for home. Willie had been driving very well and they had been within sighting distance of Steeles' when he turned the car over. That car had been turned over so often that the roof would have been the more logical place for the bumper. However, the luck of the Irish always hovered round Willie and neither passengers nor driver were ever hurt.

This time he had pulled over right on the edge of a steep grassy bank to allow a tractor coming towards him to pass, got into an argument with my father about the identity of the tractor driver and put his foot on the accelerator instead of the brake. The car shot down the bank and turned over. The door on my father's side had swung open on impact and he practically fell out, but the driver's door had jammed shut and in my father's words: 'Willie was squashed between the back of the seat and the top of the car like a big bluebottle' (meat fly).

He pushed and shoved his friend's considerable bulk out of the car and told us that at that stage he really thought that Willie had breathed his last.

'Once the air hit him he started to twitch and moan and then he opened his eyes,' said my father. 'Then at last he stood up, a bit unsteadily and obviously very put about; he was mouthing something at me but I couldn't understand him, so I asked him to point to where the pain was.'

'Bejasus, Norman, don't bother me about pain at a time like this,' he answered. 'Go and make sure that the bottles are OK!'

Willie had only been winded but, as usual, he knew where his priorities lay.

I left my parents speculating on how many more rollovers the '*cars beag*' (Willie's Irish version of little car) and its driver could survive, and went off to finish my painting job. As it happened, the Austin was scrapped shortly after that and Willie bought a shiny green van. He was so enamoured of it that he drove it to St Peter's Church and got the priest to bless it. On the way out of the driveway, he ran down two of the priest's hens and caused the housekeeper to have a rant at him.

Willie as usual had an answer: 'Sure, and I only sacrificed the poor craythurs in thanks for the blessing!'

The van didn't get treated any better than the Austin, but actually outlived Willie.

When I arrived at Steeles' on that Sunday morning, Mary Ann was doing something round the byre, and as Hebridean houses, even now, are seldom locked, I just went straight on in and got on with painting the ceiling. I noticed that the door had been painted earlier on that morning, probably by one of the sons, and I decided that they could also do the window frames, as I didn't like working with gloss paint. The second coat of paint covered the ceiling well and I worked more slowly with the roller this time to ensure a more even finish. I expected a nice quiet morning with the lodger safely tucked up in his own room with his stash and I nearly fell off the ladder when he appeared at the foot, bottle in one hand and glass in the other, and began to extol my virtues.

'*Ciorstaidh nighean Tormod, 's e naomh à Flathanas tha innte. Bidh Donald James cho toilichte às na rooms beag brèagha seo 's gum bih i beò gu bràth!*' ('Christina, Norman's daughter, she is a saint from heaven. Donald James will be so happy in these little pretty rooms that she will live for ever').

Nobody could attempt a correct translation of Willie's pidgin Irish/Scottish Gaelic, but that is a fair attempt. His long association with the island had resulted in his speaking a peculiar dialect of his own, with gender confusion and bits of English thrown in. Once you caught the gist it was fairly easy to follow, and to correct him earned you a glare worthy of the Princess Royal, followed by what can only be described as a long sulk.

When I got over the initial shock of his presence and refused the offer of a whisky to give me strength, I got on with my job and Willie, delighted to have a truly captive audience, started to fill me in on his version of the previous day's adventure. He was very annoyed about a woman who had come to the scene of the accident to see if she could be of any help: according to Willie, she was just being nosy.

'Mrs Morrison, he was very worried. He thought we were dead. When she saw that we were alive, did he try to help us? Not a finger did he lift to try and get the car back on the road. He just kept telling me that it was time I stayed at home and behaved myself. He said that I could have hit a cow or killed a child or even sent Norman and myself to the other side. I told him that when I was driving planes back in the old country I could land one on Barnacle Rock if the tide was out. My driving has never been better. Sure, and if I do go in a ditch now and then, I do it slowly, and if people keep their cows off the road I won't go into the byres and try to kill them.'

I had heard most of Willie's stories several times and thought, 'This is where he tells me the story of the cattle rustler his father caught and killed by throwing a bull at him,' so I tried to head him off by saying, 'So you and Mrs Morrison won't be friends any more then.'

'No, not at all! That's not the way of it, sure, I made it up with him. I was busy trying to get the car sorted, so I put my arm round her and told her to go home, sit down on a nice soft chair and smoke a pipe.'

Mrs Morrison was very much a proper lady and the thought of her smoking even a cigarette made me laugh so much that I nearly fell off the ladder. Unfortunately, Willie took this as encouragement and joined in with his own wheezy laugh punctuated with fits of coughing and embarked on further stories till Mary Ann came in and added her own bits of information about the accident. Willie didn't like sharing a platform and left us to it as he dragged himself off the newly painted door, which now bore the perfect imprint of his back in Harris Tweed fibres. Needless to say, the jacket had not fared any better than the door, and although he sent it to the cleaners later on that month, they could not remove the pink paint and it had to be thrown away in the end.

Mary Ann and Donald James had three children, and my young brother Donald shared many teenage scrapes with their eldest son Calum, who worked in a garage and had an old motorbike. Although his mother was pretty unflappable about most things, she really worried about his safety on the bike, and we talked about this as we cleared up the bits of wallpaper, deciding to leave Calum to repair the damage inflicted by Willie on the door.

A few nights before, the boys had crashed the bike. The lights had failed and they had run into a sheep, which had been wandering about on the main Daliburgh–Kilpheder road, between the crossroads and A. C. MacDonald's shop. I think the poor sheep was killed but both the boys were extremely lucky, as one was thrown into a ditch and the other landed on some packing material outside MacDonald's store; the first boy was extremely wet and smelly and the other had a few scratches, but had they landed on the tarred road they would have shared the same fate as the sheep.

I pretended to know nothing about the incident, as I had only heard my brother's story and I wanted to hear what Calum had told his mother. Mary Ann went on to tell me his version, which although close enough to the truth was still far enough away from it to make me realise that some of Willie Jordan's gift for exaggeration had indeed rubbed off on his godson.

'Calum told me,' she said, 'that Donald shot off the pillion, over his shoulders, and landed inside a tea chest by A. C. MacDonald's shop, standing on his head. The crash was not their fault at all. They were riding very slowly as the lights were bad, only doing ten miles an hour, and along came this sheep doing sixty . . .'

I'm afraid I was more inclined to believe that Willie Jordan had been an airline pilot in Ireland than that tale of supersonic sheep, but that was before I became a mother myself and learned how gullible you can be when your child spins a tale.

The closet was a great success and Donald James was

really pleased to be so near the rest of the family and less trouble to anyone. He was an exceedingly gentle, dignified man, and the thought of putting anyone out was only marginally less hurtful to him than being seen to be in such a helpless state. Even on days when he was not well enough to leave his bed, everyone who came to the house had to pass by his door and he would call out *'Tha latha math!'* ('It's a fine day'), the Hebridean equivalent of 'Hello!', so he had a steady stream of visitors and kept up with the comings and goings in what was always a busy house.

In the evenings, especially, Steeles' house was always full of people. Willie, being the Marks and Spencers of Kilpheder, kept his packs in his bedroom and there were always plenty of customers wanting to buy goods which were not available elsewhere. The bench was never empty and Mary Ann greeted each newcomer cheerfully and moved the kettle to the hottest part of the stove ready for the next cup of tea. She had lived her life and brought up her family with a lack of privacy which would have driven most of us mad, but seemed none the worse for it. When business with Willie was over and done with, the evening usually ended with a few hands of cards, and the game was always 'Catch The Ten'.

I have spent many years telling people that 'Catch The Ten' is a game played only in the Hebrides until I looked at a book of card games last year and found it as the subtitle for a game called 'Scotch Whist'. That should have alerted me, as we all know that all things belonging to Scotland are either Scottish or Scots and that Scotch comes in a bottle. On reading the rules of play, however, I came back to my original conclusion: 'Catch The Ten' is a game played only in the Hebrides.

I have no idea where the game originated and I have

never seen it played away from the islands, but in the Uists of the 1960s and before, even the oldest card player knew of it and could play it with razor-sharp skill. Think Partner Whist played with a depleted pack and a bucketful of added rules and you've got it. Add a Tilley lamp and a few drams and you are practically winning the game: you play only with cards numbered 6 and above. If there are six or eight players you need two packs. Players play as partners, and if there is an odd number, a dummy hand is dealt. The player who is the dummy's partner plays its hand, but keeps it closed. The general pattern of play is similar to whist, but there are differences both in strategy and scoring.

The Trump face cards all carry points: Ace 4, King 3 and Queen 2. The Jack of Trumps is the strongest card in the pack, carrying a score of 13, unless it is the only Trump card on the table at the end of a round, when it is 'Hung' and only scores 1 point. (This is usually accompanied by much jeering and crowing from the opposition.) The Ten carries 10 points but can be overtrumped by any of the face cards. (If it is done by an opponent the jeering and crowing are again brought into play.) If the player on your right slips the Ten in and you are also short-suited, then you can risk trying to 'catch' it with a Trump face card. Make it a good one, however, as the player on your left can be in a similar situation to your own and by playing an even stronger face card take your points scorer and keep his partner's Ten safe.

The first pair to reach a score of 42 points wins the game. The number of tricks gained by each pair also counts, and you can score 5, 6 or 10 by cards, but the greatest feat of all, as rare and prestigious as a golfer's 'hole in one', is a 'Vaul'. This happens when one pair gain all the honours and all the tricks. Even if their opponents have had the better score up till then, their scores are wiped out and the couple that have successfully engineered the 'Vaul' are undisputed winners. Forgive me if I have got any of the details wrong. It has indeed been a very long time since I 'tried this at home', and it is a great but quite complicated game.

I think every member of our family played cards at Steeles' at one time or another. There was never any money involved: we simply enjoyed pitting our wits against the skill and strategic play of the masters. My father claimed to know when Mary Ann had the Jack in her hand; she would tell the dealer off for giving her rubbish and whistle 'Hò rò, 's gur tù mo rùn', an old Gaelic melody, under her breath, he said. However, she found out what he'd been saying and, like all good poker players, used the tune to confound the opposition when she really did hold a handful of rubbish.

Cards were played mostly on winter evenings when it was dark early and outside work no longer possible. Now we have streetlights on various roads, but in the old days when the sun went down the darkness was so total that you could feel it. A torch was a necessity if you were going out. If the wind was really howling outside, a ghost story or two would follow the card game at Steeles'. Everybody knew one, and as people drew closer to the stove they tried to put off the moment when walking home in the dark made the stories at which they had scoffed a few minutes previously seem ever more credible.

On such a night my mother was walking home having done some business with Willie Jordan. It was a wild night, and as there had been a funeral that morning, the card game had been suspended, so she stayed for a chat with the family and Willie came down to join them. He kept talking about a light which he had seen hovering over the crossroads between our house and theirs. He said that he had seen it several times hovering above the crossroads, then moving on down over the canal bridge and past the church to the cemetery on the machair. Mary Ann said, 'Away with you, Willie, it was probably the priest's housekeeper going home from somewhere that you saw, and then maybe some Daliburgh boys were out on the machair rabbiting.'

Talk went on to the funeral and how old people still believed that a spade which was to be used to dig a grave always moved around by itself a few days before the person died. This was common belief in my grandparents' day. If you saw a spade jumping about you, got the black shawl out. There were many other ways of forecasting death – a cockerel crowing in the middle of the night, a dog howling for no reason and the absolutely foolproof one: someone seeing a vision of you wearing a shroud.

Mary Ann had been talking about a woman from Boisdale from days gone by who had been saying farewell to her son before he went off fishing in his boat. She saw his clothes change into a winding sheet before her eyes, and when she tried to touch him her hand felt wet as if water separated them. She begged him not to go out on his boat that day, and after he heard what she had seen he agreed to stay at home. As he couldn't go fishing, he did some jobs around the byre and cleaned the little house used by the chickens and ducks. When it was time for him to come in for his dinner, his mother went to fetch him and found her son lying face down in the duck pond. He'd tripped and fallen in, hitting his head on a rock, and had drowned in six inches of water. Other ghoulish topics were touched upon, and by the time my mother, always a nervous person in the dark, left for home she was well and truly spooked.

The torch was a good strong twin-cell bicycle lamp and my mother walked along using the light to avoid puddles as she braced herself against the strong wind. The thought of Willie's phantom light made her nervous, and as she approached the crossroads she tried to think of anything in the world except ghosts. When she felt two hands in the small of her back she was so terrified that she couldn't even scream. The torch fell crashing to the ground and she ran faster than she ever thought she could, losing both her shoes and caring nothing for puddles. She ran right past our house and only slowed down when she saw the headlights of a car coming towards her. Drawing courage from the strong beam of light, she turned and looked over her shoulder. There lolloping after her was Collie, our old dog. He had been waiting for her at the crossroads and when she'd hurried past him he'd given her a gentle push with his paws to let her know that he was there to guard her. Judging by the colour of my mother's face when she came in all bedraggled and shoeless, I think a few spades in Kilpheder had been taking tentative little jumps that night.

Chapter Four

THE MACHAIR WHERE Willie Jordan's phantom torches were last seen was originally bordered by a stretch of high sand dunes along the west side of the island, sheltering the good growing soil behind it and providing a buffer between the crofts and the winds blowing in off the Atlantic. Once the tall craggy outline had been a distinctive feature of the Uist coastline; over the years, however, natural erosion and the needs of island builders have decimated the dunes where we used to play our sliding games and have Sunday picnics in the white hollows.

Each crofter had an acreage of machair land designated as part of his croft and in my childhood years it formed a valuable section of our own crop-growing land. Wheat, barley, oats and potatoes thrived there, needing little maintenance. The parts of the croft closest to the house were used for haymaking, growing more potatoes and vegetables, and a large area was used solely for cattle grazing. The crofters also had some land out in the wetter areas where they dug peat for fuel and the hills were common grazing ground for their flocks of sturdy little black-faced sheep.

The machair croft had a magical quality when we were children. We went down there to help with the harvest and could play in the sand and wade in the sea when the work was done. Later, when Dr Kissling and Tom Lethebridge unearthed the remains of an early civilisation with their local helpers, we joined the many tourists marvelling at this piece of the past which had turned up on our doorstep, so to speak. Sadly, neither the owners of the island nor any other establishment have organised any means of preserving that valuable historical find, and now the fine white sand of the machair is once again giving the second-century wheelhouse a decent burial.

Once tourism took hold, we had the odd hippy-type camper trying to have a 'back-to-nature' holiday experience on the machair and giving up the second or third time he had to retrieve his tent from a wildly frothing Atlantic in the middle of the night. Pitching a tent in a hollow was no answer either. The shelter of the dunes would keep the tent from blowing away, but as night storms are generally accompanied by torrential rain, the hollow would soon become a little loch and the camper and his worldly goods would get very soggy. Neither of these weather conditions were enough to deter the British army, however, and shortly after the plans for a Guided Weapons Range in Iochdar had passed muster and a small barracks had been established in Benbecula, we had soldiers swarming all over Kilpheder machair.

The island had already seen a temporary influx of RAF personnel during the Second World War years and many fond memories of the 'airmen' remained. They had been based at Balivanich in Benbecula and had played a very important part in the defence of Britain's North Atlantic coast. The Air Ministry had bought the north end of Benbecula in 1942, and the airport and the work it provides have served the islands well over the years.

Despite this favourable history, the islanders were not too impressed when the Ministry of Defence first started making plans for their range. Aided by Father John Morrison, parish priest in Iochdar, himself born and bred in Kilpheder, people were made more aware of their rights and the crofters could see that the testing of guided missiles on the island could have many negative aspects. The main objection was that machair crofting land would be lost in Gerinish and Iochdar where the range and its maintenance buildings would be situated. Benbecula people did not want Balivanich to become militarised and the local business community were anxious in case their livelihoods would be under threat if the army built their customary large NAAFI shops and opened the doors to the general public.

Over a period of time, agreements were, however, reached, people were compensated and assurances were given that the range and camp were not going to be used as a military training base as such. A small friendly presence of personnel, testing the 'rockets', didn't pose any threat and so the Army moved in. Well, over the years Balivanich did become militarised and the sprawling monolith of the army barracks changed the township's character and appearance dramatically, and, certainly during the Falklands conflict, troops were trained there.

Still, there were many positive aspects to the second coming of the men in uniform: better roads, more jobs, more children for the schools, the first cinema and a real chemist's shop in Balivanich, to mention but a few. As far as my father and his peers were concerned, the most positive effect the soldiers on Kilpheder machair had on their lives was that their bar tent was open to all and sundry, with drinks at NAAFI prices, seven days a week.

I was living in Glendale from Monday till Friday and was far too concerned with doing my job and coping with inspectors, while taking an active part in the social activities of my islander peer group, to have much in-depth knowledge of what the soldiers were actually doing. From the road I could see many large green marquee-type tents of the kind that shall be moved neither by gale nor rainstorm. Camouflaged jeeps and other wagons were a common sight thundering past our house and my mother complained that the dog was in perpetual danger of being flattened. My father remarked that the time to worry would be when tanks with guns and Communist flags started rolling by.

'These are our boys, God bless them!'

He didn't mention the beer but I'm sure it fuelled his patriotic fervour. Our neighbour, John, reported that 'They are always having a kind of Highland Games and cooking curry.'

I still don't know what they were doing on the machair, but assume that it was part of some protracted survival exercise.

I doubt if anybody actually asked the soldiers what the purpose of their presence was. We islanders had become so used to people of all kinds coming to the island and doing exactly as they wanted without consulting us. Our ancestors had been looked upon purely as a financial investment, firstly for the clan chief and then – when he had bankrupted himself through his passion for gambling and a certain Mrs Hall (no relation!) – the subsequent owners followed the same pattern. The original islanders were there to cut and process kelp, which their masters sold for huge sums of money. The workforce had to be kept alive, so each family was given a small piece of land, enough to sustain one cow and one calf. The bottom fell out of the kelp industry and the people were 'cleared' to make room for the masters' new investment, sheep. It was not until the end of the First World War that the people of the Uists eventually won the right to rent a proper croft-sized piece of the country for which they had fought so bravely. With that kind of history, it took a long time for us islanders to start asking questions of strangers, in or out of uniforms.

The soldiers didn't bother the people of Kilpheder; they were very friendly and courteous. I am sure they must have been amused by the groups of children who rushed down to the machair after school every day to 'look at the Army'. One little local lad in particular used to entertain them by singing songs for bottles of Coca-Cola. He had a voice like an angel and knew every popular English and Gaelic song going, so the show would last as long as the Cokes kept coming. By now the local shops had improved vastly but still tended towards the basics, and although the shop owners could be very generous to people in real need, I doubt if the little lad would have got anything out of them by offering to sing for it.

Before long the bar tent was as popular as any of the local pubs, and on a Sunday when the other bars were closed, men from the north end of the island would be taken by a sudden urge to travel south and make the 'boys' feel welcome. I would have liked to have been a fly on the tent wall, as I am sure that the soldiers were told many 'facts' of island life that could not always bear scrutiny. Winding up incomers, especially the more gullible ones, has long been a common ploy among some of the younger island men and I'm sure the soldiers came in for their share.

Let me give you a fairly recent example, which took place in the bar of Lochboisdale Hotel, haunt of anglers and gillies during the fishing season. A visiting angler had just finished his dinner and was having a brandy at the bar, when he spotted his gillie drinking with his friends at a nearby table. The gillie is a very valuable asset to any keen fisherman, as he knows where the trout can be found and can row the angler to the best spot. Theirs is a relationship involving mutual respect and often genuine friendship, but not in this case. It was more of a master–servant scenario and the gillie quite rightly resented this. It was the last night of the angler's holiday, so when he came over to their table, second brandy in his hand, to enthuse about the excellence of the prawns he had just eaten, the gillie saw a chance to get his own back. 'Yes,' he said. 'Our prawns are the best in the world. It's because of the corn, but you probably know that.'

'The corn?' queried the angler.

'Yes, indeed. The prawns they serve here come from the sea down by the machair. At night when the moon comes up they crawl along the shore and wander on to the machair to eat the corn. There's nothing in the world as tasty as a corn-fed prawn.'

'Well, I'll be blowed!' said the angler. 'I never knew that.'

'Ach, it's got to be a real problem for the poor crofters,' said the gillie. 'But things are looking up. The EEC has just approved a grant for Prawn Fences to be put up all along the machair.'

The angler wandered off to pass on this nugget of information and the gillie and his friends tried to keep a straight face until he was safely out of sight.

The soldiers survived their first taste of Uist and the locals survived the beer. Soon the temporary accommodation was dismantled and the site left, with the efficiency of the Army, as they had found it. The green wagons headed northwards to Benbecula to establish a more permanent base for their rapidly swelling numbers.

Many of the islanders found work with the contractors building the camp in Benbecula, and also in Gerinish and Iochdar, where the firing range was beginning to take shape. Work was also going on in St Kilda, a remote archipelago far out in the west, separated from the Outer Isles by 50 miles of rough sea and populated mainly by rare sheep and seabirds. There the army required a road, a camp and two missile-tracking stations, and my young brother Donald joined some other local men on St Kilda working for the contractors. It was a bit similar to the South Georgia whaling situation, as they lived in a very isolated place for the duration of their contract and came home with a nice lot of money.

Our family had already started to scatter itself far from the croft, and although they all kept in touch, it was a much quieter household than it had been in the days of my childhood. The two older boys, Donald Angus and Donald John, were both in England, now young men establishing themselves in the outside world. Donald Angus's hopes of a Naval career had ended at the age of sixteen, when an accident aboard his first ship resulted in the loss of his left hand. After the rehabilitation period, when the inevitable realisation of all he had lost hit him, he went through a dark time. He was awarded a pitiful sum of money as compensation and used it to blot out the images of what might have been by spending much time in Monte Carlo. On his return he had the good fortune to meet a man who was recruiting trainee management staff for the Railway Hotel syndicate, and although his disability meant that he could never achieve full manager status within that organisation, the training he received put his feet on the right path and gave him a new belief in himself.

Donald John had finished his National Service and joined the Metropolitan Police. He was engaged to an English girl, Brenda Cranstone, from Eweshott. My father had just finished making scathing comments about Scots 'marrying out' when Donald Angus phoned to say that he had been seeing a great girl, Sheila Collins, for some time and they were soon to be married.

'From the north, I hope,' said my father.

'Yes,' said Donald Angus. 'Manchester.'

Once my father met them they all got along just fine, but he always managed at least one rendition of 'Flower of Scotland' during their visits. The twins had also left home: Alick was a horticultural apprentice in a nursery in Carmunnock outside Glasgow, while Mary Flora worked and lived at Daliburgh Hospital for a while and then moved down south to work in Devon.

The custom of naming your children after relatives meant that my mother had three Donalds to commemorate, and she did this by naming her first three sons Donald Angus, Donald John and Donald. The situation was fairly common on an island where many of the people were descendants of the Clan Donald, and as the second names were always used, there was never any confusion.

Young Donald had always been the most helpful member of our family around the croft, and sometimes I feel that much of the work he shouldered, starting as a schoolboy, went unnoticed by my parents, as they always seemed to make much of the ones who had left. Donald was content to take whatever work he could get and fill his spare time with croft work and his music. I was glad of his company when he came home for a while after finishing a job, and when, after a few years, he left home to join the London Fire Brigade, I think my parents finally realised just how much of a support he had been to them.

The accordion was Donald's favourite instrument, although he could pick up any instrument and play it and even make his own. He and two other friends formed a band and called themselves 'The Pioneers'. Donald found a tea chest and painted a logo on the front – a flaming torch, I think it was – with the name of the band painted around it. One night they were practising in our front room and I could hear a new sound, which blended in very well although it wasn't instantly recognisable: Donald had attached a broomstick and a piece of string to the tea chest and was playing it as a double bass.

The other lads from that practice of long ago are still playing music in Uist, and have established themselves as *Na Deasaich* (The Southerners), a band of some repute. Donald went on to compose the music for '*Tioram air Tir*', his brother Donald John's best-known song, and other melodies. Although still living and working in London, he likes nothing better than to play the lovely Highland tunes with a couple of bands in his spare time. He still plays a diverse number of instruments, the latest being the banjo, although the accordion is still his first love.

While I was at Glendale my father was still as busy as ever with concerts and recording, and one occasion he bullied me into my own first public performance as an adult. He finished his last song and announced that I would sing the next one. I was sitting in the audience at St Peter's Hall and will never forget the way my knees trembled all the way up to the stage. I think anger made my voice strong and I actually enjoyed the applause at the end; I was hooked. After that I performed many times but I never got over the stage fright. However, the backstage camaraderie, and the applause and the buzz of being one of the performers, were fantastic. My father and I often appeared at the same concerts up and down the islands, and often Donald and his friends would also be on the programme or playing for the dance that followed.

My mother, the best singer and musician of us all, sat in the audience. Although she had been a very popular singer in her youth and had won a medal and was also a natural pianist, she suffered from stage fright and quite early on in her married life refused to put herself through the ordeal of being on stage ever again. A pity, really, because I recently came across a song of hers which had been recorded as a filler on one of my father's School of Scottish Studies tapes and the clear sweetness of her voice was pitch-perfect.

I think I realised what a consummate performer my father was when I started to share the circuit with him. He could sing anything, from the oldest, heaviest song to the light little satirical topical ditties that he composed himself, almost on the spot, and his memory was amazing. Although he scorned the use of notes or prompts, he never forgot a word or a sequence of verses and could honestly not understand the meaning of stage fright or any kind of nervous reaction to an audience.

One Friday evening I had come home from school and he was outside fixing a stall in the byre. We were both going to Balivanich Hall that night to take part in a concert. Calum Kennedy was touring the islands and was top of the bill. To this day I would walk over hot coals for a chance to see a young Calum Kennedy performing, so I was practically tongue-tied with terror at the thought of singing on the same stage. I went out to see if my father could give me any tips on conquering my nerves. I'd had my two songs ready for weeks and had been singing them lustily and experimenting with different keys as I walked across the hill to school, to the astonishment of the Glendale sheep. When I approached him, my father was genuinely astonished at my timid attitude.

'What's to be afraid of?' he said. 'Just fix your eye on someone in the audience, give them a big smile, open your mouth and get on with it.' (It worked.)

I did not disgrace myself that evening and Calum's performance, as usual, was a perfect mix of a great-looking young man, born to wear Highland dress, singing beautiful songs with a voice like velvet soaked in honey. My father, who came on immediately after Calum, got as much applause as the Mod medallist. The audience started laughing and enjoying the prospect of hearing his introductory patter and jokes even before he appeared on the stage. He always gave the audience what he called a 'good stirring up' before singing a song, and they loved it. I had asked him what he was going to do, earlier, and had been told, 'Good God! I don't know. It's not until this evening and I still have work to do here.'

I realised then that, with the exception of a few established stories and songs which he used from time to time, he made it all up as he went along.

That evening he walked on to the stage to resounding applause and waved to someone in the audience. The effect was immediate. Applause faded into silence as they waited to hear what he had to say. He fixed his eye on a woman called Morag and said (in Gaelic) something along the lines of: 'It's good to see you here tonight, Morag. I've been meaning to call on you and give you a message from Angus' (the woman's sailor son).

Morag giggled and blushed, knowing that there had been no message but more than willing to be part of the act. After a few moments, when everyone had had a chance to see who Morag was and twitter a little, he carried on: 'You thought he was going to South Georgia – well, there was a change of plan. He's just finished a trip way up to the far North.' (Another short pause.) 'Didn't tell me where, but he's bringing you a penguin, so you'd better put another box in the henhouse and tell the cockerel that he's in for a surprise.' (This would get a minor laugh, as the audience knew that there was more to come.)

'Oh, there was another thing: the jersey you knitted for him was lovely. But don't use the hairy Highland wool again. It gives him a terrible itch.' Another pause while the audience let their imagination lead them into laughter again.

'He had to throw it away in the end and a polar bear picked it up. I asked him what the bear had done with the jersey. He said that he didn't know where it ended up. The last time he saw it the bear was wearing it and scratching his back against the North Pole.'

As the audience, Morag included, laughed away, I could see him looking around for the next target.

Hardly anyone on the island had a television at that time and so I suppose that he was their first experience of audience participation, and they liked it. He'd probably go on to someone else or tell a story with amusing allusions to something that he had just done that day. A bit like Ben Elton's skit about emptying a swing bin, my father found humour in ordinary Hebridean happenings, and as he delivered his version, in his own style, it left the audience speechless with laughter. He was a great singer of traditional songs but he will always be remembered best for his way of 'giving the audience a good stir'.

On another occasion I was singing at a concert in Iochdar Hall and had finished my encore. The song was 'O Mhàiri', a rather slow mournful song that I loved, better suited to a first number. When I was more experienced I realised that the audience prefer a short, fast, light song with a swinging chorus for an encore. There were many young people in the hall, so I dumped a few verses in case they got bored. The next person on the programme was a young lady called Rena MacLean. She was late arriving and had just walked into the back room, where we waited for our turn to go on stage, as the MC was announcing her name. She'd had no time to find out what had gone before, and so she went straight up on to the stage and launched into 'O Mhàiri', singing every verse. Rena had a voice of great beauty and in other circumstances it would have been a pleasure to listen to her rendition of the song, but the audience, having just heard it once already, could hardly bring themselves to clap at the end and she came off the stage looking very hurt. I told her what had happened and we were both very embarrassed and dreading the thought of returning to the stage to sing '*Soraidh Leibh is Oidhche Mhath Leibh*' ('Goodnight and farewell') with the other artistes at the end of the concert.

Next on was my father. He walked to the centre of the stage and said, 'With the help of my assistants I am very pleased to bring you something new tonight.'

The audience sat back and waited, thinking that some conjuring trick was coming, as he had done that once or twice. He composed his features into a solemn mask and started, 'O Mhàiri . . .', singing the first verse, while the whole hall, artistes included, erupted with laughter. Then he stopped and signalled for Rena and me to join him on the stage and we sang the last verse of the song together with a great flourish while the audience joined in. When we left him to go on with his usual 'stirring up' we heard him say, 'Now the next time I'm here, I am going to test you on that song.'

I don't think the audience were ever sure whether it had been deliberately staged or not, but it certainly made us feel better about the whole thing.

One of the most memorable concerts in which I was involved was organised by a young lad called Roderick Morrison, and it took place in Castlebay Hall on the Isle of Barra. He gathered a troupe of us together and under the name of 'South Uist Concert Party' arranged the venue and transportation across to Barra in Neil Campbell's boat. There were singers, myself included, Highland dancers and a piper. The accordionists were there, my father came along and I had written a short play for the occasion and some of the performers were doubling as actors. It was taking place on a Friday evening and I was to meet the rest of the gang at Ludag jetty after Glendale School had closed for the weekend.

Roderick looked after all the technical details and had everything planned to perfection, but the one thing he could not control was the weather. On Friday morning we woke up to a blanket of snow. The salty air soon turned that to slush, and looking out of the school windows into driving sleet, I could hardly see across Glendale Bay. Things did not look good for the Barra concert and I was very disappointed.

By the afternoon the cloud had lifted a little but the wind was still strong and the sleet showers persisted. Calum and Flora MacIntyre were full of concern and tried their best to make me stay out in Glendale for the night, refusing to believe that even Neil Campbell would attempt to cross the Sound in that weather. It is the only time I remember them talking to me without the usual deference to 'the teacher'. They were more like parents advising a none-too-bright child.

'You'll be drenched before you're halfway across the hill.' 'You'll get to Ludag and you'll be the only one there.' 'You'll have missed the school bus and then you'll be walking home, in this weather, in the dark.'

Kate Ann listened with a twinkle in her eye but didn't join in until they had finished, and then she said the thing that nearly swung the balance.

'They say that drowning is a terrible way to die.'

Well, all the advice fell on my deaf ears and I struggled against the wind and battled through the slushy heather carrying my bag of stage clothes behind my back to keep the sleet out of it. I slipped and slithered my way across the hill, and as I arrived at Ludag I saw that I was not the only lunatic abroad on that dismal evening. In a parked van singing 'Show me the way to go home' was the entire complement of the South Uist Concert Party, and leaning against a shed in his oilskins and waders, grinning from ear to ear, stood Neil Campbell.

'Ach, it's only a shower. It's a warm summer's day in Barra,' he said.

I don't know how he did it, but he chugged his boat through the wind and sleet and landed us in Barra and I never once felt a twinge of fear.

The weather in Barra was indeed better, and by the time we had dried off and eaten a big meal prepared for us by the Castlebay School canteen staff we were all ready for action. It was a memorable evening, enjoyed by everyone, and the dance which followed went on well into the night. Even my father, veteran of many a concert, said that he had seldom enjoyed an evening as much, as he danced the canteen ladies off their feet. We passed the few hours until dawn in the hall, talking and dozing on hard chairs, until the good ladies came back to give us some breakfast and wave us off on our way back to Neil's boat. In true Hebridean style, Saturday morning was bright and calm and the sail back uneventful, as we told Neil about the great time we'd had.

The people of Castlebay had packed the hall until it could hold no more, and some had to sit outside on top of a wall to watch the concert through the windows; many had stayed on in the hall after the dance to keep us company and had waved us off clapping and cheering. It's the closest I ever came to knowing what being one of the Beatles must have felt like. All in all, we were all very glad that we had risked life and limb getting there.

With all this going on, I am not surprised that I did not know much about the Army's business on Kilpheder machair. In fact I didn't really notice the Army much at all during the first few years of its existence in Benbecula.

Chapter Five

I SUPPOSE THE MOST prestigious person ever to drive past our house in Kilpheder must have been the Queen. It was before my return to Uist as a teacher but during the time when I was home from college on holiday, so I'm glad that I was there to witness such an occasion. There was much talk and excitement in advance of the visit and rumours abounded about the possibility of herself and Prince Philip dropping in to have tea in a crofthouse; I think that one was started by housewives who wanted some new furniture, as nothing came of it. The new school at Daliburgh had a nice big hall and this was chosen as the venue for a royal ball.

I would love to be able to say that some of the Royals attended the ball, but I think they preferred to party on the Royal Yacht, as none of them turned up to grace the glittering event. Still, it was a huge success, and I have never seen so many evening dresses and kilts worn to an island dance before or after. The hall was decorated with streamers of red, white and blue and festooned with lights and balloons of the same patriotic colours. We all sang 'God Save the Queen' lustily at the beginning and the end. It's a pity they missed it, really.

We were glad that they had chosen to drive through Kilpheder on the way up to the Alginate Industries factory and the Wheelhouses, as it meant that for the first time ever, the Council managed to find the funds necessary to give us a properly tarred road. Previously the road had just been gravelled and in the winter it got very rutted and messy. In the summer cars would send up a cloud of dust, and I doubt if the Queen would have liked that. So the roadmen had to work hard, and when the great day came we were able to stand by the roadside outside our house and stare through the car windows as they glided slowly by. I remember my mother hissing at us 'Wave, wave!'

It seemed a bit silly to wave at someone who was just a few inches away from you, but we did it anyway and they waved back, and we stared at them and they stared back. Then we watched as the car glided on over the shiny empty road towards the next group of people standing by their gate in the distance. My mother said 'I've just waved to the Queen, outside our house, in Kilpheder.'

Her voice was filled with awe, but I had just felt awkward and a little bit embarrassed by it all. I thought that the Queen's complexion was the most perfect I had ever seen and that she was very small and detached-looking. Prince Philip was gorgeous and he looked at us, as we stood there awkwardly, with an expression of curiosity and faint amusement on his patrician face.

My father had a much closer look, as he was presented to the royal couple and had a few words with them. We heard about little else for days, and to hear him speak about the Queen you'd think that she was someone much to be pitied for having such a boring job. Perhaps he was right, and when he impressed upon us the fact that we had been present at the making of history, he wasn't just referring to the fact that the roadmen had actually finished their work on time.

I considered real history to be something that had happened long ago and it had always interested me. I have seldom found a historic time more fascinating than when tales are recounted by people who have actually lived through it. During my time in Glendale I had the pleasure of listening to many old people talking about days gone by. Calum and Flora MacIntyre were fascinating raconteurs, as were their neighbours who came in to visit them and pass the long winter evenings talking. Having spent my childhood being passed from pillar to post between Uist, Benbecula and Barra, my knowledge of what had gone on before my time was sketchy to say the least, and I loved to hear stories of the old days.

The Clearances and the Emigrants were often spoken of, and there were always little interesting bits of information about the tough lives that some relative had faced when landing on the inhospitable coast of a strange country. I began to think about taking up a teaching post in Canada, and trying to track down some descendants of the original emigrants in Cape Breton and Nova Scotia, to see if they could add to the picture, but all plans like that had to be put on hold at least until my probationary period was over. In those days you could not apply for any permanent teaching position if you had not successfully completed your two years of evaluated work. Years later, when I applied for a job in England, despite being qualified, evaluated and much experienced, I had to do another year on probation. Nowadays burglars serve less.

Some of the Glendale families had originally come from Eriskay. Its being a very small island meant that available crofting land was limited and so, when they had married, they moved over to Glendale and set up their own crofts. Naturally they often spoke of the island, reminiscing about the old days and the Eriskay of their parents' era. The legendary Father Allan McDonald's name always cropped up, and although I knew a bit about him, it was from Calum MacIntyre and his neighbours that I learned the most.

Father Allan had come to Daliburgh in 1884 to look after a large and scattered parish, which at that time included Eriskay. Altogether he was responsible for the moral welfare of roughly 2500 people. After ten years of tireless work, trying to improve conditions for his parishioners and their children, his health broke down and the bishop sent him to Eriskay, where the slower pace of life might be more suited to his ailing health. There he continued to be 'all things to all men'. Apart from conducting religious services in the small ramshackle thatched church of the time, he helped to ensure that proper educational provision was made for the children, visited the sick and needy and was ever mindful of the hazardous occupation of the fishermen.

He battled non-stop to have the church replaced by a stout stone building with a strong slate roof which could withstand the winter storms. The church of St Michael built on top of Cnoc nan Sgrath was opened in 1903 and the fishermen returning home used it as a landmark. Father Allan was always looking to find ways to bring spiritual comfort to the fishermen and on the Feast of Our Lady, in May, he'd have them assemble all the fishing fleet in the harbour and say Mass on board one of the boats.

Sadly, his health did not improve, and two years after the completion of the new church, he died. The anecdote that most moved me was the story about Father Allan's funeral. When the coffin had been laid in the grave, the people of Eriskay told the men who were preparing to finish the job to put their spades down. Father Allan's parishioners moved forward as one and with their cupped hands filled the grave with earth, gently patting the last squares of grass over the top. Such was the love this young man, who died at the age of forty-two, inspired in his people.

Father Allan's life has been well documented, and amongst his many legacies is his own large collection of songs, stories and folklore. The present-day church of St Michael, with its bell rescued from the German battleship *Derflinger* and its altar resting on the bow of a lifeboat from the aircraft carrier *Hermes,* still stands on Cnoc nan Sgrath.

Stories about 'Weaver's Castle' or *Stac a' Bhreabadair*, an island off the coast of Eriskay in the Sound of Barra, little more than a rock with the remains of a ruined fort or castle on its summit, were also told, but as there are already many variations of the legend already in circulation, I will leave it at that. It is said to have been a place of banishment and I could imagine no prison more formidable than the tiny rocky island surrounded by crashing waves. Calum and his neighbour used to tease me by making up stories about its history, but always gave themselves away by including a teacher in the grisly ending. Obviously they had perfected this system over the years, with my predecessors.

In addition to historical folklore, they used to talk about strange creatures that could never have existed such as an *each-uisge* (water-horse). The name is similar to sea-horse, but the mythical creature that they spoke of bore no resemblance to the pretty little fairytale sea-horses you find in any good aquarium. The *each-uisge* was half-man, half-horse; he lived in deep lochs and spent his time trying to lure unsuspecting maidens to join him in their murky depths, never to be seen again. He was definitely thought to be a close relative of Satan, and if you should see one in an aquarium, call Security. The old folk told me, with perfectly straight faces, that one lived in a loch between Glendale and South Lochboisdale, on the Hartabhagh side. The last time he had surfaced was long, long ago; I couldn't pin them down on a century, but got the impression that they had all been told the story by their parents.

A young man was herding sheep near the loch, so the story goes, and his sister had gone out to the remote moor-land spot to bring him some food. When she approached the loch she saw a young man whom she took to be her brother wading waist-deep in the loch, near the edge of the water. The part of his body she could see was unclothed, and to avoid any impropriety, should he be naked, she called out that she would leave the bundle of food at the water's edge. He did not reply and kept his back to her until she was standing at the very edge of the loch. She called again, and when the man turned around slowly, she could see that it was not her brother but another young man. He had a face like a god and as soon as she met his eyes she was under his spell. She spent some time just gazing into his eyes and then leaned forward to stroke his hair. As she did so she noticed that his thick black hair gradually changed into reeds at the roots. At that moment she heard her brother calling out, '*Each-uisge, Each-uisge!*' ('Water-horse, Water-horse!') The spell was broken and the girl ran back to safety. The

Water-horse turned his back on them and sank slowly beneath the water, never to be seen again.

Of course, I didn't believe that story any more than you do, but it still gave me the shivers to think of the reeds. As far as I can make out, the loch they were talking about is one now used as a part of a salmon farm, so if he's still down there the *each-uisge* is well fed.

One night the postman, a man from South Lochboisdale, was over at MacIntyres' and I asked him if he believed in the stories about the *each-uisge*. He said that his mother had told him about it and she never lied to him, so he sort of believed in it. Then he went on to tell me about a man from Daliburgh (again from long, long ago) who was taking his corn to the mill to be ground. The mill was in Milton near the middle of the island. On the way there the man led the horses, as there wasn't enough room for him in the cart with all the corn. When they got to a bend in the road, the horses stopped dead and no amount of coaxing would make them move. They were whinnying and rolling their eyes and he could see they were very distressed. The crofter himself could see nothing unusual. There was a large rock at the side of the road and the man thought that the dark shadow it cast was the cause of alarm, so he took his coat off and put it over the horses' heads, covering their eyes. The horses immediately calmed down and he was then able to go on his way.

When he arrived at Milton he related the story to the miller, who told him that it could have been some supernatural sighting which made the horses nervous. He said that horses have a much more highly developed sense of sight than humans and that it was quite possible that they could see something from another world. The crofter was sceptical and laughed at such nonsense. The miller told him that if it happened again, he should look over the head of one horse, focus out between the ears and he too would see whatever it was. The crofter still refused to believe him. It was gathering dusk and he didn't want to be on the road too late. The cart was now half-empty, as the miller had taken some of the corn as payment, so he climbed into it and urged the horses homewards.

Sure enough, when they came to the bend in the road where the horses had acted strangely, the same thing happened again. By now it was fully dark, and although there were no shadows visible, the horses stopped and began to buck and whinny. The crofter took his coat off and leaned forwards so that he could reach the horses' heads and cover their eyes again. In so doing he just happened to look between the ears of the nearest horse, and there blocking their path was the Devil. With great presence of mind the crofter started to shout out prayers, and in a flash of light the Devil shot into the rock with such force that a crack appeared in the middle, and he disappeared.

Donald, the postman, couldn't tell me what the Devil looked like, but he did tell me where the rock was situated and I checked it out. There was a large crack just where he had told me it would be – not starting or ending at any specific edge as cracks normally do, but just there, as if a knife had been stuck in and pulled downwards and then taken out. I'm certainly not implying that I believed this or any other stories about demonic sightings in South Uist, but remember this rock, as I shall be coming back to it.

Apart from telling ghost stories the, postman had another very important function in my life: he brought me the letters which helped me to keep in touch with my good friends from college days. I had two special friends, Mary and Pat, who had been students in my year group at Notre Dame, and as they were also starting out in their careers, albeit in city schools, it was very interesting to share experiences with them. I must admit that most of our letters were about more frivolous matters, but we also wrote about our jobs and passed on a few tips about teaching.

I really looked forward to hearing from them, as they sent me news of other 'Old Girls' and kept up a link with the immediate past. In Glendale the hustle of the city seemed very far away, and although I can't say that I ever missed it all that much, it was nice to keep up with the happenings there. I learnt that our old college was closing down; it had been given university status and was being moved, lock, stock and barrel, out to Bearsden. That made me sad, as I had some good memories of my time there, and often as I walked alone backwards and forwards over the hill, my mind would drift back to student days.

Although the convent atmosphere was nowhere near as all-prevailing as it had been in with the Sisters of Notre Dame in Fort William, the regime was still fairly strict as far as coming in at night went. After all, nuns will be nuns. We had to be in at 7.30 p.m. on weekdays and 9 p.m. at weekends. Residency was compulsory unless you were a final year student or were over twenty-one. You could get an overnight pass if some relative phoned in and vouched that you were staying at their house for the night, and as the nuns were pretty gullible, that wasn't too difficult to arrange. Suffice it to say that it wasn't as restrictive as it sounds.

The faculty consisted of nuns who were highly qualified in the teaching profession and some lay lecturers, all women. It was constantly impressed upon us that we were going to be in charge of fresh young minds entrusted to us by their parents and we should never forget that responsibility. If we didn't feel up to it, we were told we should leave and try something else. Standards expected in both written and practical subjects were very high, and if you failed in one subject, then failed the resit, out you went. One student in my group failed Psychology in this way towards the end of her final year and got no mercy – she was out. It was a lot more difficult to get into that place than it was to leave it.

Criticism lessons were my own pet hate. During the period that you spent doing teaching practice in a school, a nun would come out and listen to you teaching and then evaluate your lesson. If your performance was deemed to be in any way below par, this could also be a one-way ticket to a job in Woolworth's. Most of the remarks were pretty constructive and I found them helpful, but I was always terrified of losing the nun on the way to school. I have a hopeless sense of direction and usually this didn't matter, as we were assigned to schools in little groups and I just followed the pack on and off buses. However, on the day of your Criticism lesson you left later than the rest of your group and escorted your nun to the school. They didn't get out much in those days and relied solely on their student for a safe journey.

One day I was taking an elderly nun out to a school on the edge of the town and I actually knew where to get the bus, where to get off and which street to walk down to find the school. On the journey the nuns usually spoke about various things and tried to put their student at ease, but I knew that Sister Mary Vianney would be interestingly different. She originally came from some wealthy trade family, chocolates or biscuits, I think, and had been a brilliant English lecturer at the college for many years. Her lectures were never boring and she always spoke like an actor, using quotations as we would use slang, in a booming voice that could be heard all over the building. At the end of a session, instead of dismissing us in everyday words, she would intone something like: 'Now fold up your tents like the Arabs and steal away into the night.'

When we set off she told me that as she had been to this school before, she would need no directions, and she set off at a brisk trot down to Byres Road where we were to catch the bus. I was trying to keep up with her, carrying my briefcase and hers, wondering how such a large nun could move so fast and trying to hear what she was saying as she kept up a flow of 'Old English', waving her big, black umbrella about to emphasise her point.

I nearly fell over her when she suddenly stopped and stuck her umbrella out in front of an approaching bus. I tried to tell her that our bus stop was on the other side of the road, but she ignored me and marched on to the bus. Although I tried again to tell her that we were heading in the wrong direction, she carried on talking about the way Glasgow was changing. The conductor was upstairs collecting fares and I prayed that he would hurry up and get to us so that I could ask him where to get the right bus, as by then we were approaching the city centre. Suddenly, this fact also dawned on the nun.

'We are not on hallowed ground, little one,' she informed me, 'there's something rotten in the state of Denmark!'

Picking up her umbrella, she marched up to the front of the bus. It was in the days when the bus driver sat in a little glass enclosure and didn't have anything to do with the passengers, as the conductor collected fares, but this was no obstacle to Sister Mary. She banged on the glass with her umbrella until the driver was forced to stop and slide his little window open.

'Coachman, thou art going the wrong way!' she boomed at him.

He looked at her for a minute and replied, 'Nah, hen, you're on the wrang bus!'

I think it's the only time I ever saw her stuck for words, and she didn't speak again until we had arrived at the school, on the right bus.

College holidays were longer than the school holidays we had been used to, and most of us took advantage of the long summer break to earn some money in any job we could find. I washed dishes in Lochboisdale Hotel during my first long break and that was a most forgettable experience. So I decided to try for something on the mainland at the end of the second year. Some of the girls were applying for jobs at Butlins holiday camp in Ayr, so Pat and I decided to fill in a form, as it all sounded quite glamorous. We did get jobs, but they weren't at all glamorous. Pat, poor girl, worked in the kitchens preparing vegetables, while I waited on tables in the dining hall.

It was very hard work, and although all the amenities laid on for the guests were available to us free of charge, we were nearly always too tired to do much at the end of our working day. Once I got used to the running around and learning to carry five plates on one arm and three on the other and being nice to guests when they were obnoxious, the waitressing bit was fun. I was only ever rude to one person while I was there, and I chose a good one.

The incident took place when a young man walked into the dining hall at the end of a long hard day and helped himself to some teaspoons off a table, which I had just set for the next day's breakfast. Teaspoons for some reason were always in very short supply there, and we waitresses guarded them carefully. The Blue Coats, as the supervisors were called, always inspected the tables before each sitting commenced and would dock our wages if there was anything amiss. I called after the young man and told him to 'Steal your spoons from someone else, the mean devils who own this place don't give us enough to go round, and then fine us if our tables are short of cutlery.'

He just kept going, but about half an hour later a tissue-wrapped package was delivered to me: six teaspoons with a little card on which was written, 'Sorry! Won't do it again. Bobby Butlin.'

At the end of each week the tips were very good, and when we got a bit more hardened to the job we used to work overtime in the 'Pig and Whistle' bar. That was good fun but also hard on the feet. It was the era of 'Hi De Hi!' and people really seemed to enjoy themselves at Butlins. I suppose I was lucky to be working in the dining hall and have close contact with the guests, so it wasn't too difficult to enter into the holiday spirit and forget about my aching feet; after all, the smile was as much part of my uniform as the apron.

Pat didn't fare so well, as she had a really disgusting chef to work for and ate hardly anything during the six weeks we were there. She told me tales of maggots being taken out of fish, which was then battered and fried, and the chef's special way of testing the fat, by spitting in it. Apparently his way of cooling off was to sit down in front of the fridge, open the door, take his shoes and socks off and stick his sweaty feet in amongst the food on the refrigerator shelves. We both lost a lot of weight at Butlins and it wasn't all due to the exercise.

We went to a few good parties and saw a lot of

celebrities, who were there as part of the entertainment team, and I was offered a Blue Coat's job if I wanted to sign up for the next season. I had already decided that once was enough, however, so I wasn't tempted, and the most lasting memory I have of the place is that of my feet jumping up and down in bed at night when I was trying to get to sleep so that I'd be up the next morning in time to put in an hour's work before the campers were awakened by the tannoy blaring 'When it's wet it's fine at Butlins'. We were able to save a nice bit of money and appreciate student life a lot more when the next term began.

Pat and I kept in touch for about a year, but she got married fairly soon after leaving college and our lives drifted apart. After all, she was still living in the big city and running around after buses every day, and I was listening to stories about an *Each-uisge*. I thought that she was unwise to tie herself down in marriage so soon after what I considered to be the beginning of her own independent life. Now I realise that as she and David, her husband, had been childhood sweethearts, an early marriage was what they had planned. Although married women were actively discouraged from trying to continue their careers at that time, there was always a teacher shortage in the cities, and if she so wished, she'd probably be able to continue with her work. Now I am very glad that she didn't waste time, as she died not too many years into her marriage. Knowing Pat, I'm sure that she had packed everything she wanted to do into her short life.

At the time of Pat's marriage I was very content to be back in South Uist, with a lovely little school, interesting friends and a very full life. It was a life in which, although a boyfriend was always a feature, marriage was something very much consigned to the distant future, way beyond things like getting a car and learning to drive it, passing my probation and going to Canada, and deciding what to wear to the next dance.

Chapter Six

K EEPING UP WITH fashion was a terribly difficult chore
if you lived in South Uist at the end of the 1950s,
until, like the Magi from the East, came the Indian
packmen. It was long before racism was invented, and as
far as I know islanders are colour-blind to this day in
their attitude to incomers. The packmen were given such
a warm welcome that their association with the island
still goes on, and at least one of their number settled in
Uist, got a job and raised a family there.

They were nearly all called Ali or Malik, but this was
no problem, as most of the island families had at least
two Donalds and probably a few boys called Angus as
well in their own households, having coped with this over
the years by using a second name or adding some
descriptive prefix. They used the same system to identify
the packmen: Tall Ali was Ali *Mòr* (Big Ali), while his
shorter fellow-countryman was known as Ali *Beag* (Little
Ali). They came to the islands from Glasgow where the
goods were made (probably in a sweat shop, but we

asked no questions) and toured the villages in vans. The stock was geared to the needs of an island where Willie Jordan and mail order were your sole means of acquiring anything which couldn't be eaten or used to put up a fence.

I remember my mother positively crooning over a plastic tablecloth, and my own joy after mentioning how difficult it was to buy stiff petticoats, so essential for the finished look of the short, full-skirted, glazed cotton dresses that were popular at the time, when Ali – *Beag* or *Mòr*, I can't remember which – went out to his van and brought in an armful of them. Whatever you wanted, they either had it, could bring it next time or, if it was an emergency they could phone the Glasgow factory and have it delivered.

It was extremely difficult to set up any kind of new business on the island, as there were many laws and restrictions. After all, the islands were still owned by a syndicate of people who were really concerned only with running them as a place where the wild and beautiful scenery attracted the shooting and fishing set, and young women wanting stiff petticoats were very low on their list of priorities.

Strangely enough, Willie Jordan, who had been our sole purveyor of clothing for so many years, didn't seem to resent this competitive invasion at all. In fact, I saw him buying a couple of ties once from one of the Indians, while regaling them with stories of his own early days in the business. Although they spoke perfect English, I doubt if they understood half of Willie's stories, but they were much too well-mannered to let him know that.

I wonder what they really thought of the place and its people. As they knew mainland attitudes to be rather less cordial to door-to-door salesmen, going to islands where they were greeted as old friends in every house, and urged to sit down and have something to eat before transacting a substantial bit of business, must have been the realisation of a packman's dream. They showed photographs of their families and spoke of the countries which they had left behind in coming to Britain to seek their fortunes, and send money back for their children. Come to think of it, many of our own young men were sailing off to foreign countries to make money for their families, and here were other families from foreign lands doing the same.

Our neighbour John and many people like him were always glad to see Ali or Malik, as they were a welcome diversion in a hard-working, relatively lonely situation. Once John brought my mother a pile of new tea towels that he didn't need. He said that every time the packmen came he bought some, as he didn't really need any of their stuff and couldn't think of anything else to buy. His towel drawer was getting so full that he couldn't close it any more, so would she do him a favour and use some of them before the packmen came back? My mother said that he should just tell them that he didn't need anything and he replied: 'I feel so sorry for them. It's a terrible job for a man going around the country selling knickers.'

John's own life was far from easy and his home devoid of luxury, but to him there were more important things in life than the quest for riches.

Attitudes towards people of a different colour were very relaxed, but unfortunately there were other areas that were still prone to a great deal of discrimination. Being a single mother at that time bore a dreadful stigma, as did marrying out of your religion; cohabiting was unheard of and gays stayed well hidden in the closet. If you hit the jackpot and married someone of another religion while in the early stages of pregnancy, it could change your life forever. A father could meet the ferry at Lochboisdale pier and tell his pregnant daughter and her new husband to get back where they came from and stay there. It happened; I knew the girl. It still makes me angry. To me that had nothing to do with Christianity or morality – it was an exercise in bigoted fanaticism.

I suppose things had improved since the real old days when a single woman who had borne a child had to crawl on her knees from the church door to the altar and beg forgiveness of the priest and congregation before being allowed to attend the services again. Still, that happened long ago, even before my mother's time, and as a prehistoric form of birth control I suppose it worked. Strange how the men were not required to take part in this public humiliation, but then I don't think I want to go down that road. Suffice it to say that in Uist, at least in the early part of the decade, the liberated sexy sixties was an era that was happening somewhere else.

Liberated is not the word I would apply to one situation in my memory of that time. I saw a young woman from the next village change overnight from a confident, independent, bubbly person, living and work-ing away from home although still on the island, into a jobless, cowering drudge living with her parents and frightened to death that her baby's cries would bring another rebuke. The first time she went out in public I had been at their house admiring the baby and she walked part of the way home with me. Some people were coming in the opposite direction, and as they approached she took my arm and I could feel that she was literally shaking at the thought of having to face them. She survived, as people do, and married the father of her child, but I ask myself if there had been any productive point at all to the anguish she'd had to suffer after the birth of her firstborn, a joyful if stressful time in any woman's life. I suppose it was an example of humanity being sacrificed on the altar of island distaste for 'causing talk'.

This profound respect for public opinion caused a lot of friction between my mother and myself on numerous occasions, but never more so than in the case of Jack Dolan. He was a young man from Glasgow who had been a boyfriend and dancing partner towards the end of my time at college. We still wrote to each other regularly when I first moved up to Uist, but we had soon realised that the distance between us was an insurmountable obstacle to any lasting commitment. He always wanted to see the islands and wrote to ask me if he could come up for a week. This engendered a panic in my mother worthy of an imminent German invasion during wartime. Jack automatically assumed that he could stay at our house, and as his family had always made me welcome, I felt that this was quite in order, but my mother would have none of it. 'What will people think if you have a man here in the same house?'

Eventually I managed to overcome her objections and Jack came to visit. He was made welcome and greatly enjoyed the Hebrides, even walking across the hill to Glendale and charming the MacIntyres. When he left, my mother – probably influenced by the fact of his being not only a good Catholic but a chartered accountant as well – pronounced him excellent son-in-law material. Unfortunately, I had been totally put off forever when the smart young man-about-town I had been used to seeing in Glasgow came off the ferry wearing a flat cap and a hairy tweed coat. Whoever had advised him on suitable attire for visiting an island had done his romantic ambitions no favours. We parted as friends but my mother was very disappointed. Shortly after my twenty-first birthday she had told me that playing the field was all very well but I'd be a lonely old woman in my old age if I didn't watch out. She had six of us to worry about, so it was a full-time job. The others were no longer within nagging distance, so I came in for more than my fair share of homilies.

The dances, which I have already mentioned, were a weekly or sometimes twice-weekly occurrence. There were several halls by now on the island and the Balivanich Gym, which was a legacy from 'airmen' days, was always a very popular venue. Ian MacLaughlin, one of the best accordionists who ever picked up a 'squeeze box', lived in Benbecula and played at the Gym. It was he who composed the tune known now as 'The Dark Island' and he had been playing the accordion and violin since he was a child. Another talented musician, Duncan MacLellan, lived in Kyles Flodda and he also played for dances. As the dances were all reels and waltzes with the exception of a few quicksteps, accordion music was ideal.

Although there was always some kind of refreshment available in the back rooms of the halls, the beverages were strictly non-alcoholic. You could have cups of tea, sandwiches and so on, served by the tea ladies, and sometimes they had soft drinks and crisps which they sold on behalf of the local shops, but as obtaining a liquor licence was necessary if they wished to serve anything more potent, it was left to people to make their own arrangements in that department.

This usually meant that some young men who needed Dutch courage before asking the ladies to dance with them took a half-bottle of whisky with them and disappeared outside from time to time with their friends to have a wee drink. Some women, too, had their own portable bar with a more ladylike quarter-bottle in their handbag. If all this sounds a bit sordid, just think of the many substances being smoked, injected and sniffed by our contemporaries in other parts of the country at that time. A quarter-bottle between four or five does not a Bacchanalian orgy make.

The Gym has painful memories for my young brother Donald, as it was there that he attended his first dance in his mid-teens. He had saved up and bought a nice suit and a new pair of shoes for the occasion. Unlike the casual attire worn by today's youth when going for a night out, our young men really dressed up for dances, and although they took their jackets off when the temperature in the hall made it necessary, their appearance at the beginning of the night would not disgrace a business convention.

Donald had high hopes of his first dance and had talked about nothing else for weeks. The suit was tried on with various shirts, and as we waited for the dance bus I felt proud of the handsome young man that my little brother had become. He was with a group of friends, and once the long journey to Benbecula was over and the dance started I was too busy enjoying myself to think about him. It was not until near the end of the evening that I realised that I had not seen him since we were on the bus, but the hall had been pretty packed that night and I thought that I had just overlooked him. I saw him sitting at the back of the bus on the way home and it was not until we got off by our house that I noticed anything amiss – as he squelched his way to the door.

The Gym was built on an area of low ground and a large drainage ditch had been dug around it to prevent flooding. In the dark, poor Donald in his new clothes had found this ditch on his way from the bus into the hall and had walked straight over the edge, ending up covered in brown sludge up to his shoulders. He had not even seen the inside of the hall but had spent the evening in the bus, waiting for the dance to finish. His new shoes survived, but the suit, especially after he'd tried to wash it in the kitchen sink before going to bed, was history. We laughed about it later, but as an entry into society, even on an island, it was a disaster of major proportions for a young man.

The mud bath didn't put Donald off dances, and I have memories of sitting in our kitchen after a dance, eating something which he had fried for us and talking about events of the evening until my father came and growled us off to bed. We were young and could survive on very little sleep, but my father always liked a good night's rest before a working day.

The Alginate Industries Factory in Boisdale was where my father had worked since it had been built, first as a casual worker cutting and transporting the seaweed from the shoreline to the factory; at the same time he kept the croft going, as this was still in full swing. For some years now he had been on the permanent staff at Alignate and so had run down the stock to make the croft more manageable. He had worked himself up to foreman at the factory, sometimes doing the manager's job, but was more than happy to put in a day's work with the other local men. Colonel Charles Cameron of Lochiel – known to us all as 'an Camshronach' (the Cameron) – owned the factory and from the first day he met my father he took to him and soon began dropping in to our house.

Colonel Cameron did not actually take up residence on the island, but stayed at Lochboisdale Hotel when he visited Uist and spent some time making sure that all was well at his factory. Many an evening he came to our house and sometimes brought other aristocratic friends, such as Viscount Fincastle, whom we knew simply as Johnny Fincastle, to meet my father and talk the evening away. When an Camshronach got married my parents were invited to the wedding, a lavish society affair on the mainland. My mother didn't want to go, but my father went and thoroughly enjoyed it. Most of the time the evening conversations would take the familiar road of folklore and talk of old times. If there was a dram about, my father would sing a few songs and Johnny would also oblige, usually with a ballad called 'My Pair of Nicky Tams'. It was written in broad Scots and, although we had difficulty understanding the words, being more familiar with pure English, he had a pleasant voice and accompanied the singing with funny actions.

The only time there was any discord was when the talk turned to politics. My father was a very staunch supporter of the Labour Party, as he considered that everything beneficial the islanders had ever received had come through our Labour MP. Charles Cameron came from a long line of Scottish clan chieftains and his political views were not of the working class. A lot of what my father said was purely for effect, but I could see that Charles Cameron took him seriously and got quite angry and I wondered if it was a wise move to antagonise one's boss in this way. My father assured me that for all his aristocratic lineage an Camshronach was a good sport and liked a lively argument.

Apart from the work engendered by the factory, there was little else in the way of job opportunities at our end of the island at that time. There were the roadmen who literally made a lifetime career of maintaining our roads. They were a gang of workers whose lack of speed was legendary, and gave rise to the saying that if you looked out of a plane flying over the island and saw something moving, it could be anything at all but not a roadman.

An egg-packing station opened in Lochboisdale and some people were employed there grading and packing the eggs. It caused a brief flurry of industry, and most of the Kilpheder housewives had crates of day-old chicks sent from the mainland and made a bit of money when the chickens matured and started to lay their eggs. The enterprise flopped and the packing station was closed and re-opened as The Outer Isles Crofters Shop, which was a most welcome establishment, as it was the closest thing to a much needed draper's shop on the island. There was some work to be had in the hotels and shops and also the schools and hospital, but there was still a constant exodus of young people going off to the mainland to seek work.

The tweed industry has had a foothold in the islands since time immemorial, and much of island folklore has been kept alive in the old waulking songs. These were songs sung to help women 'waulking' or shrinking the tweed by banging it on a wooden table, to keep the rhythm going. In my Glendale days there was a tweed mill in Iochdar and some of the south-end men worked there on the looms. There were also some families who were outworkers for the mill. They had their own looms and had the wool delivered and the finished tweed collected by a van from the mill on a weekly basis.

A *breabadair* (weaver) toured the island schools and held evening classes where you could learn the various stages that cloth went through from sheep to shop. The isolated situation of Glendale School was no hindrance to the *breabadair's* devotion to the ancient craft, and every autumn he would arrive there with a large loom, several small handlooms, carding paddles, a couple of spinning wheels, bags of wool and anything else he needed to conduct his weaving classes in the school. Neil Campbell transported it all from Ludag to Glendale in his boat and the MacIntyres had another lodger for a couple of weeks. The *breabadair* had been doing his rounds for many years and they knew each other well. Now old age was approaching and he feared that nobody else would want to take on the job when he retired, as it was a demanding task heaving all the equipment about in addition to needing knowledge and skill to teach the craft.

He talked about the history of weaving and how Harris Tweed was in great demand all over the world, and that our own royal family wore it during their visits to Balmoral. From him I learned that although Harris is part of the Hebrides the wool from Hebridean sheep is not used for the tweed, as it is too coarse and only suitable for carpets. The wool must be from sheep bred in mainland Scotland, and only the best and finest pure, virgin wool is used. At that time, to qualify for the orb stamp which showed that the tweed was genuine, the weaving had to be done on one of the Outer Hebridean islands and it had to be woven by Hebrideans. I don't know if those regulations are still in place but it all sounded very romantic.

All the Glendale villagers attended the weaving class, and as they had all done it before, many scarves and small blankets were produced in a short time. I had never even seen a loom before and was quite fascinated by the whole process; carding was good fun. This was when the wool was combed between two spiky bats ready for spinning. I learned how to make a *rolag* (a little pad of carded sheep's wool), and tease it out with one hand while keeping the tension on the spinning wheel steady with the other and moving my foot up and down on a pedal to keep the wheel spinning. I never quite got all the movements co-ordinated and my finished wool was fat in places and very fine in others, but at least I knew the theory.

When the wool came off the wheel we had to attach two strands to a kind of spindle, which was used to weight the ends. By the wool being flicked between finger and thumb in a winding movement the two strands were wound evenly around each other. Again, the pressure used had to be consistent, as if you wound too fast the finished wool would be too loose to be of any use, and if you went the other way and wound too tightly you could end up with a coil of yarn resembling a corkscrew. The older people made it all look so easy, and even the children, having been attending the classes since they could walk, were proficient. I will draw a veil over my own prowess; at least I had entertainment value.

Weaving on the small looms was not difficult, as all you had to do was learn to thread the wool correctly and keep your tension even as you pulled the horizontal crossbar down to fill up the warp – the vertically threaded wool – with weft, the strands that intersected the warp horizontally. The large loom was a little bit more complicated and produced wide pieces of cloth in a variety of patterns according to the skill of the operator. It involved the use of foot pedals, and I had already learned that my hands and feet weren't too good at co-ordinating their movements, so I learned the theory and left the practical exercises to the skilled weavers of Glendale.

October was one month when I could not go home during the week, as that was the month of the Rosary. Each evening the little school became a chapel as the villagers congregated to say the rosary and sing hymns to Our Lady. I had to lead the prayers and the school children led the singing. I have never been particularly religious, probably as a result of overkill while being brought up by my very religious aunts, but I liked the October evenings, and seeing all members of that isolated little community come together to pray for the rest of the world with genuine devotion was a good experience. Once a month the Eriskay priest came over to say Mass in the school, and that was particularly for the benefit of the older villagers who found going further afield to church arduous. The normal school timetable was suspended on that morning, and while the children sang hymns I took on the role usually served by an altar boy, giving responses and so on. Afterwards the priest would chat to the children and sometimes test them on their knowledge of the catechism and saints' days. So the little school behind the hill was a very valuable part of that little community, and its use for purposes other than academic work had become traditional over the years.

Chapter Seven

Is truagh fhèin an-dràsta
Mar thàing an galair ud:
Am machair is gach àite
A b' àbhaist bhith cur thairis leo –
Chan eil an donas earball
Eadar Orasaigh is Gramasdal;
Ach nì an seagal fàs
On bhàsaich an coineanach.

How sad the situation since
that plague came amongst us:
The machair and the places
that used to be full of them –
The devil a tail is to be seen
between Orosay and Gramsdale;
But the rye will grow up high
since the rabbit has been massacred.

Gur olc an obair-là rinn fear
A thug don àite 'n toiseach e,
Toirt a leithid seo de phian
Do na h-ainmhidhean neoichiontach;
'S cinnteach gum bi mìothlachd
Air Dia ann am Flathanas
Nuair ruigeas e an t–sìorrachd
'S a dh'iarras e mathanas.

What a bad day's work was done
by the man who imported it,
To give such untold pain
to the innocent creatures;
Surely God in His heaven
will treat him with contempt
When he reaches eternity
and begs to get forgiveness.

These are the first and last verses of a poem my brother Donald John wrote expressing his views on the releasing of the myxomatosis virus to cull the rabbit population of the Uists. In his youth he and his brothers assisted in a kinder form of reducing the threat posed to the machair grain crops, but the old dog and torch method was no longer enough, and so there began an extermination programme which to my mind was one of the cruellest forms of death I have ever witnessed. Even hardened crofters were moved by the scenes of suffering that they saw, and could hardly bear to go near the machair until it was all over.

If you didn't have to worry about crop damage it was easy to be beguiled by the vision of rabbit families cavorting around their burrows, but they were just another type of vermin to the folk whose livelihood they threatened. Even so, the reality of seeing eyeless rabbits beating themselves against the ground, and tearing chunks of flesh from their own bodies as they writhed about with heads swollen to the size of footballs, was not easy to stomach. It took a long time to get rid of them all, and throughout that time the stench of death hung around the machair, and you could smell the rotting bodies of rabbits from the dunes when you attended a funeral in Hallin cemetery.

Rabbits are hardy creatures and after a few years they began to appear again, but for a long time they were considered unfit to eat lest traces of the virus might have been passed on. I think there are still some people around who remember the sad sights of the myxomatosis days and I hope that when the time comes for another cull the methods used are more humane. Nature is in itself a cruel thing and I don't suppose the rabbits enjoyed being hunted very much either, but at least they stood a sporting chance against the dog and torch.

Sadness also touched the MacIntyre family during my last year in Glendale. Flora, the slight figure I had grown used to seeing, running around feeding chickens and doing things around the byre, no matter how early it was when I topped the rise and saw the house and the bay on a Monday morning, was taken ill. She collapsed and was taken to hospital suffering from internal haemorrhaging. As she was stretchered into Neil Campbell's boat her face looked as if were made out of white tissue paper, and it appeared for all the world as if she had already left us.

The house went quiet and Calum took to sitting by the stove looking at his hands and sighing. He seemed to shrink into himself and hardly ate a bite when Kate Ann cooked her usual hearty dinners; when she tried to get him to go out cockling to take his mind off things, he'd say: 'Later. There might be word . . .'

I realised that for all his gruff independent bluster when Flora was around, he was lost without his companion of many years. Happily, Flora responded to treatment. A blood transfusion helped her to regain her strength and she was running around the house again in a matter of weeks. Calum didn't make any public fuss of her when she came back, but he started eating and telling his stories again.

Flora was most amused that Norman MacKinnon, a Daliburgh man who had been the blood donor for her transfusion, came from a staunch Protestant family. Just about every time she mentioned him, she'd shut her eyes and say: 'And may God bless the good man and reward him for what he did for me.'

Now and then if she disagreed with Kate Ann over something she'd laugh and say: 'I don't know if I'm right or not, maybe it's just the Protestant in me coming out.'

Although religion had always been a dominant force

on the islands, and its observance rigidly in place, people of differing creeds lived alongside each other in peace and harmony. It was only in the case of intermarriage and other controversial situations that family disagreements arose.

Life went on as before and Flora returned to full health, then, in what seemed a pitifully short time, fate struck again. Calum collapsed with a stroke, and after a couple of days and nights during which the whole village took turns to sit by his bedside, he died. I was there when he breathed his last and one of his neighbours turned to me and said, *'Gabhaibh a' "Verse Anamana", a Chiorstaidh'* ('Say the "Soul Verse", Christina'). This was a traditional prayer, said on behalf of a dying person at the point of death, asking for the soul's safe conduct out of this world. I put my finger on Calum's cold lips and recited the ancient prayer, and I couldn't believe that I was actually doing this for Calum, my dear old friend. It was a dark period in the house by the bay. It didn't seem possible that life could be so cruel to two of the nicest people I had ever met. At the age of twenty-one I still had a lot to learn.

Despite looking as if a strong breeze could blow her away, Flora had always had a core of steel and, although obviously devastated, bore her loss with calm dignity. She had seen her daughter, Kate Ann, left a widow with three young children while no more than a girl herself, and had given her comfort and support, which was now being repaid. The house was very quiet for a time and then gradually returned to normal, or at least as normal as any house can be when a loved one has gone forever. They spoke about him often and I really think that helped; just talking about how he'd react to different things that were happening, and reminiscing about funny things he used to say, made his absence that little bit easier to bear.

At school the inspector had made his final intimidating visit, and as he had unbent sufficiently to say 'Perhaps we can get you a bit closer to home in your next school', I had the feeling that my parchment (the certificate given at the end of a successful probationary period) was forthcoming and that a transfer was also on the cards. It was a funny system in those days: you didn't have much choice in the matter of schools. You were given a list of vacancies and could apply for them, but at the end of the day the Education Authority decided where you should go and personal preference had little to do with it.

I hoped that my move would be to Daliburgh School, a large school in the next village to Kilpheder. I had attended the junior secondary department as a child, but that little corrugated iron building and the old primary school, an imposing stone-built structure next to it, had been closed for some time. The primary school was used as a council office and the old junior secondary school was now used to store building supplies. The large modern school which replaced the old building, incorporating primary and secondary departments, now stood further south on the Daliburgh–Kilpheder road, next to the old technical school, which had also changed its function and had become part of the school canteen.

Changes were happening very rapidly on the island. Time had stood still for a number of post-war years, but then it was as if the world suddenly decided that the islands could do with an update. The coming of electricity and running water to houses had transformed many lives earlier on, and now most of the little thatched houses stood empty as the new houses were built and crofting, never really a paying proposition, became more of a secondary occupation. Crofts had to be worked to some extent to guarantee tenancy, but a lot of the men found other means of providing the money necessary to exist in an increasingly materialistic environment.

The ever-expanding Army population was making its presence felt and many of the children in Benbecula were adopting English as their language of choice. Soon this spread to the south: you could address a child in Gaelic and be answered in English. Many of our young people found work in some capacity within the far-reaching administration and maintenance structure of the army garrison. Another source of employment round about that period had been the construction of the causeway, joining Gramsdale in Benbecula to Carinish in North Uist, and forming the one long island which the three separate islands have now become.

In 1960 the North Ford Causeway was opened by the Queen Mother and for the first time ever you could drive the seventy-odd miles from Lochmaddy to Ludag. The South Ford that separated South Uist from Benbecula had been bridged in 1942 to facilitate access to the port of Lochboisdale, but for many years North Uist had retained its island status, an unknown section of the universe to many South Uist people, even to those of them who had travelled the world.

Although North Uist had a thriving port in Lochmaddy, access from the Benbecula side, even as far as Grimsay, was arduous. You could see it but you could only get there with difficulty. Even at low tide, the North Ford was intimidating and full of quicksands which could swallow an unwary horse and rider in minutes if they strayed off the cairn-marked route. There were two routes you could take; the one which led on to the Ford at Uachdar and wound its way round the north end of Sùnamul to be joined by the second route, which started from Gramsdale and then curved its way round islets to the east before coming back to the west and ending up in Carinish Bay.

I remember my father telling me a story that he had heard in his young days. A man from Benbecula, a priest or doctor, I can't remember which, had been out on a sick call to Carinish late at night. Although it was night time there was a full moon and he decided to risk crossing the Ford, as the tide was still low. The moonlight completely changed the appearance of the Ford, and as it cast shimmers and shadows over the sand and rocks, the man lost his way. The quicksands claimed his horse and trap, and he himself was washed away by the incoming tide. Somehow he managed to swim to one of the small islands and was rescued the next day by fishermen, but such had been his terror that, although he was a young man, his hair had turned completely white.

As soon as the causeway opened, a tour bus from the south started going to Lochmaddy on Sundays and many people went to take a look at this island that they had not seen before. They were probably surprised to find that it did not differ from their own island in many respects, but were interested to see the villages that had only been unfamiliar names to them before the opening of the causeway. One of the North Uist hotels provided a comfort and refreshment stop, and as the people on the bus were classed as bona fide travellers, drinks were available.

There was a story going the rounds at the time that some of the North Uist people objected to people from the Papist south coming to disturb the peace of their strict Sabbath observance, especially as drink was involved. It is said that some families closed their curtains when they saw the bus approaching. I don't know if the story is true or not; my own experiences of the people of North Uist, gained at concerts and dances, were all very cordial.

When A.A. McGregor wrote of the possibility that one day the islands would be joined together, he had said that he couldn't imagine that the islanders would benefit in any way. Well, I think that he's been proven wrong. Having the dangerous fords bridged has brought benefits aplenty to all the islands concerned; not only has it cut down on accidents and loss of life through drowning, but ease of transportation, tourism, the opening up of hitherto isolated communities, the benefit to businesses and the intermingling of three separate cultures have been some of the good results of this difficult but very worthwhile undertaking.

We young people were very pleased to have a whole new community of our peers coming to our dances and found no difficulty in travelling the long distance to *their* dances, over the causeway. I must admit that Lochmaddy was a bit too far away for me, but the village hall at Carinish brings back many memories.

Although better roads and more money brought more cars, most of us young people could still not afford to run one, and although boys with cars were always the most popular, the bulk of the dance-going generation depended on a bus. There were bus services that ran during the day. MacBraynes ran buses to Benbecula geared to connect with the plane and ferry services, but the buses that served the more rural routes and did dance runs were from Fraser MacDonald's fleet in Howmore. Fraser was the son of A.C. MacDonald, the merchant who had a shop in Daliburgh and whose family have carried on the tradition over the years. He had married the daughter of another businessman from further north and had started his own shop, transport and garage business, and it was one of his buses that we used on dance nights.

Angus, who was Fraser's bus driver, knew us all and,

although not a dancer himself, he could always be prevailed upon to do a dance run no matter how tired he was after all his normal day's driving duties. He would go out to Lochboisdale and wait until the young people had had a few drinks in the hotel and then drive along to Daliburgh crossroads picking up more people there, then on along through the townships, picking up as he went along, over the causeway and up (or down, as we used to say) north to Benbecula.

It was always a very merry bus as we sang our way to the dance. Old traditional songs were followed by pop songs of the era and we didn't feel the time passing. The journey to Benbecula usually took a little over an hour, and longer if we were going to Carinish. As some of the young men might have been drinking beer in the hotel, they might require a comfort stop, which Angus was willing to provide at a convenient rock or hillock. Once, he caught a group of young men relieving themselves against the back of the bus and he drove off and left them, forcing them to do a very hasty covering-up operation as the people on the back seat jeered and catcalled at them. He was very good-natured but he did have his standards.

His busy working day caught up with him once we got to the hall and he would sleep on the back seat until we came out again. This seemed to be enough rest for him to feel sufficiently refreshed for the long drive back, but one night our merry little gang had a near-death experience in the dance bus.

We had been to the Balivanich Gym and it had been an excellent evening, as usual starting late and going on into the small hours of the morning. We noticed nothing amiss with Angus as we boarded the bus and settled down to sleep the miles away. Angus always remembered where everyone lived and would stop the bus and call out to wake you up when he got to your stop. About halfway home the bus came over the top of a rise in the road: the wheels turned to negotiate a bend but didn't turn back when the road straightened out. In the quiet bus full of sleeping passengers, while watching the wipers clear the windscreen of drizzle, Angus had fallen asleep at the wheel.

The first inkling I had that all was not well was when there was an almighty crashing noise as the bus hit a telegraph pole and snapped it in half. Glass showered in from the broken windscreen and the bus came to a halt in a semi-vertical position with its back-end up in the air. After the initial shocked silence all the lights went out and everybody started screaming at the same time. There was a mad scramble to get out, resulting in a jam about the middle of the bus, as the people at the front seemed reluctant to move. I put on my best teacher manner and called out, 'There's no need to panic, take your time and we'll all get off safely.'

Then I noticed the water creeping up about my feet. Angus had driven the bus into a loch. I have always had an almost pathological fear of drowning and I thought that my time had come. I am ashamed to admit that the calm person urging the rest of the people not to panic disappeared, and I think I stepped on my sister's head and walked on water to do it, but I was one of the first people off that bus and scrambling up the bank on to the road.

We all lost our handbags and other things, which were on seats and on the floor, as the bus was almost totally submerged before long, but had Angus been driving at a greater speed, or had the pole not slowed the bus down, we could have easily lost our lives. There are some who say that Angus was drunk, but my own opinion, for what it's worth, is that he was simply worn out with tiredness and that in a way we who were always urging him to do dance runs for us were as much to blame for the accident as he was.

Alternative transport was summoned to take us home, and although we were cold, wet and covered in diesel and mud, miraculously nobody was hurt. My father had scant sympathy for us and told us that he was sure we'd be off to a dance on the moon if there was a bus going there the next night. The same old routine started as soon as Angus got another bus, so perhaps my father was right.

Shortly after that, my brother Donald and I pooled our resources to buy a car. It was a green Morris Traveller, the kind with wooden bits all round it, of the type which is now a cherished vintage classic, but to us it was our key to independent motoring – if only one of us could pass our test. It used to belong to Theresa MacPhee, who was our next-door neighbour's daughter, so we were confident that it was a good buy. The registration number was PUS 85, and although I have had many cars over the years and would be hard-pressed to tell you the registration number of the current one, I'll never forget PUS. Why do I remember it so well? The first time Donald drove it he ran over my sister's cat.

It was not as heartless as it sounds. Most of the Hebridean dogs, cats and sheep of the time were on a constant suicide mission. Dogs considered that cars were there to chase, while the cats were very fond of falling asleep under a car and, becoming confused on waking, would dart out in front of a wheel. Sheep were fairly sensible, unless one of their lambs was on the far side of the road, when the mothering instinct could make them rush across to defend it. So learning to drive in South Uist at that time was quite an adventure.

Donald had been driving various vehicles since he was old enough to climb on to a tractor, and apart from the cat he had a clean record, even if he hadn't bothered with the formality of applying for a provisional driving licence. The police on the island at the time were fairly lenient, but once a matter was brought to their attention they had to act on it. In other words, if you didn't cause any problems with your car and nobody reported you, the road was yours as long as you could get away with it. The driving test was only held once a year, as examiners came from the mainland to conduct it. They had to fail a certain quota each time and were pretty terrified of Uist roads themselves, so getting a licence was a long hard slog.

I think Donald eventually took his test in London, where, with very little instruction, he passed first time, but while he drove PUS he did so while playing cat and mouse with the South Uist police. One night he was outside one of the dance halls and was just locking the car when he saw the two Lochboisdale policemen walking up. He dropped his keys on the ground and called to them, 'Am I glad to see you! I've just dropped the keys to this car and my friend, the driver, will be very angry if I don't find them. Could you please shine your torch down here for a minute?'

The policemen got down on their hands and knees and found the keys for him. Handing them back to him, they said, 'There you are, sir. Look after them now!'

Donald was not known to the police, so he got away with it for a long time and eventually left the island still without a driving licence. I was more conventional and went through the proper channels. The Highway Code book became my Bible as I struggled with motorway lane procedure, right-of-way on a roundabout and other facts of driving life which, although I could learn them, I would not be able to practise on single-track roads, where the main hazard was a maternally inclined sheep. My father tried to give me driving lessons, but his instincts for self-preservation were strong. As he had never sat a driving test but had been presented with a licence to drive everything under the sun during the war, so that he could drive the Ministry of Agriculture's tractor in the village, he was not really the right person to cope with my nervous attempts.

I had a few lessons with other drivers and applied for my driving test. I failed it, of course. I thought that I should have passed and couldn't agree that I had reversed on to the wrong side of a road when the road in question was only marginally wider than the car in the first place. The examiner was writing my Fail report as he asked me the Highway Code questions, so I didn't even try to give sensible answers. The worst thing about my driving test failure was that it was actually documented in a published book, for anyone who could afford 18 shillings to read it. I refer to *Scotch on the Rocks* by Arthur Swinson, Chapter 3, page 80: after describing his first meeting with my father, the author goes on to say

> His elder daughter was quite depressed, having failed her driving test that afternoon, so we spent a few moments commiserating with her about the finer points of the Highway Code.

It wasn't the Highway Code that had caused my failure. I just wasn't anywhere near confident enough to drive, and would have been a danger to myself and others if I had passed, but with the arrogance of youth I wasn't ready to admit that.

The great day dawned, my parchment arrived and I was free of probationary status. In the same post came a letter confirming my appointment to the staff of Daliburgh Primary School, and so I said a final farewell to the little community living around Glendale Bay. The life skills which I had been privileged to acquire while teaching and living there have stood me in good stead over the years, and there was no inspection or certificate for those. Nowadays, young teachers have mentors to guide them through their first few years. I could have asked for no better mentors and educators in every aspect of life, and even death itself, than the MacIntyre family of Bay View, South Glendale. They are all gone now, but I am sure that many of the teachers who spent time with them share my views.

Chapter Eight

IT HAD BEEN A YEAR of enlightenment for my father. Not only had he crossed the causeway to North Uist, but also in the same year he actually crossed the Border and took his first real peek over Hadrian's Wall as a tourist, when he went down to England to attend Donald John and Brenda's wedding in the Hampshire village of Eweshott. He had rushed down to England once before, to the Liverpool area when Donald Angus was hospitalised there, but grief and worry had occupied his mind and he spent most of the time in and out of hospitals, so he could remember few details about the place.

His croft work and the factory had left little time for travel in previous years, although he knew Glasgow well, as he went there frequently to work with the BBC and the School of Scottish Studies. England was a place that he often reviled as a country where men ran baths for their wives and crept around their own homes in aprons, although he had little first-hand knowledge of the country or its people. His view, often shared by people who have never travelled, is that if you haven't been there it couldn't possibly be worth visiting anyway. Scotland and especially the islands were Utopia as far as he was concerned.

The reason for his and other people of his generation's antipathy towards the English goes back to their history lessons in school, where they learned that as far back as they could care to remember they would find the English committing dastardly deeds against the Scots. My father could quote them all: there was Edward I, the Hammer of the Scots, who gave Wallace and Bruce much grief, and then came his son Edward II, the very first Prince of Wales, who also tried to tame the Scots and got his come-uppance at the Battle of Bannockburn. When his wife Isabella had him brought to a sticky end in Berkeley Castle, along came the next Edward. What was his first outing after his coronation? A nice trip to Halidon Hill to knock seven bells out of the Scots. On and on my father would drone: the first Queen Elizabeth dealt very badly with Mary, Queen of Scots, and so on. From Tin Hat Cromwell to Butcher Cumberland, leaping out from the pages of his school history book and enshrined forever in his amazing memory, there they all were, with most of them clutching a severed Scot's head in their fist. Not exactly the best basis for good cross-border relations. However, as far as his own family marrying the enemy was concerned, he agreed to keep an open mind, as he had no option.

My mother, my father and I went to Donald John's wedding together. I was to be bridesmaid and, as it was such a special occasion, we splashed out and travelled to Glasgow by plane. This was another new experience for him, as had always shunned air travel even when the BBC paid his expenses, preferring the boat and train journey.

He would say, 'I'm not afraid of flying, just afraid of dying. If anything happens to the boat I can swim, but if anything happens to the plane I can't fly.'

Fortunately, his first flight was a short turbulence-free experience, and although he clutched the arm rests and went white when the plane revved up on the runway, he soon relaxed.

Seen from the air for the first time, the Uists can make you wonder how people can survive amongst so much water. If the Earth from space looks like a blue planet, then the Uists from the air look like a blue island interspersed with specks of brown land. As the winding ribbon of road running from north to south disappeared under a cloud, my father turned to me and said, 'If we crash now, the swimming will still come in handy.'

Looking out of the window until the tiny little dot that was Canna disappeared soon took his mind off the miles of fresh air between him and the ground, and when we landed at the old Renfrew Airport, he was amazed that the journey had taken so little time. From that moment on he was a confirmed flyer and the BBC had to provide for an airfare in his expenses from then on.

The long train journey down to England was a source of great interest to my father, as he marvelled at the neat green fields with their tidy brown and white cows, all looking as if some sculptor had placed them there. He kept saying, 'It all looks so well scrubbed. Is the whole of England as clean as this?'

It was my own first trip across the Border, so I couldn't give him an answer. I realised that he was worried about the impression he was going to make on his son's future in-laws when he said, 'What will they make of my hands?'

My father had large square hands and, although he

was very particular cleaning them, his hard work over the years was reflected in the scars and callouses on his palms. My mother by this time was getting nervous herself, so she snapped at him, 'I'll knit you a pair of gloves and you can wear them all the time you're there if you're so vain.'

The whole wedding episode went very well, with Brenda's family and ours forging a lasting friendship and, although they owned a substantial part of Eweshott, they were no strangers to hard work. So my father's misgivings about their reaction to a working man's hands were unfounded, and he spent much time talking about different breeds of cows and things like that with Brenda's Uncle Ed, a man whose hands showed a remarkable similarity to his own.

The wedding itself went off without a hitch, although when Susie Cranstone, the other bridesmaid, and I went back to the house to change out of our finery into more casual wear for the evening dance we found that neither of us had brought a key. There was a bathroom window open, and we ended up climbing a ladder and squeezing in through the little window in our beautiful bridesmaids' dresses.

On his return home my father was full of praise for England, but of course there was the odd barb as well: 'When they offer you a cup of tea that's all they're offering. You get a cup of tea, no scone, no sandwich, no oatcake, no nothing. Imagine! Just a cup of bad tea!'

He liked his tea strong and practically stewed and served as a mere accompaniment to a substantial plate of goodies. Donald John and Brenda spent their honeymoon in Uist and we saw the other side of the coin when she'd been taken on the usual tour of friends and relatives. After the obligatory cup of tea with all the trimmings in every house, she declared that she would never eat again.

Donald Angus also married his English girl that year, in London, but it was a small quiet wedding as he'd just spent time in hospital with a stomach ulcer. We didn't manage to attend the wedding, but when he brought Sheila home she and my father got on very well, and although he would still poke fun at the English and call my mother 'dahling' in an affected English voice from time to time, I think his association with some of the nicer members of the country made him view England in a better light.

After the summer holidays I started working at Daliburgh School, and it was a strange experience sharing a staffroom with some of the teachers who had taught me in my own schooldays, in the not too distant past. It must have been a bit strange for them too, but they didn't seem to mind and were very good colleagues. One of my old secondary teachers lost track of time one day and called out to me to stop running in the corridor. We laughed about it afterwards and the easy camaraderie that developed between us made me forget about the old days when she had not been my favourite teacher.

'Porky', as we used to call her, was from another island and had often been the butt of practical jokes and pranks played on her by the little beasts we were in those days, in the old corrugated-iron school by the loch. During that time we had not made her life easy and she retaliated by using her belt quite frequently. Fortunately her aim was bad and she often missed most of your hand. The more she lost her temper, the wilder her aim became, and I remember going home one day with the imprint of the Lochgelly's three fingers all the way up my arm.

On that particular day long ago, she had been supervising two classes, as the teacher in the classroom next door had to go home because of illness. The Headmaster asked her to leave the connecting door open and set the other class some work, as it was near the end of the morning, and he'd take the class himself in the afternoon. When she had done a bit of teaching with her own class, she went into the room next door and came back with a white face, as there wasn't a single child to be seen. The other classroom was completely empty and it had no outside door, so she couldn't figure out where the children had got to. She looked very worried.

Worry changed to anger, however, when the lost children entered her classroom through the outside door, filing solemnly past her, the boys saluting and the girls bowing their heads as they each bade her 'Good morning, Miss' and, going silently through to their own room, sat down at their desks. They had all jumped out of the window, then closed it after them, and had walked round the school and back in, to give her a fright. Her own class was delighted with this diversion and shouted with laughter. The belt was well used that morning, and as I was in her class and my two older brothers in the pranksters' class and she punished us all, the MacMillans scored a hat-trick that day.

Fortunately, none of my pupils at the new Daliburgh Primary School tried any tricks like that on me, and although I had a class of Top Juniors larger than the entire number of pupils at my previous school, we got on well together. Not having been an angel myself during my schooldays actually helped, as I could spot trouble coming a mile away and take steps to avert it. I had to call 'Porky' by her Christian name when we met in the staffroom and, as she was a nice gentle person in real life, I felt quite sorry for the trouble she'd had to put up with in the old days.

Now that I was living at home, it was easier to get on

with my driving lessons. My closest friend was Jean, daughter of A.C. Macdonald, and when we weren't doing anything else I'd pick her up in PUS and we'd drive all over the island. She had been driving since she was old enough to take her test and as an instructor she was the best. If she ever felt any panic, she never showed it, and that built up my confidence.

On a fine Saturday we would drive out to isolated parts of the island to avoid traffic and practise hill-starts and emergency stops and all that. The long winding road out to Loch Skipport was a favourite route, and when the rhododendrons were in bloom we'd pick bunches of them to bring home. If we were lucky, when we reached the end of the road and stopped to give the Highway Code a going over, we could park on the old pier and watch porpoises at play out in the harbour.

During this time A.C. or Ailean Mòr (Big Alan), as he was known, was in poor health. He was getting on in years and his declining health forced him to leave the running of the business to his son and daughters, and spend most of his time sitting around the house. When Jean and I had finished our driving I'd go in with her to have a cup of tea and A.C. would come into the kitchen to enquire about our progress. I got to see another side of the aloof astute business image he had always presented to his customers and remember him as a very nice person full of local knowledge and always glad of a chance to talk.

My parents had always thought highly of him and his wife since the time when, as a teenaged naval apprentice, my brother Donald Angus had the dreadful accident which cost him his hand. My father left home immediately to be with his injured son, but first he had to go to A.C.'s shop to buy a new suitcase, as the ones we had at home were all falling to bits. It was a Sunday when we got the news and my father was very apologetic as he asked A.C. if he would open the shop and sell him a bag. Not only did he open the shop, but he and his wife filled the suitcase with everything my father would require for his journey and food for the family. When he tried to pay for it all, they would not accept a penny in payment.

Having heard about A.C.'s generosity in our time of need, I wasn't at all surprised to find that he was such a human person, but I was very impressed by his deep knowledge of the island and its history. From him I learned that the pier we used as our pit stop in Loch Skipport had been built by Lady Gordon Cathcart in the 1870s and that at the time there had been whispers that she'd had it built, not for the purpose of bringing in supplies to the island, but to make it easier to ship emigrants out. He also told me about the history of Lochboisdale Hotel and that it had been a much larger building when it was built in the reign of Queen Victoria, until fire had destroyed part of it a few years after the end of the First World War, and that the new building was therefore not as large as the old one. We heard the story about the building of Daliburgh Hospital, and although I'd heard it before from my Auntie Chirsty, Alan gave it a different flavour and I didn't mind hearing it again.

Many were the war stories he told us, having lived through two world wars. It chilled my blood to hear how the Highland Pipers were always the first on to a battlefield, on the assumption that the weird noise of the pipes might strike terror into the enemy, and remind their own ranks that they were fighting for Scotland as well as England. As a weapon the pipes were not too effective and the band was often decimated. Alan shook his head sadly as he told us that the drummer boy, never more than a schoolboy, was nearly always killed. Many of the pipers came from the Highlands and Islands and he could recite lists of young men who left home proudly and came back in a box or not at all.

From Lochmaddy or Loch nam Madadh (Loch of the Hounds), which he told us was named for watchdogs and had been a port where pirates used to congregate in the seventeenth century, through Benbecula and all the way to the Standing Stones at Pollachar, he had a rich fund of stories and information to which we would listen while the cups of tea by our elbows went cold.

There were many old people like Alan in Uist at that time, people who had had many experiences of life on the island and elsewhere. They had many stories and would tell them to anybody who wanted to listen, as their knowledge of folklore was immense. Writers, mostly from the mainland, who would come to the island for a few days and record or write notes, and then go away and write a book, often tapped this fund. Although he himself often helped people with their research, my father deplored the situation and expressed a wish that 'someone should tell our story from the inside'.

He was a great admirer of Margaret Fay Shaw, who had spent some years in South Lochboisdale gathering folklore and actually living with the people about whom she was writing.

He also got on well with Arthur Swinson, who, although not only an incomer but an Englishman, spent much time at our house recording stories and facts about the wreck of the *Politician*. It was he who included my driving test failure in his book, but apart from that he was a nice man. A veteran of the infantry, having served in India, Burma and Malaya, Arthur would sometimes be telling the stories instead of recording them. He had several plays and books to his credit at that time and was just finishing a long association with the BBC as a producer and writer; he was an accomplished man who felt quite at home in our crofthouse. We eagerly awaited the publication of his book and knew that he would not 'rubbish' the island.

I was still planning to go over to Canada to teach once I'd done a year at my new school, and I asked the headmaster if he could advise me on the best way to go about it. He was quite enthusiastic and said that, as long as I could promise him a year's unbroken service, he would be happy to arrange a teacher exchange with the Canadian government. The Teacher-Exchange programme had just started and I think that he was quite excited at the thought of having a Canadian at Daliburgh School. We would each teach at the other's school for two years and then swap back again.

It all seemed very simple, but when I mentioned this to my friend Mary Dalzell from college days, with whom I was still in close touch, she told me not to do it. She knew Glasgow teachers who had gone over as part of the exchange programme and they had not been very happy. The teacher was paid by the Education Authority in her own country and also paid tax at that country's rate. The cost of living in Canada at that time was very high and teachers were highly paid to compensate for that. Canadian taxation was low, so the Canadian teachers coming over were well pleased with their lot, while British teachers had a struggle trying to make ends meet, trying to balance a low British salary against the high cost of Canadian living.

Armed with this knowledge, I decided that I would emigrate for a couple of years and see how it went. If I did that, at least I would be paid the same as Canadian teachers. I made enquiries and established that there would be no problems with this plan, and my tentative enquiries about jobs in Canada got very encouraging replies. I would have to spend at least three months in Glasgow when the time came, sorting out all the paperwork, and then I'd be on my way.

Meanwhile, I still had to complete my year at Daliburgh and the headmaster asked me if I would add another term to that and leave at the following Christmas holidays, so that the new Top Junior class could be settled in by a teacher already familiar with the school. So, with much time still in hand before having to start the preparations, I got on with life and pushed Canada to the back of my mind, feeling that I had done well getting it all planned well in advance.

Although there was still some time to go before the next driving tests, I kept up the lessons, and as always there was plenty going on in the evenings. There was a spate of Beauty Queen competitions and these usually took place at dances. I had no ambitions in that direction myself, especially as I was as blind as a bat without my glasses and I had never seen a bespectacled Beauty Queen, but Jean was a very pretty, tall, slim, blue-eyed blonde and had once won the Cameron Queen competition, an annual event held by the Queen's Own Cameron Highlanders, at a dance on Benbecula, so we went to most of the Beauty Queen dances and I rooted for her. There were a lot of pretty blonde blue-eyed girls around at that time, and as far as I can recall she did not repeat her success, but we enjoyed the dances anyway.

The way the contests were run was a bit strange. The girls couldn't enter their names and be eliminated, as happens in other contests I had seen. (At Butlins we used to have a queen chosen every week and the prestigious

Miss United Kingdom competition, with the winner automatically qualifying for an entry into the Miss World competion, was staged there.) In the Gym all the would-be contestants were asked to take the floor with their partners and dance an elimination dance, while the judges walked amongst the dancers, giving some girls a ticket. If you were given a ticket, you left the floor when the music stopped. So it went on until only one couple was left and the lucky female was then pronounced as Queen of the May, or Cameron Queen, or whatever. I suppose it beats the swimsuit parade, but to my mind being given a ticket and told to leave the floor must have been the equivalent of 'Hop it, you're ugly!' Horrible.

There were weekly dances at the Sergeants' Mess in Balivanich and we went there from time to time. The Officers' Mess also had functions but less frequently, and they tended to be strictly Invitation Only evenings. I had cousins in Benbecula who invited me to stay now and then, and we'd go to the Mess if there was something going on. I enjoyed it, but was a bit wary of any soldiers showing an interest in me, as I always had a sneaking suspicion that there might be a lonely wife looking after some children in some other country. Homegrown talent was fine by me: it was easier to check out.

Chapter Nine

THE AUNTIES, my foster parents for many of my childhood years, had left Barra while I was at college. They were getting close to retirement age, so the teacher auntie Catherine took an assistant's post at Garrynamonie School; they both wanted to spend their retirement years in Uist and they considered that it would be easier to make their plans if they were actually on the right island when the time came to set up their own home. Although Aunt Catherine was no longer a headteacher, as she had been at all her previous schools, accommodation came with the job, and by the time I came back to Uist they had been in their little house for some time.

Before each college autumn term started we had to do a three-week course of practical work, teaching and observing at one of our local schools, and I had chosen Garrynamonie School for my practice ground one year, actually teaching and observing in the same classroom as my auntie. This was a strange situation for me, and I think we both felt a bit awkward teaching in the same room. However, I learned a lot from her and she gave me some sound advice. Although I still felt very much a child when she was around, we both survived the experience.

Garrynamonie School was familiar territory to Auntie Catherine, as she had attended it as a child and had gone on to become a pupil teacher there before leaving the island for Glasgow to complete her training at Notre Dame Training College. It was a strange twist of fate that she should end her career where it had all begun, so many years ago. Frederick Rea, author of *A School in South Uist*, had been her headmaster when she first taught there as a student, and whenever I pick up the book in which he describes his time there, I see her pretty young face on the cover standing next to the great Rea himself, dark-eyed and earnest, looking for all the world like a more serious version of my own daughter.

During my teaching years on the island I often visited the aunties in their little schoolhouse and I heard many tales that Aunt Catherine remembered from her earlier time at the school. Apart from the hen story which I have already related, there were many more about her pupils. However, I was more interested in the changes in attitude in the workplace between the current time and the days when Aunt Catherine first started out. I had noticed the extremely deferential attitude she adopted when addressing the headmaster of Garrynamonie School and realised that this was a consequence of the island perception of people in authority that had prevailed in her young days. In those days the headmaster was only marginally less powerful than God. The idea of any kind of equality between the sexes had never been heard of and would have raised a good laugh if it had.

In the Garrynamonie School of Aunt Catherine's young

days, when she had attended as a pupil, there was no National Dried Milk being served, and certainly no school dinners. The children often took a hot potato to school in their pocket and warmed their hands on it until they ate it at playtime. The peat fires in the classroom had to be fed too, and each child was supposed to bring a peat to school each day to supplement the school peat. Sometimes a family couldn't spare any peat, or a child would forget to bring it, so some of the children worked out a strategy to avoid censure.

The 'peatless' child would stand outside the building, under the classroom window which was next to the peat box, and wait. Meanwhile, in the classroom, when the teacher had her back turned, another child would go to the peat box and, on the pretext of stoking the fire, would open the window to let the draught fan the flames. He would take a peat and throw it out of the window to his waiting classmate. The child could then come into the classroom, apologise for being late, and put 'his' peat in the box. I could see that even in those far off days a canny child could be a match for any teacher.

The aunties continued their love–hate relationship with my father. He, poor man, did his best to be a good brother-in-law, helping them with their moves and trying to keep his temper under control when Auntie Chirsty referred to his home as 'the house that should have been mine'. To her he was still the incomer from Benbecula who had taken her croft. The feud went on till the very end, with my mother doing a constant peacekeeping job worthy of the UN.

As retirement approached, Auntie Chirsty kept dropping hints that she would like our old thatched croft house renovated for their retirement cottage, but, fortunately for my father's sanity, they got one of the newly built pensioners' bungalows on the Daliburgh–Lochboisdale road instead. They moved in and lived there for many years.

I have always considered it a great pity that Aunty Chirsty had never allowed herself to get to know my father properly. She had kept her resentment against him alive all her life, and yet, had she allowed it to happen, I'm sure that they could have become friends. Not as serious as her sister, she had a wicked sense of humour which he appreciated and they both loved songs and stories; in fact, they had much in common and it was an opportunity wasted. Land disputes have caused many family rifts on the island, even though much of the land is still only held in tenancy.

Religious bigotry, also the cause of many a war, has always been my own pet hate. As far as I'm concerned, we are all trying to get to the same place and how we travel there and whether we choose a leader to follow is a matter of choice for the individual. One of the instances of this nasty curse against God and humanity in which I happened to be personally involved took place during the time when I was teaching at Daliburgh School.

The parish priest had asked me if I would consider helping to organise a Youth Club with some other members of the parish, and I agreed. We were always organising concerts and dances in St Peter's Hall anyway and it seemed a good idea. It was the largest hall in the area, and when we talked about it we decided that we could start off a drama group and a country dancing class, some piping classes and other activities, without any problems. We needed some props for the drama group and records for the country dancing and a few other things, so we decided to hold a small *Cèilidh Cruinn* in the hall to raise funds. *Cèilidh Cruinn,* literally translated as Round Ceilidh, was a very informal type of concert where the audience and performers were not segregated but sat in a circle round the hall. It was easy to organise, and you could start off with only a few performers and pick out people from the audience to contribute songs and poems as the evening went along.

We had a very good evening and raised a fair sum of money. Before the people left we announced that the new Youth Club would be starting on the following Wednesday and that all young people would be welcome to attend. Many of the younger ones stayed behind to ask questions and get further details. A girl from Daliburgh had come to the ceilidh and had sung some songs. She had a lovely voice and we all enjoyed her performance. Before she left I asked her if she was interested in joining the Youth Club and helping us to form a small choir. She said that she'd love to, as she lived near the church and, there being no young people of her own age living near her, it got a bit lonely at times.

When the hall had cleared and we were ready to lock up I was chatting to the priest, and he mentioned how much he had enjoyed the girl's singing, so I told him that I had already asked her to join the Youth Club. I was horrified at his reaction.

'You must tell her that you made a mistake,' he said. 'She can't join. This is a Catholic Youth Club and she's a Protestant.'

I was really shocked and angry, but I had to comply with his wishes. She was very good about it and said, 'Don't worry about it, the minister's just as bad.' At that moment I felt like being very rude to him and leaving him to run his own club, but I didn't want to let the others down, so I held my tongue.

I am not decrying any religion, but that priest's

interpretation of Christianity, at least on that occasion, just didn't tie up with the things I had heard about previous priests who had lived in that house and had given their lives to improve the lot of *all* the islanders. Not only Father Allan McDonald, who had worked himself to death, but his successor Father George Rigg, another true Christian who had caught typhoid while nursing a sick family and had died after four years in the parish, still a young man. I doubt if the policy of exclusion had any place in their dealings with the people. I know that discrimination can be found in many places but sometimes you are made aware of it only when it touches your own life.

The Youth Club started and it was much enjoyed by all involved in it, as there was little else in the way of organised activities available to the younger teenagers at the time. The various classes were a way of keeping the island tradition of music alive, and we were fortunate to have a great piper, Pipe Major John MacDonald, living in retirement next door to the church. He was only too pleased to give piping lessons to the youngsters and would stay on to watch the country dancing and other activities.

There were only a few television sets on the island at the time and reception was poor. If we wanted to travel to Benbecula, we could go to the cinema in the Army camp and watch films in comfort, but our own local arrangements for seeing films were still locked in the dark ages of the church hall, hard wooden chairs, a portable screen and a projector which frequently broke down. There was always a break in the story when the reels had to be changed, and if something went wrong with the projector the heroine would suddenly start talking in a deep gruff voice.

The old ceilidhs where people from your village came to your house in winter and sang and told stories were already dying out. People say that TV killed the ceilidh culture, but I think that its demise started when the thatched houses gave way to the modern ones and the cosy atmosphere with its black stove and Tilley lamp went with them. In the old days croft work used to be relaxed in winter, and this meant that the families could sit up late and have a lie-in in the mornings. As more crofters got day jobs and had to be up early to get to their place of work, the difference between summer and winter habits diminished and the ceilidhs gradually stopped.

We still had the Games days and Sales days and there was a fair amount of jollification at New Year, but nothing like the protracted celebrations of my childhood. People stayed closer to home and families tended to have their own little parties much the same way as their counterparts on the mainland. The old ways had already begun to give way to a new order. The travelling shop came to your door if you didn't want to walk to Daliburgh to do your shopping, and life in general was easier for the housewife.

John and Hector, our neighbours and my father's lifelong friends, came to see us from time to time, but Hector was no longer a bachelor and his new responsibilities kept him closer to home. When he did visit he seemed to spend his time talking about sheep and cows and the new 'buck rake', whatever that was. John had health problems and tried to stop drinking altogether, but now and then he would break out and nearly always end up at our house afterwards. Whether it was the absence of his sidekick Hector or not I don't know, but now and again he'd end up in some strange situation, ranging from sleeping in the wrong house to getting arrested. He mistook our old house for his own on one occasion and spent the night there. The fact that the thatched roof was half gone and most of the floor space taken up by sacks of potatoes must have alerted him to his mistake, but by then he couldn't summon the energy to go home and he slept among the potatoes till morning.

One morning he called in to our house looking very dishevelled and white-faced, informing us that he now had a police record. My parents were very surprised, as we all knew that, although he didn't take as much care of himself as he should, there wasn't a criminal bone in his body. So he told us of the events of the previous day. He had heard that the Outer Isles Crofters Shop had some good shoes for sale, and as his Sunday ones were past their best, he'd cycled out to Lochboisdale when he'd finished his afternoon chores and bought a nice pair of black brogues.

Just as he was about to set off homewards, he met an old friend who persuaded him to go up the brae to the Lochboisdale hotel for a pint. As time passed he discovered many old friends, and by the time he got on his bike to come back home he was feeling no pain. He made a few attempts to ride his bike, steering with one hand while holding the shoebox tucked under his arm in the other, but before he got very far he realised that he was practically going round in circles. So he got off the bike, discarded the shoebox and, after tying the laces together, he slung the shoes round his neck and got back on the bike. This was much better, and with two hands now free for steering he pedalled his slightly erratic way homewards along the dark Lochboisdale road.

The dynamo light on his bike needed some stronger pedal power than John in his inebriated state could supply, so it just flickered about, but he got along fine until he saw a car approaching at some speed. On pulling over to the side of the road, he felt the front wheel skidding on a pile of gravel left there by the roadmen and he went head over handlebars into the ditch.

As ill luck would have it, the oncoming car was the Lochboisdale police car, and when the driver saw the bicycle lying on the gravel with its wheels still spinning, he stopped to investigate. The occupants of the car were not our usual policemen, who had grown used to the custom of sometimes turning a blind eye, but two young mainland policemen who were relieving them over the holiday period, and as they helped John out of the ditch and on to his feet one of them exclaimed: 'You've been drinking. I can smell it!'

Scenting danger, John turned round sharply to deny the charge, and as he did so one of the shoes, still slung around his neck, whizzed round and hit the policeman in the eye! Thinking that he had been assaulted, the policeman and his colleague bundled John and his bike into the back of the police car and without further ado took him to the police station, where he had spent a soggy, frightened night in the cells.

In the morning the policemen decided to drop the charges after hearing John's explanation and abject apologies, and he was let off with a caution. John was much chastened and vowed never to touch another drop – and we all said, 'Till next time'.

One of his main fears was that his escapade would be reported in the newspapers, but as I was the local reporter for the *Oban Times* and *Stornoway Gazette* at the time, I was able to reassure him on that score. Maybe I should have teased him a little, but I didn't have the heart for it; he had suffered enough.

John carried on dropping in occasionally, and if other

members of his family were home from the mainland, they would all come over to our house and we would have a ceilidh, just like the old days. Sometimes we'd also have visitors from Canada, Australia and New Zealand, people whose ancestors had been born in Uist and had emigrated, by choice or otherwise. Most of our visitors had traced their roots back to the island and had some connection to our family, either through blood or friendship. As I have found out myself, wherever you are in the world, if you are an Islander, 'home' means your native isle, so these people came to see the place which their ancestors had spoken of and sung about and had always called 'home'.

Many of the Scots-Canadian visitors were proud to demonstrate that they could make themselves understood in Gaelic and they told us that the original emigrants had kept the language and culture alive through the generations in many parts of the country. There were Gaelic Societies and piping competitions in many of the provinces, particularly in Vancouver and Nova Scotia, they said. They advised me to forget about Nova Scotia for my own plans, as the climate in winter was very tough, and they said that I should try for Vancouver instead as it had a more temperate climate and exiled Scots and their descendants made up a large percentage of the population. They also said that it would be easy for me to get a good job there, as Scottish-trained teachers were very highly thought of, and that if I needed a sponsor they would speak for me.

At school we had a new member of staff, an art teacher from Kirkcudbright in the south of Scotland. Dorothy was about my age, the only child of a middle-class mainland family, and although it was her first experience of living on an island she quickly settled in. Soon she was going to dances on the bus with Jean and myself and becoming involved in all aspects of the local social life. Although she loved the island and her art, she really hated teaching; her favourite saying was 'Teaching would be just great if it wasn't for the blasted kids.'

I don't know what the problem was, but I do know that if you don't at least like children, teaching must be torture, as they can smell the fear a mile away and make your life even more miserable. However, Dorothy decided to give it a year and then try for something else. Meanwhile, she concentrated on all the entertainment that Uist had to offer and joined Jean in her efforts to persuade me to abandon my plans for leaving the island. Jean always changed the subject when I mentioned Canada, and although I insisted that I was only going for two years or so and would be back, she'd say:

'Don't you believe it, you'll be married to a Mountie and living in a log cabin eating maple syrup with everything before you know it.'

I wasn't in the least bit interested in anyone in uniform on the island, unlike Dorothy, who had a soldier boyfriend, and Jean, who was being romanced by one of our young policemen, so I'd point this out to her, but she still didn't like the idea of my leaving. Jean's own future was very much tied up with the family business and she was quite content with that.

Dorothy soon became familiar with the various families and learned not to talk too much about her pupils in a staffroom where you could be talking in derogatory terms about a child and one of your colleagues would say, 'He's my nephew'.

But even with her improved knowledge she sometimes made mistakes. One day she was talking about a child in one of her classes who had a pronounced Glasgow accent and one of the other teachers said, 'That'll be one of the Homers.'

Later that day Dorothy remarked to the teacher in question that the child was not a Homer, as there was no family with that surname on her register. She didn't know that this was the collective label given to the many children from the Homes who were fostered by island parents.

I don't know when the policy of bringing groups of mainland children to the island and dishing them out to any family who volunteered to give them a home started. As there were many Homers of my parents' ages around, I suppose it had been in place since before the Second World War, if not even earlier. By my time the regulations had been tightened up but the Homer tag still remained. The children seemed happy enough, becoming members of their new families very quickly, learning the language and helping out around the crofts of their foster families. They were soon accepted by their peers and didn't seem to mind being known as Homers, although, looking back, it wasn't very politically correct. I've often heard the children introducing themselves to someone and adding 'I'm a Homer'. They didn't appear to consider the term demeaning in any way. Many of them made the island their home and few went back to their birth families, but some went the way of the island youth, leaving to work on the mainland when they left school. In the days when they were brought to the island and offered around to whoever wanted them, it must have been a really traumatic experience for them, but it all seemed to work out all right in the end. They were brought up in good caring homes and I never heard of any being sent back.

In the spring of my year at Daliburgh School, the annual driving test loomed up again. I was desperately anxious to pass so that I could have a little experience of driving my car before it fell to pieces from old age. The police were getting more careful about checking licences, and as I knew them personally there was a strong chance of my being caught if I took the risk of driving by myself. When the time came, I took the test and passed it, but to this day I'm not quite sure if I did so on my own merits or not. I do know that on the evening before the test, several brawny young men of my acquaintance sought the examiner out in the hotel bar and treated him to a few drinks. They mentioned that a friend of theirs was taking her test the next day and that they hoped she was going to pass it.

The next day in Lochboisdale, just before I got into the car to start my test drive, these young men turned up, greeting the examiner and wishing me luck, and they were leaning against the wall of The Outer Isles Crofters Shop when we returned to do the final Highway Code test. They folded their arms across their chests and stared at Mr Veitch, the examiner, when he produced the pink Fail slips and the green Pass slips. When he started writing on the much-valued piece of green paper, they applauded loudly and I was not the only one who looked relieved. I had nothing to do with that exercise and was quite annoyed when they told me about the drinking session the night before. Perhaps I would have passed anyway – Jean's tuition would have seen to that – and as I have been driving for many years in many countries without ever causing an accident, I don't think that the intimidation of the examiner, if that is what was intended, had been necessary.

There was much jubilation that night and we had an invitation to a party at the police station. I have a hazy recollection of being locked in one of the cells for refusing to drink a vile concoction that someone had mixed for me, and thinking that I'd hate to spend time in that dark damp smelly place. The party continued at Jean's house until dawn, when we got Ian, Jean's brother, out of bed to drive us all down to the Kilpheder sands in his big van to watch the sunrise. There was quite a crowd of us, all young people, walking along the white, white sands on a clear early morning watching the sun come up over the horizon and listening to the stillness broken only by the lapping of the waves and the lonely bark of a seal calf from the colony on the rocks in the distance. I remember someone starting to sing 'Stranger on the Shore' and Dorothy saying: 'If I could paint this, I'd never have to teach another child, ever.'

And Ian, ever the voice of reason, shouting at us, 'God, you're mad, the lot of you! Get back in the van and I'll take you home, I'm freezing.'

When I got up the next morning, my first day as a qualified driver, I couldn't even remember where I had left the car.

Ali Mór and Ali Beag '. . . like the Magi from the East came the Indian Packmen.'

Niall Mór Campbell '. . . the ferryman who had spent most of his adult life on the water.'

Donald James Steele '. . . Donald James Steele was an elderly man.'

Mary Ann Steele
' . . . Mary Ann coped with it all
and never lost her sense of humour.'

Norman at the BBC
' . . . we wondered if he would be able to take
part in the recording at all with no teeth.'

South Glendale Primary School (now demolished)
' . . . I could look out of my bedroom window and see it silhouetted against the bay.'

Factory workers, left to right:
Domhnull Bhròdie, Tormad Ruadh,
Dommhnull Aonaghais Chalain,
Archie Beag ' . . . working with smelly
seaweed and inhaling the white dust
from the processed tangles'

Christina and Mary Flora
' . . . in later years we discovered parallels in
our tastes such as a love of the outdoors.'

The Old House (now renovated) ' . . . memories centred round the sustaining constant
of the little croft house.'

Young Donald on Kilpheder Machair (summer 2000) ' . . . the accordion is still his first love.'

Colin on St Kilda, ' . . . I did something totally out of character and gave the time of day to an English soldier.'

Alan Macphee, binding corn ' . . . Making the land pay is difficult.'

Army Camp, Village Bay St Kilda, ' . . . most of the buildings used by the soldiers were purpose built.'

Chapter Ten

A UNTIE CATHERINE WANTED a holiday. She and Auntie Chirsty had moved from the schoolhouse some time previously, on her retirement, and were living in their little pensioners' bungalow in Leonard Place, Daliburgh, and I think she felt that after her long years of teaching she was free to have a bit of fun. So, almost as soon as the boxes were unpacked, she had taken my mother on a pilgrimage. This outing had not been an unqualified success, as my mother got a bad case of food poisoning during the journey to Lourdes, and very nearly reversed the whole Lourdes claim of curing all ills by going there healthy and coming back half-dead.

Now Auntie Catherine wanted me to go to Allington Castle, a Carmelite priory in Aylesham, Kent, and join her on a fortnight's prayer, fasting and retreat holiday. My auntie's capacity for enjoyment knew no bounds. I don't think she was in any way trying to improve my moral welfare; she just didn't want to be on her own, especially with all the Brothers about.

In her later years Auntie Chirsty had developed a tendency to take to her bed frequently and sleep a lot. She called her ailment *an ruaidh* and I have no translation for that – stress, perhaps? Maybe she thought that after her years as her sister's housekeeper and helping to bring up our family, she deserved a bit of mollycoddling, I don't know. It didn't seem to bother Auntie Catherine and, as they were both pretty old, they deserved to live their lives as they wished. She had flatly refused to join Catherine on any of her jaunts and my mother had decided that one brush with death was enough, and in future would confine herself to solo shopping trips to Glasgow, so that's how I became the chosen one.

My summer holidays had already been planned, so I put up quite a struggle. My young sister Mary Flora was working at the Castle Rock Hotel in Woolacombe, Devon, and I wanted to go down there to see her and have a proper resort holiday at the same time. My two brothers Donald Angus and Donald John and their wives had produced baby daughters, so a visit to London *en route* was also a possibility. When Auntie approached me with her request I was less than enthusiastic; at first I flatly refused, but she looked so disappointed and there were a lot of 'You wouldn't be where you are today ... ' comments coming from Auntie Chirsty's bedroom, so eventually I gave in.

Much haggling ensued, and eventually we agreed that we would go to London to see the babies for a few days, then on to Aylesford for a week. She could retreat and fast as much as she liked, but I would just have a quiet holiday, 'forgetting the cares of the outside world, watching the swans on the moat and reading in the tranquil garden.' (This alternative to the holy holiday was also offered in the brochure.) Then we'd go on to

Devon, where Auntie Catherine could read in a tranquil garden while I would join my sister in a kind of anti-retreat. My father found endless amusement in this unlikely pairing of holiday companions, but as it turned out it was a very enjoyable trip.

The little ones, Catherine and Kay, were very sweet and our time in London too short, although Sheila took us to see the sights and Auntie loved St Paul's and the Brompton Oratory. We had a picnic in St James's Park and fed the ducks by the pond; outside Buckingham Palace she echoed many people's reservations about the need of one family for so many imposing residences, but, being a genuinely humble person all her life, she qualified the observation by saying 'But it is not for the likes of us to find fault with the likes of them.'

It was good to see my two older brothers again and to see that they were well and happy. As always, they were hungry for news of the island and we spent much time talking and laughing about the old days. Donald John showed me his latest songs and poems and I was pleased to see that he didn't let his busy life interfere with his talent. Brenda told me that she was always finding bits of paper around the house covered in his writing and she had learnt not to throw anything out if it was written in Gaelic. Although he lived and worked in London, he always wrote about Uist and events that took place there, and always in Gaelic. I think his writing was a kind of antidote to the city and the often stressful work of a policeman.

Leaving London, we took the train through the lush summer countryside of Kent to Aylesford. Brenda and Sheila decided to come with us, and they brought the little girls, who charmed everyone near us on the train. They had heard of the Carmelite priory, but until now had not visited it and were eager to know what it was like inside. Aunt Catherine phoned ahead and booked them in to have their evening meal with us before returning home.

Allington Castle was very interesting, imposing and mediaeval-looking from the outside. Inside the old moated castle a hooded monk showed us to a room devoid of all luxury, with the original stone walls unadorned by any form of concession to the twentieth century, and I must say that I had misgivings at first. There were two narrow wooden beds, flanked by washstands, each with a basin and a jug on top, and I thought 'I've been here before'; it looked like a more austere version of the Convent.

Sheila was horrified at the starkness of it all, and Brenda said, 'I suppose they are trying to keep everything authentic.'

They stayed for the evening meal, which was very palatable, but as all the guests sat at an enormous refectory table and a monk said a ten-minute grace before we could eat, then proceeded to sit at the top of the table throughout the meal, conversation was stilted. When Brenda and Sheila were taking leave of us with their babes, Sheila whispered in my ear:

'Listen, girl, if you get desperate, send up a smoke signal and we'll come and break you out.' She was an ex-WREN, so I suppose it looked a bit like a prison to her, but to me, an ex-convent girl, it didn't look so bad.

I spent the week watching a pair of swans building their nest on a little island in the moat and did a lot of reading in gardens that were tranquil indeed. Although I took no part in imposed silences or fasting, sometimes the beautiful plainsong hymns drew me into the chapel and I shall always remember that week as an oasis of calm in a life which I thought I had planned to perfection but which, unbeknown to me at the time, was about to spin well out of its intended orbit.

Devon was great. I saw a lot of my sister, Mary Flora, and as we had seen very little of each other hitherto, with me being at home while she was with the aunties, her being back home when I was in Glasgow and Fort William, and then my living at home and teaching locally when she had left, it was good to make a start on getting to know each other. In later years we discovered many common interests and parallels in our tastes, such as liking the same books and enjoying the outdoors. For sisters, having no childhood baggage probably helps, and we get along very well.

There were other island girls working at the Castle Rock Hotel, including the daughter of Mary by the Canal, the dear departed old friend of my childhood days, and the week just flew by. We talked, went to Ilfracombe to see the donkeys, were invited to a beach barbecue and did touristy things.

Auntie Catherine didn't go too far from the hotel, as she was scandalised by the sight of all the young people in shorts and swimsuits walking around, or, as she described them, 'Half-naked folk. Have they no shame?'

Still, she enjoyed sitting in the sun and talking to some other silver-haired residents who were intrigued by her accent. I'm sure that when she returned to Auntie Chirsty she probably told her that Mary Flora was working in a place that was a cross between Sodom and Gomorrah.

On the way back we stopped off in Glasgow to see Alick, and he seemed to be getting on well with his plants and things and had a good circle of friends, so we could give my parents a favourable report on all their far-flung children. I took the opportunity to meet with the Director of Education at Glasgow Corporation headquarters, to ask about the possibility of employment while I was tying up the paperwork for Canada. He immediately offered me a job at St Jude's Primary School in Barlanark, as a teacher at that school was retiring and about to start her final term.

Before I left the Director's office I had signed a contract to start there at the beginning of the following January. He understood that I was only going to be in Glasgow until my emigration papers and passport business was sorted out, so he said that we could review the situation at the end of my first term. I was well pleased and on my return to Uist I sent off a letter to Inverness Education Authority giving them a term's notice.

Now that it was all beginning to look real, my parents were sighing a little as they watched me start to sort things out in my room and put things to one side for packing, but they had grown used to seeing their children going off to work elsewhere, so they didn't put up any objections. My mother had given up her crusade to get me to 'settle down', and as my longest running romance had been with a boy from North Uist and it had raised a bit of the old religious controversy, I think she may have been secretly relieved when that ended. I must admit that the thought of all the raised eyebrows on both sides of the North Ford probably kept that association going longer than it might have done otherwise, but it was fun while it lasted.

Dorothy had given up on the teaching profession and was pursuing an application to join Pan American Airways as a hostess. She was accepted almost immediately and was also working a term's notice at Daliburgh School. There we got our classes ready for handing over to our successors, who had already been appointed. The Youth Club was still going strong, and although I had started to drop out of the concert circuit, I went when I had the time. We still went to dances with Jean and the gang and it was all going along just fine, until one night at a dance in the Balivanich Gym when I did something totally out of character and gave the time of day to an English soldier, a REME Warrant Officer. Three weeks later I was engaged to him. Canadian plans went out of the window, at least for the moment, and the future was nothing if not uncertain. As our Ruby Wedding approaches, neither of us can explain how two sane people could have reached such an important decision so rapidly and why it should have happened at that time in our lives, but whatever the reason, we are not sorry that it did.

Love at first sight? No way. We spent our first evening together having a huge argument, and when he asked if he could see me again, my answer was 'Not if I see you first.'

He was very persistent, however, and, as you can gather, things improved between us. Colin had been in Benbecula for three years and was due for posting out in a few months, but our paths had never crossed; I was just about to leave the island for Glasgow and then move on to Canada, and now this had happened. It was all very inconvenient. My parents took it all in their stride and were quite taken with Colin when they met him, although my father gave him a grilling worthy of any Victorian patriarch and then told me: 'He'll do, but are you sure that he's not too sensible for you?'

My mother was all pleased and twittery about planning a wedding. She liked Colin but I have the sneaking suspicion that she would have embraced Willie Jordan as a son-in-law if it made me 'stop gallivanting and behave like a proper teacher'.

I was never sure what that meant, but I think it involved wearing a fur coat and a hat to church and praying a lot.

Jean was delighted and Dorothy claimed some responsibility, as she had mentioned Colin to me several times and had actually introduced us. However neither of them could see how it was all going to end, as I was working my final month of notice at Daliburgh and there was a teacher's desk in Barlanark, many miles of land and sea away, with my name on it. With the mad optimism of youth, I was sure that we could work things out as we went along – after all, my long-term planning had not exactly proved foolproof.

There was a lot of toing and froing between Benbecula and Kilpheder as Colin got to know my family and friends. It wasn't too easy for him, as he had no car of his own and had to rely on the generosity of car-owning friends. When the friends were using their cars themselves, one of the Benbecula shopkeepers, Charlie MacLeod, a friend of both my parents with whom Colin was acquainted, told him to borrow his van whenever he liked. Charlie had been one of my mother's admirers in her carefree single days while she had been living with Aunt Catherine in Benbecula. He was happy to be involved in the present turn of events and seldom used the van in the evening himself, as he was getting on in years.

Colin's journeys from Benbecula to Kilpheder went smoothly as a rule, but once or twice he found out that sheep were not the only hazard on island roads. One evening he was coming down fairly late and it was already dark when he picked up the keys and thanked Charlie.

'Watch out for the dog, now,' said Charlie.

As Colin manoeuvred the van out of its tight parking space between the shop and a stone wall he kept a sharp lookout through the windscreen, in case he should run the dog over. He couldn't see any sign of the animal and, putting the gear into reverse, he looked over his shoulder. As he did so two bright eyes looked straight into his and a wet tongue slathered its way from his forehead to his chin. Charlie's dog had been sleeping on the back seat of the van. Charlie came running out when he heard the van crashing into the wall, but as there was no lasting damage to wall, vehicle, driver or furry passenger, all he said was 'I'm sorry, Colin, I should have told you he was sleeping in the van.'

I expect the story went down well in the bar of Creagorry Hotel that night. My father enjoyed it too.

On another night Colin didn't seem to be his usual self, looking preoccupied and being very quiet. Most of the time, if he and my father were in the same room, I couldn't get a word in edgeways and as I had been out when he'd arrived at the house, I thought that they'd had a falling-out over something and left it at that. My father thought that Colin and I had had a disagreement over the phone earlier, and waited for me to come home and hopefully sort things out, as there was a definite atmosphere. When I'd been there for a while and things were still strained, my mother said: 'What's up, Colin, aren't you feeling well? You look as if you've seen a ghost.'

'I didn't see one,' he replied, ' but I definitely think I've felt one around me.'

When he was driving down the South Uist road, past Beinn na Coraraidh and the big rock that stood there, he felt the hairs on the back of his neck stand up and a cold draught from the back of the car made a shiver go through his whole body. He could feel a presence in the back of the car but was too scared to look in the rear-view mirror. His mind told him to stop the car and investigate, but his body wouldn't obey it and a few minutes later the atmosphere changed back to normal. He stopped and checked the car but there was nothing on the back seat and the windows were closed.

'I felt as if something really evil was in there with me,' he said.

He had just passed a big rock. Remember the rock with the crack in it that had featured in Donald the Glendale postman's story? That was the one. Colin swore that he had never heard that story until we told him about it after we'd heard of his experience, and I believed him, as he's not the type to bother making things up for effect. Although he drove home in the dark that night and many other nights, it never happened again.

Our neighbour John was full of misgivings about my taking up with a soldier and told me many dark tales of women who had got into trouble with the servicemen during the war. All left penniless and shoeless, with a houseful of babies, when the rascally airmen went back to their English wives, he said. I don't know where he got his information from, as he had never stirred too far from his croft and I couldn't think of any Kilpheder women fitting his description. When he met the soldier in question, he declared him far too much like an Islander to be an Englishman, let alone a soldier. Praise indeed.

Another fan club started when Colin met the aunties. They had invited us to tea and had bought a new china teaset for the occasion. Now, if you've seen the comedy *Father Ted*, in which the housekeeper's plates of sandwiches are like the Cairngorms, the aunties always produced a table that would make Mrs Doyle's efforts pale into insignificance, and on this occasion they had excelled themselves. Fortunately, Colin has a very good appetite and, being forewarned, had starved himself for most of the day in preparation, so he just ate and ate and ate. The cups of tea kept coming and he kept putting them away. The aunties were mightily impressed. When we were leaving, Auntie Chirsty presented him with a pair of the special socks, grey ones, knitted in the finest soft two-ply wool, which she always made for my brothers. He had eaten his way into her good books on that occasion, but on future visits he had cause to regret his enthusiasm for the table, as the food began to take over most of the room.

At the end of the term and my final days at Daliburgh School I felt very sad. I had loved it there and was sure that no Glasgow school could ever come up to its standards either in terms of friendly staff or well-behaved, bright pupils. Dorothy was also leaving and she, Jean and I had a little 'wake' for the days of yore. Jean was a bit brighter about my departure than she had been: first because I wasn't going straight to Canada now, but there was also another reason – one of Colin's army friends, John McDonnell, had expressed an interest in meeting her, and as she had admired him from afar for some time but they both seemed a bit shy about making a move, we thought we'd play Cupid and arrange a foursome. It was an unqualified success and I think they are about three years behind us in their wedding anniversaries. Not as precipitous as our engagement, but Jean came from a canny family.

Talking of families, I still had to meet my prospective in-laws, so after taking leave of Daliburgh School, Colin and I went to Bristol to meet his family and stay for Christmas. From there I would go straight to Glasgow, where I had arranged lodgings with my college friend

Mary Dalzell's family. Colin would leave me there with all my worldly goods and continue his journey on to Uist.

We sailed on the *Claymore*, the larger and more stable successor to the awful *Lochness*, but still not a drive-on, drive-off ferry. The cars were driven on to a big net, the driver got out and the net was gathered up and winched on board by a crane. We hadn't brought a car, as I doubt if PUS would have survived the net, let alone the journey. Instead we took the train from Oban to Buchanan Street Station in Glasgow and then transferred to Central Station to catch the Bristol train. We were late getting in to Buchanan Street and didn't have much time in hand before the Bristol train left, so we were not too happy to see the taxi rank completely devoid of taxis. As I was effectively moving house at the end of the holiday, we were loaded down with luggage, and as we puffed our way as fast as we could up the incline towards Central Station, I thought that we were both going to die. We made it to the station, just before the whistle blew, but it was a good ten minutes before either of us could speak.

The visit was good. No strangeness at all right from the moment Colin's mother opened the door, and a little later when he had left the room, she whispered to me:

'I've always been afraid that he'd come back from foreign parts with a black wife, it makes it so difficult for the poor children.'

So I was of an acceptable colour at least. At that moment she reminded me of my own mother and her strange ways of evaluating people. I loved Bristol: it was such a clean bright city, and although it was a very cold winter with much snow about, we did a lot of sight-seeing. Theatres, cathedrals, docks and the beautiful old university at the top of Park Street, Brunel's station and suspension bridge, the Nails – large metal objects rising from a cobbled square on whose surface the slavers would place their money when a bargain had been struck over some unlucky slave, thus giving rise to the saying 'paid on the nail' – so much history held within a few square miles; I liked it all. We also paid a visit to a jeweller's and Colin bought me a lovely diamond ring and I liked that too, and he bought himself a car.

I had my first experience of an English Christmas, which we spent with Colin's brother and his family. Then his mother hired a hall and arranged a huge party where I met what seemed like more relatives than the entire population of South Uist in one evening. All too soon it was time to head north again.

The weather had deteriorated steadily over Christmas and New Year, and the whole country was in the grip of one of the worst winters it had hitherto known. We left early in the morning, and although it had taken us nearly an hour to dig the car out of the snow before we set off, it wasn't too bad once we got onto the major roads. There were no motorways then, so Shap was rather dicey, as a blizzard blew up just as we were approaching the summit. It was a frightful journey from then on: the weather got worse and worse, and after a brief overnight stop and an early start, it was evening of the next day before we made it to Glasgow.

The Dalzell family lived on the borders of Springburn and Balornock in a solid old tenement house which was like a haven of warmth after the howling blizzard and ice storm conditions through which we had been driving for the best part of two days. I was at the end of my journey, but Colin only had time for a hot drink and a sandwich before having to turn the car around and head out of Glasgow towards Oban to catch the boat for Lochboisdale.

I really didn't envy him one bit, and knowing the narrow unlit roads he had to travel once he was out of the city, I was concerned for his safety in the worst driving conditions imaginable. The route from Glasgow to Oban, even in those days long before the construction of the present-day road, was still one of the prettiest in the country. In good weather you drove between towering mountains reflected in clear lochs and a picture postcard view awaited round every bend. In winter darkness, in a blizzard, when one wiper is frozen to the windscreen and the other has been whipped off by the howling wind, it's a different story. I could imagine all sorts of different scenarios, all resulting in my being single again before I'd even got used to the weight of the engagement ring on my finger.

When Colin called me the next evening, I found out that my fears had not been unfounded. It had been a hazardous journey. Under the narrow old roads of the time there were gulleys for drainage to stop the water cascading off the high ground on either side of the roads during rainstorms and causing flooding. The freezing cold wind had iced up the water in the gullies, resulting in a blockage, and the water, then free to gush across the roads, had gradually frozen. The water running down the sides had also frozen and great slabs of ice had fallen on to the road here and there. Not ideal conditions for someone driving that road for the first time, in the dark.

To make matters even worse, the signpost at the Tarbet intersection, which should have pointed him in the right direction for Crianlarich and the turn-off for Oban, had been turned around by the high wind and was pointing to the left instead of the right. Colin had followed this road for half an hour before he stopped at Arrochar to check the map, found out his mistake and had to turn back.

Eventually, within sight of Oban, he saw a pub in the distance; hoping that it would still be open and have a bed available, he went up the side road and parked outside. The pub was open, and such was the landlord's astonishment that someone had actually driven from Bristol in that weather that Colin was treated to free drinks all night. He sat there with only the landlord for company till he could summon enough energy to drag himself off to bed for a few hours' sleep, as he had to be up in time for the early morning sailing of the *Claymore*. Back in Balornock, I'd worried for a bit, but Mary and I had much to catch up on and we burned a bit of midnight oil till I started falling asleep in my chair.

Chapter Eleven

How do you know when a friendship begins? My first memory of Mary Dalzell is quite clear. We were both in our first year at college and it was the Wednesday morning Speech Class.

I am not quite sure what the purpose of this class was: maybe it was a means of giving us an opportunity to build up our public-speaking skills so that we'd be able to make ourselves heard as we yelled 'Put him down!' across a Glasgow playground. We were allocated topics on the spot, and we spoke about them for a couple of minutes. It was torture for some students and they died a thousand deaths while stumbling through some boring little homily on 'How to Iron a Shirt' or 'My Best Day' with a dry mouth. Any MacMillan can talk for Scotland, so I didn't mind Speech Class at all.

On that particular day I had been given the subject 'It Makes My Blood Boil' to talk about, and for my speech I'd chosen to castigate Elizabeth Taylor, who had just stolen Eddie Fisher from cute little Debbie Reynolds, causing her to go into a decline. I had been reading about Ms Taylor in a downmarket rag and my tirade was quite informative. Across the room I caught Mary's eye. She gave me a wicked grin and pointed to the lecturer, who was hanging on to my every word. She then pointed to the clock and gave me a cautious 'thumbs up'. The message was implicit: 'Keep going as long as you can and it won't get round to my turn.'

No problem – when I ran out of facts, I just made it up as I went along and had to conclude after a while, as it was getting tiring. The lecturer only had time to say, 'Well, that was different!' before the bell went, and so began a friendship.

At college we didn't really have the exclusive 'best friend' kind of relationships that schoolchildren have: you were more likely to be a member of several different groups. There were always one or two people with whom you found more common ground than others, and during the final year you already knew which of the friendships would endure; for me Pat Plunkett and Mary Dalzell fell into this category. Soon after leaving college Pat had married and contact was gradually lost, but wherever Mary and I have been in the world, and although there can be years between meetings, our friendship has spanned the decades and is still strong.

So when I started lodging with the Dalzells during my teaching time in Glasgow I was already familiar with the house and its occupants. Mary's mother was a tall, dark-haired woman with a commanding presence who originally came from Dalry in Ayrshire. Her father was an equally tall, equally dark-haired man from Belfast in Northern Ireland and one whom I always think of as a quiet, very calm man. Mary, their only child, was small and fair-haired, and to my mind bore little resemblance to either of them in looks or manner. She was not as strident as her mother and certainly not as calm as her father, but always either on the brink of gloomy disaster or ecstatic exuberance. I suppose dramatic is the word I'm looking for. It was an interesting household.

Mary had come to Uist with me during one or two breaks and had a dalliance with one of my older brothers for a short while, but it didn't last. She loved the island and all the social life of the time. As she had no brothers or sisters, mixing with our large, diverse, mobile family must have been a novel experience for her, very different to her own ordered existence as a cherished only child. I think her mother considered me as a calming influence on Mary and had always treated me as a second daughter during my college days, so when she invited me to use their spare bedroom during my spell at St Jude's I had no qualms about accepting the offer.

Christmas holidays are short, so I barely had time to sleep the arduous journey from Bristol out of my bones before I was trudging through the snow to the bus stop to catch the first of two buses that would take me to my new school on the outskirts of the city. There had been no time to arrange a preliminary visit, as the school had been closed for the holidays, and in those days there was no such thing as the present-day system of holding in-service training, giving teachers a couple of child-free days to sort things out before the pupils arrive to begin a new term. Then we all arrived together on the first day of term with varying degrees of reluctance.

St Jude's was a very large school and a harassed headmaster greeted me with relief and gratitude. One of his new appointees had not turned up, but had left a note in his mailbox telling him that she had changed her mind and would not be joining his staff, so he was glad to see that he had at least one of his two new teachers on site.

He told me that a large percentage of his pupils came from a vast block of high-rise council flats nearby, into which – and this is a direct quote – 'the Corporation decanted the families when they tarted up the Gorbals and Cowcaddens'.

Both areas mentioned were slums, so that explained the speed with which I had been offered the job. I wondered if walking through the playground had been enough to make the other incumbent take to her heels. My own ears were still ringing from the ripe language I had heard as I had fought my way through the squabbling crowd to get into the school building, but as at that point at least the children were directing their abuse at each other, I was apprehensive but willing to give it a try. I was a bit concerned, however, when he asked me if I would mind leaving my classroom door open and supervising the teacherless class, which was in the room next to mine, until he could arrange cover. I had a vision of poor old Porky's missing class scenario being re-enacted.

My concern was well justified when I found that I had forty ten-year-olds on my own register and a composite class of forty-two nine- and ten-year-olds next door. How do you teach eighty-two children? There is only one answer: you can't. You can set them lessons and mark their work, but forget any thoughts of getting to know their individual needs. Hearing each child read and helping anyone with difficulties could take the whole school day. It took a month to get a long-term supply teacher in, and my job description for that period could have been written in two words: crowd control. One thing surprised me, however: discipline was not a problem.

The children of that time, especially in the poorer areas, still had a healthy respect for authority, and once they came into the school building their teachers' word was law. Marking their work took many hours, but as ignoring the work that a child has struggled to complete is pretty cruel, it took care of many evenings at the Dalzell table.

Mary was teaching at St Aloysius Primary, a Springburn school within walking distance from her home, and we saw little of each other during the week, as our work kept us so busy, and my working day involved so much travelling. She was on the point of becoming engaged herself, to Charles Boyle, a medical student, and when we did have time to talk it was mostly about future hopes and past memories. One memory in particular caused us some amusement, the holiday on the Isle of Man after our graduation.

Mary's mother had bought a raffle ticket at the doctor's surgery where she worked and, as the raffle was for charity and she had never won a prize in her life, she had even not bothered to check the list of prizes on offer. Some weeks later she was delighted to find that she had won a holiday for two on the Isle of Man, which she very generously gave to Mary and myself to celebrate the end of our student days.

We had a wonderful first week, going to see Ivy Benson's All Girl Orchestra who played in the pavilion at the sea front, swimming and sunbathing, sightseeing and shopping. In many ways it was a great week, but on the Friday, with one week to go, we both felt a bit disappointed, as our money was nearly all gone and we hadn't met any boys. The clientele of the boarding house were all blue-rinsed couples and most of the boys we'd seen appeared to be holidaying with their girlfriends. Then, on the Saturday morning, after we'd gone up to our room to get our stuff together for the beach, there was a knock on our bedroom door and there stood two young men with porcelain chamberpots on their heads asking:

'Do you have THESE under your beds?'

It's the first and last time that I had ever heard that chat-up line being used. Bob and Hugh were lads from Aberdeen who had checked in that morning, seen us as they were passing through the dining room, and had been trying to work out how to introduce themselves. They were quite mad but they certainly livened up our final week. We were able to show them around, have a lot of laughs and generally have the holiday that we thought we were going to have in the first place. At the end of the week, as they waved us off on the plane, we wondered if any young girls were booking in to our boarding house so that they could model the pots again.

The Glasgow of my teaching days was a million light years away from our present 'City of Culture'. Then it embraced many cultures, and some of them specialised in the use of razors, so you were careful where you walked after dark. The buildings were tall, gloomy and grimy in many areas, and although the more affluent districts were pleasant, even the snow couldn't improve parts of it. The dreadful winter continued as the snow settled and froze and fresh flurries fell on top of that to become a grey slush as we all slipped and slithered through it, trying to remain upright as best we could. It was dark when I went to catch the bus in the morning, and by the time I got back after school the yellow glow from the streetlamps was again lighting up the gloomy scene. Then I got jaundice, through eating some 'iffy' meat dressed up as a curry, and was very ill and pretty yellow myself for two weeks.

When I had recovered and rejoined the staff of St

Jude's, the weather had changed for the better and I was able to go out more at weekends. Sometimes I met my brother Alick, who was still working at the Carmunnock nurseries, and we'd have a day out together. I also saw something of my aunt Mary Margaret, my father's sister, who lived with her husband and family in Govanhill. My father came from a large family of seven boys and one girl and, with one exception, Uncle Allan who worked the old family croft in Benbecula, they were scattered about from Glasgow to Fort William, so I never got round them all. There were many ex-Islanders in the city and at my mother's instigation I managed to visit a few of her old friends.

Islanders who lived and worked in Glasgow have always kept up the links with their heritage, and in the early 60s there were many places in the city where they congregated. There were organised groups like the Uist and Barra Association, and one for Mull and Iona etc, where people from specific island groups met and held concerts and dances to keep up their contacts and sustain the Gaelic culture. There were also many meeting places in the city such as the Hielanman's Umbrella and Paisley Road Toll where you could find Islanders talking Gaelic in animated groups, especially after dances in St Margaret's Hall, Kinning Park.

Mary and I had some nights out, dancing at the Highlanders' Institute and Govan Town Hall mainly, but the weather and our respective jobs often made an evening in watching television a more attractive alternative. Mary's father often had meetings in the evenings and her mother would join us to watch *Come Dancing*, her favourite programme. If we wanted a snack before going to bed, we took turns to prepare it, and it soon became apparent that Mrs Dalzell was the only one amongst us who could produce anything half-edible. I couldn't even make something on toast properly. The toast was either burnt or tough and chewy because I had made it too soon and it had time to get cold before I'd made the topping. My scrambled eggs were grey and granular and so rubbery that they refused to stay on the toast.

Mary's mother decided that, as both her daughter and I were in great danger of poisoning our husbands when the time came that we would have to cook for them, we should look for an evening class which would at least teach us how to produce a survival diet. She said:

'I know Colin's in the army and he won't be fussy, but there are limits, and Charles will soon be a doctor and he can cure himself, but think of your children.'

She herself had a full-time job and had no time to teach us, and anyway she told us that as her own cooking skills had just been picked up as she was growing up, she couldn't teach them to anyone else.

'I just taste it and add a pinch of this and a handful of that.'

It was all Greek to us, so we agreed to give the thought of an evening class some consideration. I suppose the fact that we had both gone to schools where you were taught academic subjects to the exclusion of all else, unless you were going to teach home economics or take an Institutional Management course at college, had added to our ignorance. I remember the appetising smells coming out of the Domestic Science building at Fort William School, and I'm sure that none of the pupils in that class needed a crash course in cookery before getting married.

Going back out to be taught something after a day's teaching didn't really appeal to either of us, so in the end it was Mary's mother who phoned around, found a suitable class and enrolled us in it. It was a six-week course and included a bit of basic instruction, but it soon became clear to us that we were the Special Needs pair in the class. We didn't know the difference between short crust and flaky pastry, and had never heard of a roux. The woman taking the class was quite horrified to see Mary banging a ball of pastry on the table and saying, 'It's just like playing with plasticine.'

'Cool fingers, cool fingers, girls! Good pastry must be cool in the making and hot in the baking!' she exhorted.

I don't know if the instructor was ever the same again after the conclusion of the classes, but at least we managed to produce a meal to take home at the end of the six weeks. It consisted of a vegetable curry and a Swiss apple tart. Mary's curry was better than mine, as I'd let the onions burn, giving the finished dish an interestingly acrid taste, but the meringue on her tart was flat, while mine was fluffy if a bit raw. So we had a very substantial supper that night, and Mr Dalzell suggested that, as our mistakes seemed to cancel each other out, perhaps we should look for houses with an adjoining kitchen when the time came to put our newly acquired skills to the test.

By the time I went home to Uist for the half-term break, I had decided that I would not renew my contract at the end of the term, but would try for a school closer to home. Colin had been sent to the St Kilda outpost of the Guided Weapons Range and so, had I still been in Uist, I wouldn't have seen much of him anyway, and with the primary purpose of moving to Glasgow, namely emigration to Canada, now abandoned, there didn't seem to be any reason for my being there.

I was not at all optimistic about getting appointed to a school on my own island. Most appointments were made at the beginning of the autumn term when the new graduates joined the profession. As the applicants usually outnumbered the posts, a job on your home island was like gold and most teachers held on to theirs pretty firmly. However, I thought that anywhere in the Highlands would at least be closer and certainly more appealing than my current Blackboard Jungle work environment. My job was fine as long as I was within the four walls of the classroom, but playground duty was tough, and patrolling the dining hall during the lunch hour made feeding time at the zoo look like a state banquet.

Letters from my parents and phone calls kept me in touch with the family, and the envelopes with the puffin stamp bearing the logo 'St Kilda, the furthest station West' were eagerly awaited. Colin didn't mind the isolation of the St Kilda camp, as he was keenly interested in birds and all kinds of natural history, and spent a lot of his spare time taking photographs of the wildlife. The island's social history also fascinated him, as many of the buildings used by the inhabitants before they were evacuated were still standing.

My own knowledge of St Kilda was very sketchy, and all I knew was that it was very remote and that the population had dwindled over the years until the few that were left had been evacuated to the mainland. We've always called the island Hiort in Gaelic, and my brother Donald, who had worked there, told me that although the English name was St Kilda, it was not actually named after a saint; in fact, there had never been a saint bearing that name. From Colin I learned that the Icelandic word *skildar*, meaning shields, had been the original name, probably a reference to the cliffs, and that over the years the name had been corrupted to become St Kilda. The Gaelic name of Hiort was also derived from the Icelandic language, from their word *hirtir* meaning deer; this was again a reference to the spiky peaks, which resembled deer's antlers when seen on the skyline.

Colin told me many interesting things about the island that had once been home to a thriving community and had its own parliament, where matters involving the inhabitants were decided. Although the island was effectively cut off from the rest of the world for eight months of the year, people had lived there for centuries, even before Roman times. At one time the population had numbered 200, but emigration and illness had gradually diminished their numbers, until in 1930, after a very bad winter, the last remaining residents decided to leave St Kilda for good.

I heard about the strange Soay sheep with their brown fleeces, the double-horned rams which still roamed the island like some exotic creatures from a far-off land and the cute brown mice that looked like small squirrels sitting up on their hind legs to eat nuts and seeds which they held in their front paws. They had no fear of the men in uniform who had come to share their island; instead, they would allow the soldiers to hand-feed them. The birds were many and varied, and they had once formed the mainstay of the indigenous population's diet. Their menfolk often scaled impossible-looking cliffs to catch gannets and fulmars, which they would store in *cleitean*, stone structures with turf roofs, against the hard days of winter. The St Kilda residents had left but the bird and plant life remained, and in 1956 the owner, the Marquis of Bute, had bequeathed the island to the National Trust for Scotland, who leased part of it to the Army. Most of the buildings used by the soldiers had been purpose-built, but the original factor's house was restored and used, and also the old Manse, which was refurbished and used as the Sergeants' Mess.

While on St Kilda, as telephone time was limited, Colin was allowed to make only two phone calls per week, each of twenty minutes' duration, and one evening he spent most of the time telling me about the haunted room in the old Manse where, by virtue of his rank, he now had his living quarters. When he had first arrived on the island he had been pleased to see that he had a room to himself – and then he found out why.

The room was at the end of the old Manse building next to the chapel wall; it was always extremely cold and there were hints from other soldiers of something other than mice appearing there at night. Someone told him not to look out of the window after dark, and he thought this was just a story made up by bored soldiers. Then one night he woke up and actually saw a black shape standing at the foot of the bed and he knew that this was no prank. The shape hovered for a while and disappeared into the air. Made of stern stuff, he continued to use that room and saw the otherworldly spectre on more than one occasion.

Once the numbers in the camp had risen, another soldier had to share his room, but he only stayed there for one night, as he too had seen the ghost and had sat up in bed white-faced and frozen with fear until morning. Then along came Dick, a Greek Cypriot sergeant who pooh-poohed the whole idea and slept there soundly, night after night, with no visitations. So, after a night's drinking at the Puff Inn, a building designated for that purpose, Colin and his friends decided to puncture Dick's pompous rejection of the ghost theory. He had gone to bed early, and, as they could see that the light had gone out in the room, they knew that he was already asleep.

They went into the ruined chapel where they had seen the harp-like remains of an ancient piano and with great difficulty manoeuvred the large frame between them, trying to move quietly and frequently collapsing on top of it in fits of alcoholic giggles, until it was under Dick's window. They then proceeded to twang the old instrument and, choking with silent laughter, accompanied the ghostly music with eerie moans and groans. Although they kept this up for some time the light in the room stayed off and they thought that Dick had slept through it all. Much disgruntled, they took the frame back and went over to the Mess to drown their disappointment. There, in his pyjamas and as white as a sheet, stood Dick, a teetotaller, gulping a large brandy. He would not admit to having seen or heard anything. Although he continued to sleep in the haunted room, he never referred to the ghost again, and when anyone tried to draw him out on the subject he went strangely quiet. When I heard that story I knew that my father's fears of my marrying a man who was too sensible for me were groundless.

The ghost may well have been the troubled spirit of a lady who had been banished to St Kilda by her husband before the '45 Rebellion and had been virtually imprisoned there for eight years. Her name was Lady Grange and her husband had been a strong supporter of the Jacobite cause; when the rebellion was being planned, she was caught eavesdropping on her husband and his plotting friends, so she was exiled to St Kilda lest she unwittingly pass on any incriminating information. Her husband had told everyone that she had died and even held a fake funeral for her, so she knew that she could never return home. She left St Kilda a few years before she died, but remained a prisoner right up until her death in 1745. I imagine that she must have been very unhappy with her situation and that her restless spirit could well be coming back to the scene of her imprisonment; however as there was no record of her ever having lived in the Manse, I can't imagine why she would choose to appear there.

Happily the half-term break at St Jude's coincided with Colin's return from St Kilda and, although I was in Uist for only a week, it was long enough for us to decide that, as his next posting could not be many months away, we would get married on Uist in the summer school holidays, regardless of whether I could get a job on the island or not. We would be leaving before long, so it was not important.

My parents were very pleased, especially my mother, who immediately began making long, long lists. The event was still six months away but she had waited a long time for this, as my elder brothers had got married on the mainland and she was raring to plan a wedding. Colin's family were also happy, as they very much wanted to come and see this strange place that they had been hearing about. The only fly in the ointment was that I was going to be stuck in Glasgow for much of the preparation time if something didn't change soon. So, as soon as I got back there I wrote a letter to J. A. MacLean, the Director of Education for Inverness-shire, explaining my situation, and awaited his answer without much hope.

I was stunned and delighted to receive his reply by return of post. My letter couldn't have come at a better time, he said. He had a school for me – the teacher was leaving unexpectedly for health reasons, and if I wanted it the school could be mine at Easter. I had specified that I would be leaving South Uist shortly after my marriage and would be available only for one term, but this suited him fine as he could appoint a new graduate for the autumn. If however, anything went wrong in my plans, I was welcome to talk to him again as and when. The formal contract was attached, and as he hadn't mentioned the school by name in his covering letter, I was apprehensive to say the least as I looked through all the legal stuff and found the name typed in. It was a small school in South Uist, South Glendale Primary! And so I became the only teacher ever to be appointed to the little school by Glendale Bay twice. I was very pleased to accept the job.

The headmaster at St Jude's was sad but understanding, and the rest of my time in Glasgow was a blur of choosing a wedding dress, bridesmaids' dresses for my sister and my friend Mary, who was now engaged to Charles and was getting married a couple of weeks after me, and for the two little nieces, one from Colin's family and one from mine, who were also going to be bridesmaids. Mary's mother was beside herself with joy at having not only one bride-to-be but two to advise on all things pertaining to marriage, and I'm sure that James Dalzell breathed a sigh of relief when I said my goodbyes to them and left him with only one set of wedding plans ringing in his ears.

Chapter Twelve

'*I*S MATH AN LONG A THUG *a-mach an cala às na dh'fhalbh i!*' ('It's a good ship that returns to its port of departure!')

Neil Campbell greeted me with a proverb and one of his big grins as I parked PUS on Ludag jetty, above his boat.

'Jump in the boat,' he said, 'and save your feet for the wedding reel. I'll even take you twice around the bay if we have time. Just be careful or that big stone on your finger will sink the boat!'

It was good to be back, to see the hill looking lonely and peaceful in the spring sunshine. A few sheep stood out against the skyline, and no doubt behind its screening bulk the villagers of Glendale were busy with their morning chores. Neil had some stores for the school to deliver and had waited to give me a lift, so on my first day back for my brief return to the school where it had all begun, I didn't even have to walk the hill. I just had to sit back and listen to Neil and take in the beautiful clean, clear views of sea, islands and wheeling birds as we chugged our way around the headland and into Glendale Bay.

'I don't think you'll find many changes,' Neil said. Then he added, 'I think Eriskay has moved six inches to the right.'

A welcome speech, engagement acknowledgement and a news update – all delivered 'Neil style'.

The old car PUS had been given a lot of attention by Colin when he was over from St Kilda; now that he had a car of his own, it was easier for him to come down to Kilpheder, and he had spent some time with my parents while I was away. He had given the car an overhaul and had also mended some of my father's implements that had been given up as beyond repair, including a small motorised tiller. Once the Major in charge of the workshops, a nasty bumptious little man, found him making a new part for the tiller and asked him which particular radar he was working on. When Colin told him what he was doing, the little Major got very angry about personal work being done in Army time. Colin reminded him that they had been instructed to 'forge and maintain friendly relations with the native population'. No more was said.

As the old car was working quite well, I no longer had to depend on the school bus and the spring weather made the hill walk pleasant, so I decided to live at home for the term that I would spend at Glendale School.

The car had always been considered as more of a family wagon than belonging to any specific member. My role in its purchase had been in partnership with Donald, and when repairs and other expenses were due whoever had the money to pay them picked up the bill. Quite often my father did this, or if it was a simple job he would tackle it himself, so we all thought of it as our car and whoever needed it drove it. While I was in Glasgow my father had been using it to get to work until a few weeks before I came back, when the unthinkable happened – he lost his job.

I was not told anything about this until the evening of my return, but I knew that something was wrong as soon as I saw him. He bore the look of someone who had suffered a loss and was sad and angry at the same time. I had only seen this air about him once before, and that was when my brother Donald Angus had his accident. I knew that something bad had happened, but as I also knew that the family were all well I kept putting the thought to one side and hoping that my being home would make him forget whatever was troubling him. Unfortunately, it all went too deep for that.

In a nutshell, he and some other men from the factory had gone for a lunchtime drink at Polachar Inn, a regular Friday thing. On this Friday they were late back to work, and before they arrived back an Camshronach, the owner, had phoned from the mainland asking to speak to one of the absent men. The manager told him the situation and the owner asked if my father was with the absentees. When he was told that that was the case, he said, 'When they come back, sack them all.'

That was that.

On the following Monday morning all the other men went back to the factory, apologised and were given their jobs back. My father went to his grave convinced that it had been all been contrived to get rid of him. He was a staunch Labour supporter who never missed a chance of backing the owner, once his good friend, into a corner on matters political, and telling the other men how many good things the Labour MP had done for the island.

According to him, his employer had political aspirations of a more upper class orientation and was looking to the Western Isles for a seat. I don't know. I wasn't there at the time, and it was probably just his injured pride talking. It certainly seemed a bit severe to sack a senior staff member for coming back late on a Friday lunchtime – after all, a seaweed factory is hardly ICI – but I suppose he who pays the piper has the right to call the tune. I just saw the terrible things that taking away a man's dignity did to my father, and through him to his family. Of course he wouldn't go and beg to be reinstated, convinced as he was that it would only lead to further humiliation. Instead he went right off the rails. If he had been sacked for drinking, then he would live up to his newfound reputation, and the man we knew and had looked up to all our lives began to disappear.

The change didn't happen overnight, but gradually over a period of years he grew more and more bitter, and whereas before a glass of whisky only made him even better company, now it only brought a morose disillusioned person to the surface. Eventually reason prevailed and he gave up drinking altogether, but I don't think he ever quite recovered his self-respect.

Of course the aunties had a field day, but to give them their due, they confined their remarks to conversations with my mother and the rest of the family and did not openly antagonise my father. A wise decision, as his diplomacy of the past might not have checked his tongue in his current mood.

There was no occupational pension provided with the factory job and the staff was paid weekly, so he had been dismissed after a lifetime of working with smelly seaweed, and inhaling the white dust from the processed tangles, with one week's wages in his pocket. Knowing that there was little money in the pot, I said that I would pay all the wedding expenses myself, but the aunties rallied round and offered to pick up some of the bills as a wedding present. I had to grit my teeth and listen to a homily about idle drunken fathers losing their jobs and not being able to do their duty towards their children, but as it was going to cost them a pretty penny, I let them have their money's worth. I knew that my father had never been idle since his early years in Benbecula, when he had worked as a ploughboy even before he left school. The drinking was a result and not the cause of his present situation, but as I had been listening to their poor opinion of him since I was four and a half, it had all become like a boring record with the needle stuck. It would take more than their malicious carping to undermine my regard for him, so I just listened and accepted their offer with as much grace as I could muster.

At home, we all got used to hearing my father going over and over the 'Why did he ask if I was with them before he gave the order?' question. It was best not to enter into any discussion on the subject and mostly we just left him to get on with it. Fortunately, getting it all off his chest seemed to help, and for the time I was with my parents in the run-up to the wedding there were no binges. My father promised me that he would do his best to look forward and not keep going back over things that troubled him, but it was very easy for me to give advice when I wasn't the person hurting. Once he told me:

'It's very difficult, it is the last thing I think about every night when I close my eyes. First thing in the morning when I wake up and look at the clock to see how much time I have to do things around the house before I leave for work, it hits me. An Camshronach sacked me.'

Poor man. There were many things to do round the

croft and he spent much time tending the cows and mending fences. Although the number of cattle had dwindled over the years, there was still enough work to keep him busy and there was also the hay and corn to harvest. Money was tight, but it had been tighter in the old days, and thanks to my mother's ingenuity there was always plenty of food on the table.

My own mind had become very much taken up with thoughts of food, and how to prepare it. When I was a child my mother had taught me how to make a rabbit stew, as she couldn't bear to touch the creatures herself, so I cooked them for the family. I could open a tin of Spam and boil a mean potato, but that's as far as it went, and my coffee was acknowledged by all our family to be the worst in the world. The cookery lessons in Glasgow meant that I could make an edible curry and a hit-or-miss apple tart, but cooking anything else or even preparing a shopping list were skills that had passed me by. Little girls usually pick up that sort of knowledge when they are children, but I had not been encouraged to interfere in Auntie Chirsty's kitchen, and so in my early twenties I had to start learning at my mother's knee, as it were.

In her youth my mother had worked for a titled family in Oban, and as Mary the cook was a Uist girl my mother had spent a lot of her spare time in the kitchen, talking to her and being co-opted into helping with meal preparations. So she had a fund of tips to pass on to me and they saved my new husband from starvation when the time came. My father commented that it was a great pity that the rabbit population had been practically wiped out by myxomatosis, as I could have introduced Colin to my one and only foolproof recipe.

One thing I could never manage was a decent pancake. I don't mean the nice fat fluffy Scots pancakes that practically make themselves and walk off the griddle. I was fine with those. The ones that gave me so much grief were the thin English pancakes, or crêpes as they call them in France. Colin's mother could produce them by the basketful, mixing and stirring and tossing, with no trouble whatsoever. They were a total disaster for me. I spent many hours trying to produce a few for him when we were first married and after my first efforts I even had to throw the frying pan out. He says that he saw a seagull eating one of my discards and the poor bird took five minutes to get off the ground. However, after a few lessons with my mother I could cook sufficient meals to keep body and soul together. Pancakes took a few more years.

Life at Glendale had indeed not changed a bit. The school roll had got even smaller and the actual teaching was more like giving a few nice children private tuition. Not like St Jude's at all. I had my lunch with Kate Ann and her mother every day and they were still the calm, sane people I had left. Although they had only met my father once when he and our neighbour John had gone over the hill to find a stray sheep on dipping day and had spent a few hours in their house before bringing the sheep back, they were full of concern for him and did their best to reassure me that his present state was just a passing phase. I drew comfort from them, as they had met adversity in their own lives and it had not destroyed them.

The MacIntyres were very excited about my forthcoming nuptials and couldn't get over how my plans had changed since leaving them.

'You were so determined to go to Canada. I thought you'd have been over there by now,' Flora said, 'but if it was meant to happen it would have happened.'

They invited Colin out to tea, to see if 'he was fit to walk the hill', as they put it, and they treated him like royalty. He thought that Glendale was a beautiful little place and really enjoyed meeting the people with whom I had spent so much time before I had met him. I only wished that old Calum had still been there – I would have liked to have heard them swapping fishing stories.

Colin loved to fish, especially if a boat was involved, and one day he and his friend Doug Braid, another Warrant Officer from the camp, had gone out from Loch Carnan pier to try and catch some of the big fish which they had heard about. They went right out into the Minch and started to use the feather line usually used for mackerel fishing. The result was spectacular – huge cod coming up three at a time. They caught so many that they were in danger of shipping water and had to stop. Colin brought his share of the catch straight down to Kilpheder, but as we had no deep freeze at the time he spent the evening going round the village dishing out free fish to all and sundry. I don't think he has ever had such a memorable day's fishing since then.

Doug Braid and his wife Barbara were old friends of Colin's and I was soon invited to meet them at their home in the married quarters of the camp at Balivanich. The house was one of the little Medway houses that had originally housed RAF officers many years ago. New officers' quarters had been built and the senior ranks were now quartered in the old Medways. The buildings didn't look like much from the outside, but inside they were surprisingly spacious and comfortable. All Army married quarters come complete with everything you and your family could possibly need, and this came as an agreeable surprise to me, as it cut out a lot of spending on furniture and other essentials. Meeting the Braids and

343

other Army couples and hearing them reminisce about mutual friends and other places where they had all been together soon made me realise that an Army unit, at least at that time, was just like a large constantly moving family, and it allayed my secret fears about the life that would be mine before long.

My friendship with Jean went on as if the months in Glasgow hadn't happened. We saw each other often but now it was a different relationship. No more parties and dawn walks on the machair. Her father had died and she was very busy with the shop, which had been much extended. Her romance with John was going well and she too contemplated a departure from the island if it should lead to marriage. Her older brother and sister were the mainstay of the business and Jean, being much younger, was not quite as deeply interested in it as they were. John was coming to the end of his Army service and did not want to sign on for a further period, so there was some uncertainty about their future. It seemed that the previous year, when we had both been so carefree, belonged to two other girls. We were both very happy but our lives had become more serious. Dorothy was still in touch and was well content with her glamorous but tiring life as an air hostess, away from the dreaded 'brats'.

My father was pleased to know that I would be living in Benbecula, his old stamping ground, at least for a short time before leaving the island, and spent many evenings telling me stories about his own young days there. He had a deep love for the old Benbecula and, like most people who thought about it at all, he feared that the Army presence would change it forever. He could see the benefits but thought that they were going to cost Benbecula and especially Balivanich, much of its croft land and all of its character.

As always, he had a fund of information to pass on about the history of various places, like Culla Bay between Aird and Griminish, a beautiful curved inlet with the whitest of sands that he recommended for picnics in the summer. It was originally called Culla Mhoire, ('Mary's Gift'), because of the legendary harvest of kelp brought in there by the tides. In the old days this was used by the people to fertilise their land and was also a source of income for the landlords.

I was intrigued by the name Columba Place which was given to a certain group of houses, and remarked that I hadn't heard of St Columba ever visiting Benbecula. He told me that there had also been a Loch Chaluim Cille ('Columba's Loch') in his young days but he thought he'd heard that it was being drained for some reason. On an island in the middle of the loch were the ruins of a little chapel called Teampall Chaluim Cille ('Columba's Temple'). It was all at least 1000 years old, he thought, and dated back to the time when one of the first monks who came to Balivanich arrived there from Ireland.

This monk had been driven out of Ireland and had asked God to lead him to a place where he could carry on his work. The tides and currents washed his little boat ashore on the coast of Benbecula and he started to build a chapel on the side of the loch. Every morning he would find that the stones had mysteriously moved out on to the island, so he deduced that he was meant to build the chapel there. When he finished his building he blessed the chapel and named it and the loch in honour of St Columba. Many monks came after him and that is how Balivanich got its name: Baile Mhanaich means 'township of monks'. It was a good story and it explained the Columba Place name, but I couldn't understand why God had wanted the chapel built on a tiny island in the middle of a loch. It didn't seem very congregation-friendly, but legends are always a bit puzzling.

It was good to see my father gradually getting back on form, and soon he was back to normal, doing concerts and even having a drink or two without becoming morbid. The first time he went on stage after the dismissal he did a kind of Dean Martin performance, staggering on to the stage and slurring his words, then tugging his forelock and saying:

'Shorry, shir, work ish the cursh of the drinking clashes. I won't do it again . . . what do you mean? I won't get the shance, because you're shacking me?'

Following this with a few caustic but funny Gaelic references to his ex-employer got him over the embarrassment and back in with his audiences – they weren't to know how much it had cost him.

His teeth had always given my father a lot of trouble, and my mother, who had followed the old tradition of having all her lovely teeth out at the first sign of toothache, had no patience with his moans and groans.

'Off to the dentist with you and out with them all!'

In the end, after having had a few out but still having recurring problems with fillings, he decided to take her advice. In days gone by he would have had to wait until a dentist came to the island, but things had improved by this time and there was a nice young dentist living in Daliburgh, so the old situation of having to grin and bear it was no excuse. Reluctantly my father went over to the surgery to have an initial inspection, and the dentist agreed with my mother's diagnosis that a clean sweep would be the best thing.

An appointment was made and he settled down to wait. The very next day he had a letter from the BBC asking him to go to Glasgow to do a recording, on a date three days after he was due to have the teeth out. He really enjoyed the trips to Glasgow and by now knew most of the production team and his fellow artistes, so he decided to go, do the recording and leave the dental work until later. He got in touch with the dentist and tried to cancel his appointment, but as the dentist knew well how bad the teeth were, he was adamant. He had a packed book of appointments stretching far into the future, and if my father broke this one it could be a full six months before he could fit him in again. By that time, said the dentist, my father would not have to worry about his teeth any more: the gums would have become infected and he would be in Hallin cemetery, having died of blood poisoning. So my father capitulated. There were no earlier appointments that he could have, but the dentist asked him to come in for impressions straight away and said that he would have the dentures made up and ready to put in as the old teeth came out.

The much-feared day arrived and it all went smoothly. Dad was quite taken with his new teeth, giving the occasional grimace, but spending most of the time admiring his reflection in the mirror. The following day he was getting ready to catch the plane and he mentioned to my mother that the top set of dentures were very tight, as his gums were swollen, so she advised a salt and water mouthwash to ease the swelling. She made up a concoction for him and off he went to the bathroom to try it out.

With the top set taken out gingerly, he carefully rinsed his mouth out with the salt water, then spat into the lavatory pan and pulled the chain hard. As he took his hand away from the wooden handgrip at the end of the chain he knocked his dentures off the top of the cistern and straight into the gushing water. When our plumbing had been done by *am Plumair Mòr* (the big plumber) much talk had ensued about the desirability of having a very strong flushing system in your cisterns if you had no mains drainage for your sewage. *Am Plumair Mòr* had excelled himself by modifying our cistern so well that the flush, if pulled hard, could dispose of a half-grown cat. So my father's last sight of his new top set was brief as they rushed away towards the septic tank.

There was much lispy cursing from the direction of the bathroom, and we all waited for him to come in and tear up his plane ticket. Not so – he just took the bottom set out and carried on with his preparations. He didn't look too bad, as his gums were still quite swollen, but we wondered if he would be able to take part in the recording at all, with no teeth. When he came back from Glasgow he said that it hadn't been a problem. He'd spent the plane journey compiling a list of songs with maximum 'Ho-ro's and minimum 's' sounds and it all went very well. He gave us a demonstration before he changed out of his travelling clothes:

Hi horò, mo nighean donn,
Hi horì, mo nighean donn,
Hi horò, mo nighean donn a' chùil rèidh,
Mhaighdean òg a bha leam,
Bha do chomhradh rium ciùin,
Tha mo chridh' an-diugh trom na do dhéidh.

Hi horò, my brown maid,
Hi horì, my brown maid,
Hi horò, my brown maid flowing-haired,
Maiden young who with me
Kept such sweet company,
My poor heart is forlorn now you've gone.

We had to agree that he sounded just fine as long as you didn't look at his mouth.

'Good job it wasn't a TV recording,' my mother said, conveniently forgetting that her advice had caused it all. If there is one thing on which my sister, brothers and I agree, it is that in an argument with my father, my mother never knew how to quit while she was ahead. Happily, on this occasion, as my father was flushed with the success of his trip, he just laughed and told us that he had been approached to take part in the first live TV broadcast of a new Gaelic programme called '*Se 'ur Beatha* ('You are Welcome') which was to take place in the near future and that he was going to see the dentist as soon as possible to make sure that he would be able to smile at the cameras.

The Glendale folk were getting all excited: men with tripods and measuring instruments had been seen on the hill and the consensus of opinion was that it must have something to do with the road. Their ongoing fight for a road had been a bone of contention for so long that they had given up believing that they would ever be able to step out of their houses and into a car. Of course, nobody told them what was going on, their letters went unanswered or got vague replies, and when one of them approached the engineers he was told that it was all just part of a survey. So that was that, again.

Kate Ann said: 'They're waiting for us all to die and then they won't have to bother.'

I must admit that, busy though I was with other things at the time, I wondered whether she might be right. It seemed such a shame. It was a really beautiful spot and the people had lived under such a disadvantage for so long, and with such good grace.

Chapter Thirteen

I SUPPOSE IT WAS ONLY natural that the final days of my life as a single daughter of the croft should make me look around at the changes that had occurred in my surroundings since I had first become aware of them. The changes in my own family had been many, some good and some not so good. Most of the changes on the island, however, had been for the better.

Many of the innovations on the Uists taking place in the early days of the 1960s were probably as a result of the rising population and the granting of housing loans for crofters. Then there were more subsidies available than there had been in previous years, and although the croft could not yet be described, as I have seen in an article I read some time ago, as a 'piece of land providing a good crop of subsidies and surrounded by a fence of regulations', things were going that way. A crofter could only have one dwelling place on his land and any usage of that land for purposes other than planting crops and raising cattle and sheep was very much frowned upon and needed so much unravelling of red tape that people didn't bother to try. The prices for cattle and sheep, although a lot better than today's derisory prices, were not good, and so making the land pay was difficult. Some crofts were just left idle as stock was run down to allow time for a day job. People visiting the island could easily think that the land should be put to some other use, but the crofter couldn't do anything about it as his hands were tied. Things have improved now and many crofters own their homes and land and some restrictions have been lifted, but not before time.

To begin with, the improvements were pretty much evenly spread over the Uists and Benbecula. However, over the years since the 1960s there has been a gradual shift in the pattern, with more and more emphasis on Benbecula, and Balivanich has become a kind of administrative capital. In my own opinion this is all very well as long as investment in other parts of the islands keeps pace and the development generated by Benbecula is spread out, and not merely drawn in and controlled there to cause economic sterility in other areas, as this would create an imbalance in the already frail social structure of the islands. However, this is all hindsight talking; in the early Sixties it still looked good.

The daily papers got to us a day after they had been on sale on the mainland, as they came on the afternoon plane, but you got used to reading 'yesterday's news' if you lived on the island. There was no way round it and the shopkeepers could only give you the papers when they got them in themselves.

The shops we used then were the same ones as had been trading when I had gone to Daliburgh School as a pupil, the Co-op and A. C. MacDonald's, both much enlarged and carrying a much larger variety of stock. In

Kilpheder we used to have a shop next door to our house run by the MacLellan family, but that had closed down and another small shop with a petrol station had been opened by Donald MacNeil out at Greybridge, on the Daliburgh–Kilpheder boundary, where there had been a shop many years ago. In addition, we had three travelling shops, the Co-op, A. C.'s and another from Boisdale owned by Finlay MacDonald, all of which came round on different days, so things had indeed improved.

The availability of a larger variety of foods brought about a change in our own family diet. In the old days we were never without a barrel of salt herring (one of my own all-time favourite meals with floury machair potatoes), which together with home-killed lamb and chicken provided our year-round sustenance. We bought beef and bacon from the shops, but more as a luxury than a necessity. Although I believe that pigs are now being kept on the island, in my young days they were not part of the crofter's stock. Perhaps the Hebridean soil was considered to be too soft for the rooting and wallowing in which a pig likes to indulge, so we never ate pork. My mother made our own butter and crowdie (cottage cheese) and also haggis and black puddings when an animal had been slaughtered. There had always been a vegetable patch on the croft where my father grew cabbage, turnips, carrots, beetroot and lettuce in season, so we were fairly self-sufficient. Now we had mince, pork chops and pies appearing on the table, and my father was introduced to tins of corned beef and spaghetti in a lurid orange sauce. Processed food had come to stay and the barrel of herring became a bucket and then disappeared altogether.

Quite a few people that I know of were diagnosed as diabetic in the years following this change. I have always wondered if there was any connection to the change in diet, as the condition had been unheard of in previous generations. Perhaps it was more a case that our doctors were better trained than before and that people may have been undiagnosed diabetics in the old days when our medical provision had been dire.

The healthcare situation had improved immensely by the 1960s. In addition to our dentist we had two excellent doctors in Daliburgh, Dr MacLean, who spoke fluent Gaelic and was very popular with the older folk, as they found it difficult to explain their aches and pains in English, and Dr Robertson, who combined the duties of GP and surgeon. The Robertson family were English-speaking but very nice and soon integrated into our community. They built a house near St Peter's Church and Mrs Robertson produced a beautiful rock garden there that was the envy of all who saw it. She and my father talked about flowers for hours, and after he'd been looking at her garden he'd say, 'Now I'm going home to dig my garden up and throw it away.'

My mother was actually a better gardener than he was, as he was used to planting things in rows, and clumps and clusters were foreign words to him. When Alick came home for a holiday, he was always trying to get new plants going, and then coming back to find that they'd been either dug up by my father, who hadn't recognised them, or been choked and overgrown because he was frightened to touch them, and had left them alone.

We still had many visitors to the house, and although an Camshronach no longer visited, Johnny Fincastle still dropped in from time to time. On the death of his father he had become the Earl of Dunmore, but apart from going a bit red in the face when he told us about it he didn't let his newly acquired exalted status make any difference to his enjoyment of my father's company. The last time I saw him he came to give me a lovely silver dish with a blue-glass lining as a wedding present, and every time I've used it I've thought what a genuinely nice young man he had been. He judged people by their character rather than their material worth and was a good ambassador for the aristocracy.

Rockets were being fired regularly from the rangehead on Iochdar machair and they generated a lot of interest locally. The rockets were unarmed Corporal missiles, and if you knew when the launching was taking place you could see them from the back of our house on a clear day. Sound travels very well in the clear Hebridean air, and we could hear a faint 'boom' as the fuels ignited and sent the rocket high up in the sky before curving out over the Atlantic to be guided to its splashdown point. Nobody called them missiles; the word 'rocket' made them sound so much less threatening and their firing was watched with curiosity, without anxiety.

One day, however, we saw what could happen if things went wrong, when one of the rockets went out of control for a few seconds and instead of following its prescribed trajectory turned round and headed back to land. The tracking team on the ground soon had the situation under control and it was blown up while still over the sea, but it made many people think of the consequences should this not have been the case. It did not carry a warhead but it could still have made a sizeable hole in the island had it exploded on land. The incident was soon forgotten and with our customary pragmatism we islanders concluded that the army knew what it was doing. There was a headline about it in one of the daily papers and my brother wrote a song about it, and that was that.

The man most violently opposed to the establishing of

the range, Father John Morrison, had some years previously had a thirty-foot high statue of Our Lady of the Isles erected on the slopes of Rueval to celebrate the Marian Year. She stands with the baby in her arms looking out over Iochdar machair, and I think a lot of the older folk believed that as long as she was keeping an eye on Army activities all would be well. They were right on that particular day at least.

My own Army activities had been curtailed slightly in the run-up to the wedding when Colin was sent over to St Kilda yet again. As he was leaving his car with me for the three-week period of his absence, I drove him to Loch Carnan pier, where he and other soldiers boarded a dreadful old boat called *The Mull* for eight hours of heaving and rolling through seas that were never calm. The passage itself was always difficult, but docking at Village Bay on the island was the real test of mettle. The island of St Kilda lies in a high wind corridor and at high tide the bay resembles a boiling cauldron if the wind blows from the east. *The Mull* anchored in the bay and the soldiers were ferried ashore in a little dory. From the heaving little wooden boat they had to jump on to a pitching raft made from planks and car tyres and attached to the pier by ropes, then climb up on to the jetty. As the raft could only be floated at high tide, nobody could predict whether actual arrival on the island would take minutes, hours or be abandoned if the wind was too high. Knowing about this made my own hillwalking seem pretty tame. However, like my fellow islanders I was confident that the army knew what it was doing, so I didn't worry too much about it, as the forthcoming wedding took up most of my thinking time.

I learned much about weddings in the run-up to my own, and I think one of the things which surprised me most was that a lot of the preparations have nothing at all to do with the actual wedding. How could painting the outside of our house be classed as a wedding preparation? I must admit that I left my parents to do what they liked, as it seemed to keep them happy. The lists were made up and lost and made up again, and I have a sneaking suspicion that when it came to making the final plans and sending out invitations, my mother never actually consulted any of her bits of paper. My own list was short: 3 July – wear white dress, go to St Peter's, get married.

As the day approached I was given a lot of advice about what not to do on my wedding day, and one little hint has stuck in my mind: do not put your wedding dress on over a pair of trousers. A cousin of mine gave me this gem of wisdom based on her own experience. On her wedding morning she'd made all the usual preparations and had a bit of time in hand, so rather than put her wedding dress on too early she had dressed in a pair of navy trousers and a top. Time had gone on and when the car arrived to take her to church she still hadn't changed, so the dress and veil were put on in a rush. As she walked up the aisle she felt something falling around her ankles, and when she looked down she could see the navy trousers bunching out from under the hem of her white satin dress. She thought that she'd taken them off, but in the rush to get dressed she had only unzipped them. There was a short pause in her progress towards the altar, while she stepped out of the trousers and kicked them under a seat.

During the twice-weekly, twenty-minute phone calls from St Kilda, much of the time was spent talking about things pertaining to the wedding, but I was interested to hear that the 'Ghostbusters' were at it again. Scattered about the island was the wreckage of several planes that had crashed on St Kilda during the war years, and this had aroused much interest and curiosity in the minds of the khaki-clad incomers. They decided to hold a kind of séance with an Ouija board to try and contact the spirits of the aircrews. The séances got going late at night, usually in conjunction with the intake of liquid spirits, and appeared to be very successful; they soon established contact with the crew of one aircraft, and got all their names, ranks and numbers and the type of aircraft that they had been flying. They also gleaned the information that one crew member had survived for two weeks before dying of his terrible injuries. As all this appeared to be an important new revelation, Colin took it upon himself to inform the Air Ministry of the facts. After some time he had a reply. It had been all rubbish – no such plane, no such people. 'Stop wasting Air Ministry time or we'll inform your Commanding Officer,' the letter said. I am relieved to say that that was the last time he dabbled in the occult.

By the time he returned from St Kilda I had some exciting news for him: the Glendale road had been approved and work would be starting any day. I don't know if all the letters written by various people had been a trigger in any way at all, but at least now the little community living round the bay could have a better life and they were all looking forward to the day when the road would finally be opened. There was a bit of poetic justice meted out by the Council, who had been bombarded with letters from generations of Glendale teachers – the first thing they did after the road was opened was to close the school. I suppose it made economic sense to bus the few children there to a larger school, but that little building had been so much more than an educational establishment. It had been a symbol of contact with the outside world and over the years had provided valuable service to the community. It had been a school, chapel, meeting-place and focal point among the scattered dwellings. Still, I suppose losing it was a small price to pay for gaining the road.

Our wedding presents were arriving and beginning to take over the house. In fact one of them was grazing away on Tobht' 'IcIlleChriòsda ('Gilchrist's Ruin'), the hillock behind our house. One of the Glendale families had given me a beautiful tray made of rosewood and inlaid with butterfly wings, which I had seen and admired when their son came home from sea, and they had also presented me with a sheep. The wedding was going to be the traditional type with all the catering and cooking done by the bride's family, but some of the meat (mainly chicken) and other goods were supplied by the guests, and the sheep was meant to be slaughtered and roasted for this purpose. However, I had strong feelings about eating anything which had been baa-ing a 'good morning' to me each day, and it remained on our croft in happy retirement, at least until I was safely off the island. I think it eventually found its way to my parents' table, as I remember my father giving us the fleece to use as a bedside rug some years later.

Any bride-to-be can tell you that in the weeks preceding her wedding someone seems to press a fast-forward button and there's never enough time to do the things that need to be done. So it was for me, and in no time at all I was laden with presents walking back over the hill for the last time. I would love to be able to say that I took a last long look at the houses and the bay, but in reality I just scuttled along as fast as I could, as I was already late for something which at the time seemed more important.

I should have taken that last look, because the next time I went out to Glendale, some years into the future, the school was gone, many of the old houses had been replaced and very few of the old people remained to admire the wide black ribbon of road along which I was driving.

Many of the wedding guests were coming over from the mainland and a party of new in-laws was also expected, so there was much to plan. Some people were spending a few days at our house and others were to be accommodated at the houses of friends. Here comes another tip about weddings: always keep your bridesmaids under the same roof on the night before the wedding. I didn't, and someone forgot to send a car for one of the small bridesmaids – it would have to be the little English niece – who had to run all the way to the church in her pretty little dress and brocade shoes. Fortunately, the house where she was sleeping wasn't too far away from St Peter's but it couldn't have given her much of a good impression of us, especially as she had been made to eat real oatmeal porridge for the first time that morning.

My friend Mary from Glasgow had volunteered to bring the wedding dress with her, as I had so much luggage to bring with me when I returned to the island. It was quite an elaborate dress, with a bustle, train and two hooped petticoats, and the last time I had seen it hanging on its satin hanger it didn't seem like too large a transportation problem. Poor Mary – when I saw her coming off the ferry with a box resembling a large coffin I knew that I should have made other arrangements. Fortunately for our continuing friendship, her fellow-passengers had given her some help.

July was a very popular month for island weddings, as

the weather is usually nice at that time, so on the day that my future in-laws travelled on the *Claymore* a lot of the passengers were coming to the island for some wedding or other. I've heard them talking about it afterwards and saying, 'Everyone on that ferry was going to the wedding.'

They are friendly folk and had really enjoyed talking to all and sundry on the boat, but in much the same way as you'll get asked in America whether you know the Smiths who live in London, they assumed that because they were going to an island everybody knew everyone else. Even in those days that was not strictly true. However, they had been to Edinburgh and had travelled through the beautiful Highlands on their way to Uist and thought that Scotland was awesome, so I didn't really mind the fact that on their arrival in Kilpheder they appeared to be rather surprised that I actually lived in a house and not in a bothy.

My mother had gone to Glasgow to buy outfits for herself and the aunties and had returned with very blue hair. She had been advised by her friends to have a blue rinse on her white hair and something had gone wrong. It was very startling. Fortunately it was the type of product that mellowed with age, and after a few shampoos she was shouting, 'For God's sake don't wash it all out, I paid good money for this!'

Her outfit was very nice, but as we lined up to receive the guests on my wedding morning, I couldn't help noticing that the dress and jacket that my new mother-in-law, a skilled dressmaker, had made for herself was almost identical, both in colour and style. Still, the hats were different. Colin and my father were exempt from all this feminine preoccupation with appearance. My father flatly refused to buy a new suit, as he insisted that his current best suit had only just been broken in, and Colin was getting married in dress uniform.

The wedding ceremony was to be held in St Peter's Church, the old building in which I had been christened and which had dominated our landscape since the mid-1800s, and as I had a history of fainting when kneeling upright, discovered in my convent days, Monsignor MacKellaig told me that he'd have the velvet chairs placed as close to the kneelers as possible. I think that was just about the full extent of my input to the actual planning of the day.

After the ceremony the bride and groom were to head a procession, led by two pipers, across the road to the church hall, where the reception would be held. The greeting of guests would take place at the inside door of the hall, and the whole of the floor would be filled with dining tables for the wedding lunch which would form the first part of the reception. Then would come speeches and the reading of greetings telegrams and a short interval during which the floor would be cleared for dancing. Tables set up on the stage would take care of remaining guests and latecomers, and the waitresses would carry on serving the lunch meal until about five o'clock, when the menu would change to a high tea, also served on the stage. Whisky and sherry were to be provided at the table for toasts, and beer would be on tap from barrels set up in the back room. This had been the format for weddings at St Peter's since the hall had first been opened, so the wedding really organised itself.

After the clearing of the hall, tradition decreed that the bride and groom led off the dancing with the Bridal Reel, but here we decided to have a slight alteration, due to the nationality of my bridegroom. He was game for anything, but I did not want him to give the assembled guests the pleasure of watching him give the usual Sassenach's version of Scots Reel steps: hopping on one foot, kicking the other in the air and shouting 'Whee!' – mean of me, I know, so we opted for a waltz instead. This was a first, and I believe it caused talk: 'Could she be hiding something under the hoops?'

Time gave the lie to that one, but my mother also told me that some people were annoyed that we left the reception before it ended. We had to do this so that we could catch the only plane that week which would make the connection to our onward flight to Norway, where we'd booked our honeymoon. It was a long time ago, but if anybody still feels offended, sorry, folks.

If it's any consolation, I was less than pleased to find that our plans for a discreet departure from the island had been scuppered by whoever arranged for two pipers in full Highland Dress to meet us at Balivanich Airport and pipe us aboard the plane to the strains of 'Highland Wedding', prompting the Captain to welcome us aboard and wish us a long and happy life together. No doubt whoever did it meant well, but it was very embarrassing as we were stared at for the whole duration of the flight.

We had chosen Norway for our honeymoon, as Colin had visited it briefly before and wanted to see more of it. I had always wanted to see the country that had once been bound to my own island, with its fjords and glaciers. The country was lovely and the people generally very hospitable, even if my brand new wedding ring went unnoticed, as the married women of Norway wear their rings on their right hands.

My wedding day, like those of most brides I've spoken to, went by in a kind of blur. Several little things have stuck in my mind, however, like the *Daily Express* reporter who kept making a thorough nuisance of himself: incensed at being banned from taking photographs inside the church, he gave Colin the headline 'Rocketing Cupid' and published a picture in which the groom had his eyes shut and the bride looked as if she was gearing up to have a good spit.

I remember seeing Colin standing with his brother Ken by the altar and thinking 'My goodness, he looks white. I hope his seat is close to the kneeler.'

My friend Jean was driving the wedding car and I can remember thinking that she was much more nervous than I was, stepping on my dress at least twice as she helped me out of the car. I remember her saying, 'Isn't this better than Canada?'

Strange the ironies of life. Both she and Dorothy, the two people who had been so much against my going there, settled in Canada themselves after they were married, and although I've had homes on three different continents over the years, it took me twenty-five years to visit Canada. Beautiful land! I have been back many times for visits and I know that, contented as I have been, had my world taken a different spin I would have found it hard to come home at the end of the intended two years.

Clearest of all my memories is that of my wedding morning, waiting for the car to arrive in a house strangely quiet and empty of people, with nobody left but my father, who, uncharacteristically, was rehearsing his wedding speech. Earlier he had told me that although I was now going to 'belong' to someone else, I would always be his daughter. He was not given to emotional speeches but I knew what he meant, and I think he also knew that I have never 'belonged' to anyone but myself since the age of four and a half and never would. Belong with, certainly, but not belong to. If the truth were known he had always remained his own person too – *am Badhlach*, the Benbecula man, as some South Uist people

363

still called him after a lifetime of living in Kilpheder. The man waiting for me at the church had needed to be self-sufficient all his adult life too, as his father had deserted the family when he was just fourteen.

So, as I stood in my room, at the window that looks directly on to the old house, my thoughts were not concerned with the future: I was confident that it was in safe hands. Instead, my eyes were filled with scenes from the past engendered by the sight of that old building with the sagging thatched roof. They were filled with memories of Hallowe'ens and Hogmanays, of long-gone people like Mary by the Canal and her old 'bad dog'. I could almost hear my mother and Donald Angus holding their music competitions before his accident had put paid to his musical achievements, and smiled as I heard again the shout of 'Goal!' on the night of the dumpling. I felt once more the feeling of warmth and security that had surrounded me when I stepped through the crofthouse door on the night that I had run away from Barra to attend my very first island wedding. Memories of childhood and young adulthood all centred round the sustaining constant of the little crofthouse and its occupants – memories that would never fade. By the time Jean arrived with the car to take me to my own island wedding, I was calmer than my father, who was still muttering his lines, and I knew that I was not saying goodbye to anything at all, and that whatever the future might bring I could always come back – back to the croft, back to the family, and back to the island.